ALL ALONE IN THE WORLD

D1153640

ALL ALONE IN THE WORLD

CHILDREN OF THE INCARCERATED

NELL BERNSTEIN

THE NEW PRESS

NEW YORK
LONDON

Copyright © 2005 by Nell Bernstein
All rights reserved.
No part of this book may be reproduced, in any form,
without written permission from the publisher.

Requests for permission to reproduce selections from this book should be mailed to:
Permissions Department, The New Press, 38 Greene Street, New York, NY 10013

Published in the United States by The New Press, New York, 2005
Distributed by W. W. Norton & Company, Inc., New York

LIBRARY OF CONGRESS CATALOGING-IN-PUBLICATION DATA

Bernstein, Nell.
All alone in the world : children of the incarcerated / Nell Bernstein.
p.   cm.
Includes bibliographical references and index.
ISBN 1-56584-952-3
1. Chidren of prisoners—United States.   2. Prisoners—United States—
Family relationships.   3. Prisoners' families—United States.   4. Custody
of children—United States.   I. Title.

HV8886.U5B47   2005
362.82'95—dc22   2005043872

The New Press was established in 1990 as a not-for-profit alternative to the large,
commercial publishing houses currently dominating the book publishing industry.
The New Press operates in the public interest rather than for private gain, and is
committed to publishing, in innovative ways, works of educational, cultural, and
community value that are often deemed insufficiently profitable.

www.thenewpress.com

Composition by dix!

Printed in the United States of America

2   4   6   8   10   9   7   5   3

For Tim

CONTENTS

ACKNOWLEDGMENTS

I had been speaking with and writing about the children of prisoners for several years when Helena Huang of the JEHT Foundation asked me, "Have you ever thought about writing a book?" She has brought empathy and rigor to the work of helping frame and focus the book, and commitment to the effort of making sure children's voices are heard.

The children and families who shared their time, stories, and insight made that effort both necessary and possible. This is, I hope, their book.

I began reporting on the children of incarcerated parents in 2000 with the support of a media fellowship from the Criminal Justice Initiative of the Open Society Institute in New York. The OSI network has provided intellectual and moral support that has lasted well beyond the fellowship term. In San Francisco, Ellen Walker of the Zellerbach Family Foundation offered crucial support for continuing the work I had begun, as did the members of the San Francisco Partnership for Incarcerated Parents.

A number of people read chapters and offered valuable comments: Sasha Abramsky, Phil Bernstein, Peter Breen, Joan

Hilty, Nancy Goldstein, Teresa Moore, and Ellen Walker. Peter Solomon read every word with precision and respect. Liz Gaynes and Emani Davis have been generous with their insight and their faith. Debbie Lewites transcribed interviews with speed and heart. At The New Press, Diane Wachtell lent a careful and empathetic eye to every page.

Sandy Close of Pacific News Service offered key advice on structure and tone, helping me down from my soapbox more than once. Before that, she raised me as a writer, teaching me that policy could only be understood, and improved, by trying to see it through the eyes of those affected. The first time I met Sandy, fifteen years ago, she told me I needed to listen more. I've been trying.

My mother, Harriet Stix, made me her first editor shortly after I learned to read. By producing newspaper and magazine features at the kitchen table, and making me part of the process, she showed me how to be a mother and a writer.

My husband, Timothy Buckwalter, has listened, read, and talked through this book so many times that he has come to live inside it along with me. My children, Ruby and Nicholas, kept me on track by endlessly repeating two key questions: "Why do people go to jail?" and "When will your book ever be finished?" They remind me every day what it means to be somebody's mother.

AUTHOR'S NOTE

Where first and last names are used, the names are real. Most first names used alone are real. The following have been changed: Ahmad, Ana, Anthony, Antonia, Christine, Christopher, Curtis, Jennifer, Keneshia, Kenyatta, Kimara, Márta, Randall, Susana, Terrence, Will.

ALL ALONE IN THE WORLD

INTRODUCTION

A CHILD IS BORN under armed guard in a public hospital in a remote rural county. After forty-eight hours, he is lifted from his mother's arms, bundled in hospital blankets, and handed to a social worker, who will drive him back to the county of his conception and deliver him to strangers.

A four-year-old peers at her father through scratched Plexiglas, shouting to be heard over a staticky telephone. "Daddy, come out of there," she roars in frustration, dropping the phone and banging her fist against the glass.

A six-year-old crouches behind his bed as armed strangers ransack his home, breaking through floorboards and throwing his parents to the ground. Downstairs, two police cars wait: one for his parents, one for him.

A nine-year-old burns his hand trying to make breakfast for himself and his baby brother. The two have been alone in an empty apartment for almost two weeks, since police removed their mother without explanation. Eventually, a neighbor will notice the boy out pushing a stroller by himself and call Child Protective Services.

An eleven-year-old struggles to reconnect with a mother who has recently been released from prison. The woman's drug conviction means she can't live in public housing, receive welfare, or obtain food stamps. After several months of fruitless job searching and sleeping in a shelter, she accepts an offer from the neighborhood cocaine dealer. This time, when the mother goes back to prison, the daughter refuses to accept her calls.

A sixteen-year-old sits in a cell inside juvenile hall, replaying in his head the words he has heard all his life: "You'll wind up like your father." He finds an odd comfort in finally fulfilling this expectation.

A twenty-two-year-old makes frantic phone calls from the county jail, trying to find someone who can help her make bail. She is pregnant, and terrified of giving birth behind bars. Her own parents were in and out of prison during her childhood years, leaving friends and relatives to raise her. She'd sworn she would give her children the life she never had, but the cycle of imprisonment and loss is beginning to feel like a tide too powerful to fight.

Two-point-four million American children have a mother or father in jail or prison right now. More than seven million, or one in ten of the nation's children, have a parent under criminal justice supervision—incarcerated, on probation, or on parole. In some neighborhoods, the numbers are so high that children will tell you just about everyone on their block has seen a mother or father locked up at one point or another.

Over the past three decades, the United States has embarked on an expansion of its penal system that is unprecedented in its scope and overwhelming in its impact on children and families. With more than 2.1 million of our citizens behind bars—a five-fold increase from thirty years ago—we have now outstripped Russia as the world's most prolific jailer. This represents not a response to an upsurge in violence—nearly three-quarters of those admitted to state prisons have been convicted of non-violent crimes—but a radical revision in our approach to those who use and sell drugs. Since 1980, the number of people behind bars for breaking the drug laws has increased twelvefold, far outstripping the growth of the prison population as a whole.

The prison boom has done more than rob individual children of the presence of a parent. It has stripped poor communities of the most valuable resource they have left: familial bonds. In neighborhoods across the country—drained first of fathers, then of mothers—children rely for care on impoverished grandmothers or a series of paid strangers. These children celebrate a parent's release with cyclical regularity, then lose hope in increments as she fights a losing battle against joblessness, untreated addiction, and the intractable stigma of a criminal record.

What it means to a child to lose a parent to prison depends, of course, on individual circumstance: whether that parent is a mother or a father; whether the child lived with that parent before the arrest, and what the family's circumstances were; why and for how long the parent will be incarcerated; who cares for the child in the parent's absence, and what supports that child obtains.

Overall, however, the picture drawn by researchers—and, in interviews, by children themselves—is bleak. The children of prisoners suffer from anxiety and attention disorders, or from post-traumatic stress. They are likely to bounce from one caregiver to another; to have and to cause trouble in school. Often poor to begin with, they get poorer once a parent is arrested. As many as half of all boys whose parents do time will wind up behind bars themselves—a formula that virtually guarantees one generation's prison boom will feed and fuel the next.

"A successful corrections system doesn't grow," criminologist Stephen Richards has observed. "If they were correcting anybody, they'd shrink." As our failing prison system continues to expand its reach, more and more of our children fall under its shadow, denied the light of parental attention they need in order to grow.

These children have committed no crime, but the penalty they are forced to pay is steep. They forfeit, too often, much of what matters to them: their homes, their safety, their public status and private self-image, their primary source of comfort and affection. Their lives and prospects are profoundly affected by the numerous institutions that lay claim to their parents—police, courts, jails and prisons, probation and parole—but they have no rights, explicit or implicit, within any of these jurisdictions. Conversely, there is no requirement that systems serving children—schools, child welfare departments, juvenile justice agencies—so much as take note of parental incarceration.

The harm children experience is sometimes referred to as one of the collateral consequences of America's policy of mass incarceration. In fact, "collateral" may be too oblique a term. The dissolution of families, the harm to children—and the resultant perpetuation of the cycle of crime and incarceration from one generation to the next—may be the most profound and damaging effect of our current penal structure.

Despite their numbers, the children of prisoners have so far remained largely invisible. But an elephant can grow only so large before people start remarking on its presence in the living room. Three in every hundred American children have a parent behind bars. The stories, if one listens for them, are everywhere.

Planning a reporting trip for this book, I called a hotel dis-

counter to reserve a room. It was late at night, and the operator
was talkative. He asked me why I was traveling, and I told him
about my research. There was a silence. Then he told me that
his brother had been picked up with five tabs of LSD at a Grateful Dead concert. The brother was in prison, and the operator,
who was twenty-nine years old, was caring for his brother's
three daughters.

"The kids are beautiful, and they're so screwed up," he said.
It was an hour and a half before he let me off the phone.

In California, I attended a legislative dinner on the issue of
children of incarcerated parents. After the dinner, two of the
waitresses approached the organizers. One was caring for the
child of an incarcerated sister. The other had a morning job as a
kindergarten teacher. The previous week, a six-year-old had
arrived at school tearful and enraged. His mother had been arrested that morning, and he had been sent off to walk to school
alone.

In the chapters that follow, young people describe the course
their lives have taken as their parents traveled through the criminal justice system. Their stories make clear that each decision
we make about how to handle lawbreaking—from arrest protocols through sentencing through policy governing the
prospects of returning prisoners—affects children's lives in
deep and lasting ways.

Decades of attachment research underscore the obvious:
kids need parents, do better in their presence, suffer when the
relationship to a parent is severed or breached. Children whose
parents have broken the law are no exception. These children
are far from blind to their parents' failings—they live with them
every day, and they have more at stake than anyone in seeing
their mothers and fathers rehabilitated, and living within the

law. But in one way or another, most say the same thing: things were hard. Mom got arrested. Things got worse.

What might an alternative look like—an approach to crime that would promote public safety while also protecting children and preserving families; that would make children's lives better rather than worse? This question is not as hard to answer as it might appear. Across the country, individual states, counties, and agencies have come up with effective approaches to meeting these dual imperatives at every stop on the criminal justice circuit. Several of these efforts are profiled in the pages that follow. Each is worthy of examination, and of replication. But as long as they remain alternatives—the exception rather than the rule—children whose parents have run afoul of the law will remain vulnerable to the wages of crime and punishment both.

These 2.4 million children cannot be kept hidden much longer. To see them—to hear them—will mean more than just the revelation of a problem or injustice. My conversations with children raised in the shadow of the prison have left me convinced that they have much more to offer than an accounting of their sorrows. Protracted experience of the impact of our current method of dealing with lawbreaking has created a generation of clear-eyed and insightful policy analysts with a profound stake in the creation of a fair and effective criminal justice system. There is not an aspect of criminal justice policy, from arrest through reentry, that does not touch children's lives; that they cannot help us understand more deeply, and make better.

1

ARREST

ANTHONY WAS A SLIGHT and restless boy of ten with pale skin and huge brown eyes. In a nearly bare office adjacent to the room where his grandmother was attending a support group, he was in and out of his chair, squirming and wriggling, his eyes wandering the room.

"I lived with my mother and her boyfriend and then they made drugs and sold them in the shed and I was in the house and they weren't even watching me," he said in one breath.

While his mother cooked methamphetamine, Anthony watched television. That is what he was doing the day the police came. Anthony was five years old. The police broke down the door, then smashed through the floorboards looking for drugs. Anthony remembers a lot of things shattered or crushed after that, things that had belonged to his grandfather. He remembers an officer putting him in the back of a police car. He was frightened, and didn't know where he was being taken.

"It's kiddie jail," he said of the children's shelter in which he found himself. "A jail for kids. Actually, it's not punishment. Actually, they punished me, though. Someone stole my watch. And they gave me clothes too small for me. They keep you in

cells—little rooms that you sleep in, and you have nothing
except for a bed, blankets, and sheets. You couldn't even go
to the bathroom in the middle of the night. They wouldn't let
you out."

At the shelter, Anthony cried for his mother and his grandmother. His grandmother came right away when she learned
what had happened, but it was two and a half weeks—and three
family court hearings—before Anthony was released from the
shelter and permitted to go home with her. She lived in another
county, and child welfare authorities insisted that she secure
local housing before they would release Anthony to her care.

"He was in so much pain," she said of the boy who met her at
the shelter. "He jumped in my arms from across the room and
said, 'Granny, get me out of here.' "

Anthony remembers the day he left the shelter. "I had a
Wolverine and an Incredible Hulk in a plastic baggie in one
hand and the other hand was holding my grandma and we ran
down the street as fast as we can, away from the shelter."

Anthony's mother is out of jail now, trying to stay clean. Anthony knows if she slips up, the police will take her away again.
He fears it will happen to him, too. Because of the way he was
taken there, and how little was explained to him, the shelter has
come to haunt Anthony.

"The third time you go in the children's shelter, you can
never go out until you're eighteen. My uncle told me, and it's
true, too."

Anthony drew from his mother's arrest a few simple lessons:
his mother was bad. He was bad. Authority was destructive. It is
difficult to imagine a scenario in which a parent's arrest would
not be wrenching for a child. But Anthony's fear and sorrow
might have been eased by steps as simple as having someone

take him into another room while his home was searched and talk to him about what was going on, or asking his mother if there were someone she might call to care for him.

These things happen, sometimes, when an individual officer thinks of them, or a chief mandates them. But the majority of police departments have no written protocol delineating officers' responsibility to the children of arrested parents, and those protocols that do exist vary widely in their wording and their implementation. A national survey by the American Bar Association (ABA) Center on Children and the Law found that only one-third of patrol officers will handle a situation differently if children are present. Of that third, only one in five will treat a suspect differently if children are present. One in ten will take special care to protect the children.

The result is that an event that is by its nature traumatic—the forcible removal by armed strangers of the person to whom children naturally look for protection—happens in ways that are virtually guaranteed to exacerbate, rather than mitigate, that trauma.

A national study found that almost 70 percent of children who were present at a parent's arrest watched their parent being handcuffed, and nearly 30 percent were confronted with drawn weapons. When researcher Christina Jose Kampfner interviewed children who had witnessed their mothers' arrests, she found that many suffered classic symptoms of post-traumatic stress syndrome—they couldn't sleep or concentrate, and they had flashbacks to the moment of arrest. If an arrested parent later returns home on parole or probation, officers often have license to enter the house at will—meaning that children may relive that trauma in their living rooms as well as their imaginations.

Police often plan raids for late-night or early-morning hours, when those they seek are most likely to be home with their families. That ups the odds that police will get their man, but also that children will awaken to see it happen. It should come as no surprise that sleep disorders follow.

Some narcotics officers report that they have children searched before releasing them to a relative or a shelter, in case they have drugs in their clothing or diaper. *Washington Post* reporter Leon Dash interviewed the son of a longtime drug dealer and prostitute who recalled being forced to strip and spread his buttocks inside his own apartment during police raids.

When police deem children in need of child protective services, the majority deliver the children in a police car rather than having a child welfare worker pick them up in a less-intimidating vehicle. About one-fourth of police departments routinely bring children first to the police station rather than to a shelter or other civilian destination. Officers who find themselves responsible for children at the time of an arrest complain that their "babysitting" responsibilities interfere with their ability to do their real job.

"It is unfair to keep young children at the police station," one officer told the ABA researchers. "This is not a good place to watch children; there is no place to eat; they can't sleep here; we often don't have the supplies to take care of them, especially infants."

A child who is picked up by police officers, transported in a police car, and deposited at the police station—where he may be deprived of food and sleep—will almost inevitably experience himself as having been arrested. To all intents and purposes, he has been.

In one jurisdiction, police supervisors described the following protocol for handling the child of an arrestee when no relative is available to pick him up: first, officers take the child to the hospital for a physical examination. Next, they transport him to the local juvenile detention center to "fill out the necessary forms." Finally, they deposit him at a foster home.

This jurisdiction was presented as a model by the researchers who visited it. Both police and child welfare workers reported that their protocol was working efficiently and congratulated themselves and each other for their smooth collaboration. But try for a moment to imagine this circuit as a child might experience it (an exercise that is necessary because the researchers did not speak with any actual children). An armed and uniformed stranger handcuffs and takes away your parent, then places you in a police car, where you are separated from your rescuer by a metal grid. From where you sit, you can hear the crackle of the dispatcher on the radio reporting crimes and crises elsewhere in town. You are driven to the hospital, where you are required to take off your clothes and be scrutinized and prodded by another stranger. Then you are taken to a jail—just as your parent has been—where you sit in silence as the adults around you process the paperwork that will determine your immediate future. Finally, you are deposited at the home of yet another stranger, where you are given someone else's pajamas and sent off to sleep in an unfamiliar bed.

It is quite likely that the various adults this child will encounter along his route will make an effort to treat him kindly. The problem is not the callousness of individuals but the mechanical indifference of multiple bureaucracies, each of which functions according to its own imperatives. These bureaucratic exigencies—rather than children's experience—become the lens through which policies and protocols are drawn up and assessed. The system is viewed as "working" when it works for the institutions that comprise it—in itself, a legitimate end. But when children's experience is not also given priority, the effect is to leave children feeling afraid, alone, and unseen.

"I just wish the police would have talked to me like I was a part of it," said Christopher, who was whisked off to a foster home in the wake of his mother's arrest—"which I was. But they acted like I wasn't."

The trauma children experience when a parent is arrested may set the tone for their subsequent relationship with the criminal justice system. A natural desire to protect oneself and defend one's family evolves into a hatred of police, and authority generally—a rage that can make it difficult for a child to grow up to respect the law or trust its representatives.

"Adult lives are shaped by childhood experience," observed San Francisco Sheriff Michael Hennessy, who said children sometimes call his jail looking for their missing parents in the wake of an arrest. "If children are abused by the criminal justice system, they will have hostility towards law enforcement as adults. If they are treated fairly, and see government as a place to receive assistance as opposed to something that takes away rights, they will be more likely to reach out to and respect government as adults."

Ana, fifteen, has been watching her mother get arrested for years, for crimes such as forgery and drug possession. Once, she saw an officer snatch the cigarette from her mother's mouth and throw it to the ground. Another time, she heard her mother crying that the handcuffs were too tight and were hurting her. "I don't care," the officer answered.

Ana's brother, now five, witnessed these gratuitous cruelties throughout his early childhood. "When he sees the cops now, he'll run, because he's scared of them," Ana said. "He's all, 'They took my mommy and they hurt her.' "

Seeing one's parent helpless and restrained at an age when one still wants and needs to see her as omnipotent can be deeply disorienting. Lorraine watched police search her house and arrest her mother for drug offenses throughout her childhood. What left her most embittered, Lorraine said, was the fact that she rarely received an acknowledgment of her presence, much less an explanation.

"I was left thinking, 'What could my mother possibly have done that they can come in my home and invade my privacy?'" Lorraine said. "I'd watch them handcuff my mother and take her to jail, thinking, 'Don't they know that she is beautiful in my eyes, and that I could help her get better? That she has a child at home who yearns for her presence?' I remember crying to the police, 'Please don't take my mother away from me.' Yet time after time, I would watch them handcuff my mother, place her in the police car, and drive away, leaving me to wonder, 'Will I see her again?' I began to hate the police."

Children who do not manage to hate the authorities are likely to blame themselves. Jennifer was twelve years old when she returned home from science camp one afternoon to find police in her home. They arrested her mother and took Jennifer to a shelter. She felt, she said, "that my life was over. That I would never see my family again. I thought I had done something wrong, because I had to go away, too. But my family says I didn't."

Jennifer was twenty-seven years old when she told this story. She still didn't sound convinced.

A parent's arrest is the moment when a child's invisibility is made visible; when it is communicated to him most explicitly how little he will matter within the systems and institutions that lay claim to his family.

With appalling regularity, young people describe being left to fend for themselves in empty apartments for weeks or even months in the wake of a parent's arrest. In most cases, these children were not present when the parent was arrested; they simply came home from school to find their parent gone and were left to draw their own conclusions—not to mention cook their own dinner. But some told of watching police handcuff and remove a parent—the only adult in the house—and simply leave them behind. These stories bring home like no others the degree to which children are simply not seen, much less considered, within the criminal justice system.

The first time I heard such a story was from Ricky, then sixteen. Ricky's mother, like one-third of all incarcerated mothers, was living alone with her children at the time of her arrest. Ricky was nine years old, and his brother was under a year.

"The police came and took my mom, and I guess they thought someone else was in the house, I don't really know," Ricky said. "But no one else was in the house. I was trying to ask them what happened and they wouldn't say. Everything went so fast. They just rushed in the house and got her and left."

After that, Ricky did his best. He cooked for himself and his brother, and he changed the baby's diapers. "Sometimes he'd cry, because he probably would want to see my mother. But he was used to me, too," Ricky said.

Ricky burned himself trying to make toast and got a blister on his hand, but he felt he was managing. He remembered that each day, his mother would take him and his brother out for a walk. So he kept to the family routine, pushing the baby down the sidewalk in a stroller every day for two weeks, until a neighbor took notice and called Child Protective Services.

Social workers came and took Ricky's brother from him, just as police had his mother. The boys were sent to separate foster homes. Ricky saw his mother only once after that, years later, when he ran into her on the street and she told him she was working on getting him back. A year after that, he received a letter from a stranger with a hospital return address, telling him his mother had died. He never found out how she died, or what had happened to her in the years following her arrest.

I spoke with Ricky again a few years after our first meeting. He was nineteen, and doing well. He had been lucky in foster care; he had landed with a loving caregiver who had made a stable home for him. As a teenager, he had been contacted by his brother's adoptive parents and had been able to forge a new relationship with him. Now he was attending a suburban junior college, where he had been recruited for his football talents.

As we walked around campus, Ricky seemed calmer than when I had met him three years earlier, confident and happy in his new role as college athlete. It was late summer, and he was registering for classes and getting ready for the upcoming season.

We talked again about the events of his childhood. He offered some new details, but the story he told was identical in its outline to the one he had told me years earlier. I was less surprised now by what I was hearing, but no less confused.

The problem with Ricky's account is that it makes no sense. Why was his mother arrested? Why didn't she call from jail, or make some arrangement for her children's care? Why were they never reunited with her, or even permitted a visit? Why was he separated from his brother? Why did his mother not return for him as she had promised? Why on earth were two small children left alone in an empty apartment?

I pressed Ricky on these questions until he grew frustrated. He did not know, because no one had ever told him. The police were in a hurry, and so were the social workers. "All I know is that they just rushed me in the system and that was that. They didn't tell me why I can't go back with my mom."

The confusion I felt trying to sort out Ricky's history, with its gaping holes and incomprehensible events, simply reflected his own. Major pieces of his autobiography—that part of it which unfolded in the days and years after his mother's arrest— were not, and likely never would be, available to him.

When I first met Ricky, I was sure his story was exceptional. But the more I spoke with young people about their parents' arrest and incarceration, the less so it appeared.

Antonia was five years old when she saw her mother arrested on the street for prostitution. "I saw the police coming at me and I just ran," Antonia recalled. "As a child, I thought maybe they might arrest me. At five years old, I should have been aware of the police as good people who help you. Not, 'My mom is in the car with them!' Not, 'My mom is handcuffed!' "

Antonia ran home and told her older brothers what had happened. The children were on their own until their mother was released from jail a week later. Antonia remembers her ten-year-old brother trying to "be like the mother" during that time.

"When we would try to get junk food at the store, he would say, 'No, put that back.' We would burn food and he would get mad at us. 'I'm supposed to do the cooking! I deal with fire!' "

When young people describe the arrest of a parent, the sense one gets is not only of unnecessary trauma but also of tremendous missed opportunity. A child whose parent is arrested is likely already a vulnerable child. Arrest, reimagined, could be an opportunity to make that vulnerable child, and her family, visible; to make a bad situation better rather than worse.

As it stands, young people's reports of being overlooked or ignored are confirmed by law enforcement accounts. "I have taken and seen hundreds of children processed throughout my years in law enforcement," wrote one investigator in a handout prepared for a seminar at the California State Legislature. "The way these children are handled after a parent is arrested varies from, ignoring them, leaving them with a neighbor, leaving them alone with the promise that someone will be back from the store shortly.

"This area is highly overlooked and uncontrolled," he continued. "This area is like spousal abuse years ago. It was taken lightly and officers took the path of least resistance, until the law required specific actions. I think this problem is in the same realm."

Another police officer told a researcher, "Most cops do not like to and will not take kids into protective custody. It takes time, puts pressure on you from your agency, creates tons of paperwork, and CPS [Child Protective Services] isn't happy because they have other cases. There are all kinds of pressures [for law enforcement] not to take the kids."

Another officer was more succinct: asking after children, he told the researchers, would be "one more thing to do."

Some officers told the ABA researchers that they did not consider it necessary to inquire about children because they felt certain arrestees would always volunteer that information, in the hope of getting off easy because they had children. In fact, arrested parents may have a strong incentive *not* to tell police about children, or seek official help, because they fear losing their children to foster care—perhaps permanently—if they do so.

The alternative—making one's own arrangements for a child's care—is often difficult. Although many women arrestees are primary caregivers to children, they generally receive little or no assistance, or even access to a telephone, to make arrangements for children's care.

In 2001, Marcus Nieto of the California Research Bureau surveyed California police and sheriff's departments about their approach to the children of arrested parents. He found what he called a "de facto 'don't ask and don't tell' policy"— children were generally not considered a police responsibility unless they were perceived to be in grave danger.

When Nieto asked law enforcement personnel for their suggestions for improving police response to children of arrestees, the most popular answer was "nothing can be done." Those respondents who did see room for improvement primarily pointed to agencies other than their own.

While there is in general no statutory mandate for police to concern themselves with children at the time of an arrest, courts have occasionally held police liable for injuries to children left alone after a caretaker is arrested. *White v. Rochford,* the 1979 case that established the precedent for such liability, is based on a set of circumstances that tax the imagination. Police left three small children alone on a highway at night after arresting their uncle for a traffic violation. One child was hit by a car while crossing the freeway. The other two were later hospitalized with severe pneumonia.

A nine-year-old left alone with a baby—or a child venturing

into traffic—does not go unnoticed indefinitely. When a Florida two-year-old spent nearly three weeks alone in an empty apartment after her mother was arrested—surviving on ketchup and dried noodles—the story made national news.

Teenagers are more likely to slip under the radar indefinitely—and most likely to be left alone in the first place. With few foster homes willing to take them, teenage children of arrestees are commonly left to fend for themselves at home. Even among police departments that told the ABA researchers they had a written policy outlining officers' responsibility for minor children of an arrested caretaker, only 55 percent defined "minor" as all children under eighteen. The rest offered definitions that ranged from sixteen and under to ten and under. In other words, children who would not be permitted to sign a lease, get a job, or enroll themselves in school because of their age were, as a matter of explicit policy, deemed old enough to be left behind in empty apartments should police find it necessary to take away their parents.

Terrence fell into this category. He was fifteen when police broke down the door of his home and arrested his drug-using mother. "'Call somebody to come watch you,'" he remembers an officer advising him on the way out.

"They were so busy trying to take my mom out, and the other people that were with her, they didn't care about me," Terrence said. "All they cared about was getting them people to jail that day."

"I was scared and angry," recalled Terrence, who had, as it happened, no one to call. "Then when I see my mama in a car, being hauled off, ain't comin' home, I'm feeling this sad feeling and angry feeling now. 'I gotta make it happen. I gotta help my mama.' I took it on me."

In his mother's absence, Terrence said, "I just cooked, cleaned, went to school. Stayed out of trouble. Really, that's all I could do. I stayed around other people a lot, 'cause I never liked being in my house all the time. It got lonely and it got scary."

Among Terrence's fears was that the police would return, this time for him. "I'm like, 'They could come kick in the door at any time again. They might think I'm doing something.'"

For a few weeks, Terrence got by on what was left of the family's food stamps. When they ran out, he could secure no more; only his mother's name was on the card required to pick them up each month. He cracked open his piggy bank, netting $56. When that was gone, he washed cars in the neighborhood and sold newspapers door to door. At fifteen, he was too young to get a real job.

"In my head I was like, 'I'm gonna be the man. I'm gonna pay the bills. I'm gonna try to do it,'" Terrence said, "but I just didn't know what to do. I just basically had to eat noodles and do what I could until my mom came home."

Terrence bought groceries with his earnings, but he couldn't keep up with the bills. The electricity got cut off, then the water and gas.

Once his apartment went dark, then cold, Terrence began spending more and more time with friends from school who lived together in a foster home nearby. When he began spending the night there, the foster father took notice and asked Terrence whether something was wrong at home. Terrence explained his situation, and the man arranged for Terrence to be placed with him on an emergency basis. Five months had passed since Terrence's mother's arrest before his solitary status registered as an "emergency" with any official entity.

Terrence was clearly a thoughtful boy with a strong sense of what he needed. Had the police simply asked him that question when they removed his mother, he likely would have told them.

He might also, had anyone asked, have offered his own vision for drug-policy reform, one that took his needs into account: "I think they shouldn't have took my mama to jail. Just made her go to court, and give her some community service, or some type of alternative, where she can go to the program down the street. Give her the opportunity to make up for what she did. Using drugs, she's hurting herself. You take her away from me, now you're hurting me."

"HASSLE, HASSLE, CAN'T YOU get in trouble for scaring little kids with toy guns?"

"Hassle, if I find a million dollars and I give it to you, what would you do?"

"Hassle, am I old enough to go to jail?"

"Hassle, if you see sixteen grown men bothering people, you'll call for backup?"

"Hassle, I know how to drive. It's just that I'm short!"

Lieutenant Ray Hassett of the New Haven Department of Police Service had pulled over in order to confiscate a cap gun from a six-year-old who was apparently unaware that it was not wise to point it at an oncoming patrol car. The boy and his siblings took the opportunity to unleash a stream of questions and commentary they seemed to have been stockpiling for just such an occasion. A tangle of hands reached in to shake Hassett's, and five radiant faces pressed inside the open passenger window. Sugary residue from one girl's lollipop dripped onto the upholstery.

Hassett has been patrolling the streets of New Haven, Con-

necticut, for eighteen years. The nickname "Hassle" was con-
ferred on him so long ago that the current crop of neighborhood kids knows him by no other. As we drove through New
Haven's Chapel Dwight neighborhood, which skirts the Yale
University campus, Hassett saw children everywhere he
looked. It is in his nature, and also his training.

Hassett is one of the founding members of the Child Development–Community Policing Program (CD-CP), a fifteen-
year-old collaboration between the New Haven Department of
Police Service and the Yale Child Study Center (YCSC). The
program is officially charged with healing the wounds that
chronic exposure to violence inflicts on children and families,
but it has reached beyond that mandate, transforming the way
the police department handles everything from a homicide arrest to a traffic accident when children are present. In New
Haven, children are now routinely seen, heard, and treated with
care at the scene of an arrest.

The program was conceived in the early 1990s, when New
Haven, like many American cities, was struggling to quell the
crack trade and the violence that accompanied it. According to
departmental legend, then–police chief Nicholas Pastore had
been called to the scene of a homicide, where he saw several
children huddled on a couch, their mother's dead body on the
floor before them. As investigators went about their business,
no one was paying attention to the clearly traumatized children.
Pastore sought guidance from Dr. Donald J. Cohen, then the
director of the Yale Child Study Center, and the CD-CP was
born.

Dr. Steven Berkowitz, a child psychiatrist and the medical director of the CD-CP, is tweedy and bearlike, with curly brown
hair and a salt-and-pepper beard. He has the kind of face that, if

you were a child and your parents had been spirited away, you might consider trusting. The scenario Pastore encountered, said Berkowitz—kids on the couch, unnoticed and unattended—remains the norm in much of the country.

"Systems don't think," Berkowitz asserted. "They're more like machines—you turn on the switch and they just keep doing what they always do. The real question is, how do you get systems to think?"

Because police are often the first "system" representatives through the door, they represent an obvious starting point. Watching a parent arrested and taken away, Berkowitz noted, is itself one of the most significant traumas a child can experience. He has seen children respond by becoming unable to eat or to sleep, losing the ability to speak or use the toilet, or reverting from walking to crawling.

Through the CD-CP, New Haven police officers receive training in child development, and police supervisors are eligible for fellowships at the YCSC. Child Study Center clinicians are on call twenty-four hours, and they will come to the scene of a crime or an arrest, crayons in hand, to offer counseling and support. New Haven police refer children to the YCSC for treatment and counseling in the wake of parental arrest and other traumas. At weekly case conferences, police, probation officers, mental health workers, school representatives, and child welfare workers meet with YCSC clinicians to review cases involving children and police.

On the morning when I visited, the case-conferencing group was working its way through a three-page agenda packed with terse descriptions of imploding families: "A twenty-five-year-old mother of two tried to commit suicide." "As a result of her daughter's victimization by bullies over the past year, a mother left a threatening message on her teacher's voice mail." "Three children were discovered to be living with their grandmother in a crack house." "An eight-year old girl witnessed a domestic incident between her parents."

A New Haven police officer offered an account of a narcotics arrest the previous night. A ten-year-old boy had been in the back seat when his grandmother was arrested at gunpoint while making a drug deal. The boy, the officer reported, was terrified; CD-CP clinicians would follow up with offers of counseling and services via the aunt who was now caring for him. The YCSC receives an average of ten such police referrals each week and has seen about seven thousand police-referred children since the program's inception.

Hassett described a call the day before in Chapel Dwight: a two-year-old had been found wandering the streets in only a diaper and socks. Police had canvassed the neighborhood with a loudspeaker and had local television stations broadcast the boy's picture, but no one had claimed him. After several hours, a neighbor told police where the child lived. When police visited the house, they found that a seventeen- and a thirteen-year-old had been left in charge of six younger siblings. The toddler had walked out while the teenagers were trying to get everyone into bed. When the parents returned home—the father had gone to pick the mother up from work—they assumed the boy was asleep, and his absence went unnoticed. By the time police tracked down the family, the child welfare department had already placed the child in a foster home.

At the CD-CP meeting, a child welfare worker interpreted this account by remarking that when he leaves his children with a babysitter, he makes sure the sitter has his cell phone and pager numbers. A police officer offered an opposing view: his daughter had once wandered a quarter-mile from the house as a toddler, and he didn't consider himself a negligent parent.

As he would throughout the meeting, YCSC psychoanalyst Dr. Steven Marans directed the conversation away from competing adult perspectives and toward a child's-eye view. "I've treated children who've had removals [from their homes] at an early age," he cautioned. "Timing is essential. Twenty-four hours in the life of a two-year-old is a lifetime. I don't fault child welfare for looking at safety, but we need to take extra steps to determine the best interest of the child. Is there a relative down the street that the kid has spent time with? From a child's perspective, that two-year-old deserves that."

The CD-CP has been replicated in thirteen cities, and New Haven police and YCSC staff regularly consult with police from other cities in the hope of sharing what they have learned and spreading the model. The day I was there, a visiting officer from Providence, Rhode Island—which is developing a program modeled on New Haven's—picked up on Marans's cue, noting that Hassett's decision not to arrest the parents for child endangerment had likely spared the boy's siblings significant trauma.

"We're not going to arrest our way out of poverty," New Haven police chief Francisco Ortiz told me after the meeting, "so we have to start here, thinking about the children."

The Chapel Dwight neighborhood was, as Hassett dryly put it, "busy" on the spring afternoon when I accompanied him on his rounds through the four-square-mile district in which he had spent the past eight years. "Wussup? Wussup?" Hassett called gamely to young men on stoops and street corners as we crawled through the neighborhood at ten miles an hour, windows open. Some offered a brisk nod. Most looked away. One grimaced visibly.

A burly white man with a bristly, Mohawk-like strip of hair dividing his otherwise-shaved head into neat halves, Hassett wore a shirt and tie underneath his uniform. His oval sunglasses sat mid-forehead, obscuring his eyebrows. Before the need for a steady paycheck drove him to police work two decades earlier, Hassett had been a stage and screen actor in London and Los Angeles. He appeared in films including *Body Double* and *The Spy Who Loved Me*, and he played one of Harrison Ford's stormtroopers in *The Empire Strikes Back*. He has been cast as a police officer more than once, but he likened his current role to that of a country doctor.

Much of Hassett's work on the afternoon I spent with him involved cleaning up the messes that had filled the agenda of the morning's CD-CP meeting. At the police station, reporters from two local television stations were awaiting comment on the stray toddler. Hassett assumed a classic cop stance for the camera—feet wide apart, hands folded—but offered the reporters little else. It was, after all, not much of a story—working parents, a houseful of kids. The reporters' questions trailed off and they packed up their equipment.

Hassett pulled up outside the neighborhood middle school—a block-sized brick square on barren grounds—as it was letting out. "Hi poleeeeeeceman!" a girl shouted. Hassett tried his "wussup" again on a crowd of boys heading for the bus. Finally, he got an audible "wussup" in return. His face offered no clue as to whether he heard the sarcasm in the boy's tone.

A school crossing guard accosted Hassett, outraged about the two-year-old: "How could you forget the baby?"

Inside, a secretary also had an opinion to share: "I wanna beat that lady up about that baby last night."

"It's not as bad as you think," Hassett told her.

"I think kids should be very closely supervised."

"It's not as bad as you think."

"A mistake? OK. But I still wanna whup her."

"Everyone was out for blood last night," Hassett told me. "They wanted to see somebody coming out in cuffs. It's a little more time-consuming to look at the real situation—a family that is overwhelmed and needs childproof locks on their door. I'm trying to bring everyone down a bit. The family is probably mortified."

The school principal stopped Hassett to confer about the mother who had left the message threatening a teacher. Hassett listened quietly as the principal offered his perspective. "She said some very inflammatory things," Hassett told me later of the middle-schooler's mother. "We certainly had enough probable cause to arrest her. Would that have solved anything? If you're looking at the child as being the focus of the behavior, would that have helped the child? I don't think so." Hassett was, however, worried about the girl, who kept getting into fights at school, and he hoped the threat of police involvement would be leverage enough to get the reluctant mother to allow her daughter to be seen at the YCSC.

On the standard New Haven police-report form, there is a space in which an officer is required to list all children present at the scene and check off whether the YCSC was consulted. If a caregiver declines services and the officer thinks the kids need them, he'll knock on the door in a day or two and extend the offer again. I asked Hassett about the view that police exist to ensure public safety, not act as "social workers" or "babysitters." Hassett bristled at the distinction. Encouraging kids to see cops as the enemy, he explained, does not enhance public safety—nor, for that matter, police safety. One of the archetypal CD-CP stories, in fact, involves a child, who had been well treated by police in the past, saving an officer's life by warning him of an imminent ambush.

"For a lot of the kids, their parents getting locked up is not new," Hassett said. "It's part of daily life. I have to go back to the house again and again. Do I wanna fight every time I go there? No. Do I wanna be able to have them open the door instead of kicking it down? Yes. Having a rapport with the family helps get the job done in a safe manner.

"The last thing I want to be seen as is the bad guy coming in there. We're the good guys. So you take a little extra time. You sit down, say, 'How you doin',' look around and ask about the toys he has—just like you would with your own kids. When you go into a house to investigate an incident, your work isn't done until you take a look at those kids."

This kind of interaction, Steven Berkowitz observed, can do more than encourage kids to open the door to the cops. "If you set it up so that authority and the police are the bad guys, then what reason would any child have to think that doing the right thing is going to be good for them?" he asked. "Now here's the supreme example of authority in society saying, 'I'm here, I'm listening, and I'm not bullshitting you.' It's a huge difference. Do I think it's going to detraumatize or heal? No. But I think it gives them a rope."

2

SENTENCING

CARL'S MOTHER HAD BEEN in prison for four years by the time Carl, then twelve, found the courage to ask her when she would be coming home.

Carl had heard rumors about his mother's sentence, but no one had ever said the words "triple life" to him before the day his mother spelled it out for him over the phone.

"I didn't even think it was real at the time," Carl said. "I thought she was kidding. I remember saying, 'You can't do triple life. You only have one.' "

Carl was eighteen when I met him—a polite and expressive African American teenager with caterpillar eyebrows and a Louisiana drawl, his small frame disappearing into oversized designer clothes. He was still struggling to make sense of the government's plan for his thirty-six-year-old mother, who had never spent a night away from him before the day the federal agents came: that she will grow old and die inside the Federal Correctional Institution in Dublin, California; that she will never see her children, or her grandchildren, or their children, outside a prison visiting room.

Carl's mother, Danielle Metz, was sentenced to triple life

plus twenty years for her involvement in her husband's crack cocaine business—an enterprise that, according to court documents, involved the distribution of over 150 kilograms of cocaine, and the murder of rivals. Danielle, for her part, does not deny that she participated in her husband's drug business. But she describes herself as an abused wife who married young and got in over her head; who did what she was told—mainly dropping off and picking up packages—because she was cowed and intimidated.

Carl was too young to understand the complexities of Danielle's trial, but he has struggled to come to terms with the outcome. "It was her first conviction," he said. "Before that, she didn't even have a traffic ticket. Why so long? Triple life on her first time. I'm not going to say I don't think that's right. I *know* that's not right."

Those who are not taught to vilify an absent parent are likely to idealize her. The mother Carl remembers is saintlike in her devotion. Long after he was able to walk, Danielle carried him everywhere, like a little prince. Carl did not know that his mother and stepfather—who is also serving multiple life sentences—were involved in the drug trade. What he knew was that his mother picked him up from school each afternoon and checked his homework after dinner; that she took him swimming on the weekends, and said "See you later, alligator" as she tucked him in at night. If he brought home an "A" from school, they went to Toys "Я" Us. This is what Carl knew, so this is what he lost.

"That's probably what hurts so much," he said—"remembering. I could remember like it was yesterday, everything we done, everything we seen. Every day I wake up in the morning, that's the first thing come in my mind, before anything: what if my mom was here?"

Some young people become cynical when they believe a parent has been unfairly punished. They conclude that they are helpless in the face of arbitrary power; that there is no point in trying to do right in an unjust world. Carl has taken the opposite approach, holding on to an intense faith in humanity's capacity for justice and his own power to tap that better instinct. Carl has had some success as a rapper, and he believes devoutly that with fame will come the capacity to liberate his mother.

"I think if somebody looked into it, they'd really have no problem helping her," Carl said. "I know if they hear this story, it's nobody in this world that thinks that's fair. You can't bring nobody on earth to me like that.

"I really want to meet the judge," Carl added—"see what he was thinking at the time."

In fact, what the judge was thinking was of little relevance to Carl's mother's fate. Danielle was sentenced under federal mandatory sentencing laws that tie judges' hands, requiring them to impose whatever term the legislature has prescribed for a particular category of offender, rather than the one they may have concluded that a specific offense merits.

At FCI Dublin, Danielle is surrounded by fellow first-time offenders serving decades-long sentences, many under mandatory sentencing laws passed in the mid-1980s, when the nation was caught up in hysteria over the spread of crack cocaine. The law that sealed Danielle's fate was the earlier Continuing Criminal Enterprise statute, a 1970 federal law that was ostensibly intended to nab mobsters and drug "kingpins." To receive the sentence Danielle did under the statute, one must be found to have been a leader in a large drug-trafficking enterprise. Once that conclusion has been reached, a life sentence is mandatory. Danielle was also convicted of money laundering, possession with intent to distribute cocaine, and conspiracy (a count that was later voided).

Danielle's sentence reflects legislative trends of recent decades, which have greatly increased the time people spend in prison and the number who will stay there forever. According to a report from the Sentencing Project, the lifer population has more than tripled in the past two decades. Today, one in every eleven federal and state prisoners is doing a life sentence. One in four is serving a sentence of twenty years or more. In six states and in the federal system—where some two thousand prisoners, including Danielle, are doing life for drug offenses—all life sentences are imposed without the possibility of parole.

The life sentence as it was primarily used until the 1970s was indeterminate (e.g., fifteen years to life). After a minimum number of years had been served, a parole board would regularly reevaluate a person's behavior and evidence of rehabilitation. An individual who was found to have been rehabilitated could be released on parole once the minimum had been served, while one deemed unrehabilitated could be kept behind bars indefinitely.

Mandatory sentencing has obliterated this distinction. If you are found to have possessed or distributed a specific amount of a particular substance, you will serve a legislatively mandated number of years, regardless of the circumstances of your crime, your character, or any other mitigating factors. Among the things judges are explicitly barred from considering are the needs of children.

Mandatory sentencing laws have helped make women prisoners the fastest-growing segment of the prison population nationwide. According to the federal General Accounting Office, their numbers increased more than sevenfold between 1980 and the end of 2003, from 13,400 to more than 100,000. Most of this increase can be traced to "tough on crime" measures such as mandatory sentencing, rather than to an increase in female criminality.

As the Sentencing Project's Marc Mauer has pointed out, the movement away from indeterminate sentencing and toward mandatory minimums reflects a shift in thinking about the purpose of incarceration, from rehabilitation to punishment. Rehabilitation, after all, is a mysterious and unpredictable process—who can say how long it will take? For that reason, a sentence intended to rehabilitate needed to have some built-in flexibility. Once lawbreakers began to be defined exclusively in terms of their criminal acts, and the function of incarceration came to be seen primarily as deterrence and punishment, such flexibility was no longer required.

Carl did not use the word "rehabilitation," but he had clearly given thought to the concept.

"I feel like your first time should be a warning," he said. " 'Cause I know if my mom come home, she'll live totally different. If you could put my head on the chopping board, and there was some kind of way you could read her mind, I would take that risk that she really was sorry."

I tried to explain to Carl how it had been legislatively determined that sorry didn't matter; that regardless of whether she would ever break the law again, his mother had committed a crime for which she could never finish paying. It made no sense to Carl that his mother's fate had been sealed not by the judge who heard her case but by a group of legislators who had reached their conclusions decades earlier and hundreds of miles away.

"Who is this person? You know him?" he asked me, still looking for a face to put on what had happened, an individual to hold accountable.

Carl needs to believe that *someone* decided to take his mother away forever; that someone would one day hear his petition and provide redress. It is part of the faith that continues to sustain him. Everyone, Carl believes—even "this person" who gave his mother three life sentences for a first offense—has the capacity for repentance, and rehabilitation.

FCI Dublin sits on the Camp Parks Army Base thirty-five miles east of San Francisco. The facility is set back so far from the road that a guard at an entrance to the compound hands visitors a map to steer them through the empty fields to the prison itself.

The buildings originally housed youthful offenders, until, as a prison spokesperson explained, the Federal Bureau of Prisons "got out of the juvenile business" and converted the site to a low-security women's prison in 1972. The low-lying stained-wood buildings with their sloped shingle roofs resemble ski condominiums, save for the view of razor wire. On the day I visited, swarms of crows screamed in a eucalyptus grove just outside the prison doors. Inside the empty lobby, an employee bulletin board announced an upcoming training opportunity: the Martin Luther King Jr. Lunch and Learn, in honor of the holiday the following week. A lone seagull circled the empty yard.

Danielle was waiting in the empty visiting room. She was tiny, in a pressed khaki shirt and pants, with warm almond eyes and the round, smooth face of a doll. She wore delicately etched gold hoop earrings, and her pressed hair had a side part. A scattering of freckles decorated her cheekbones. She spoke quietly—a prison representative waited in a chair a few yards away—and sat with rounded shoulders, as if to consume as little space as possible in the chilly, echoing room.

Danielle was eighteen when she began dating then-thirty-year-old Glenn Metz, and a single parent to Carl, whose father had died when Carl was six months old. Glenn told Danielle he admired her devotion to her son, Danielle said; that he cared for Carl, too, and would help her to raise him. Danielle moved out of her parents' house and into Glenn's. At first, Danielle said, she believed his income derived from his auto-towing business. Later, she learned he was selling drugs.

Danielle said her husband was a good father to Carl and to Gleneisha, the daughter they had together. For years, she told herself that was why she stayed, even, she said, after he became abusive toward her. When her husband asked her to pick up drugs or drop off money, Danielle said, she did not ask questions. "He didn't force me," she said, "but I still was intimidated. I couldn't say no."

At twenty-five, Danielle decided she'd had enough. She gathered up her children, left Las Vegas—where the family had been living—and flew home to her mother in New Orleans. By the time police came looking for her, Danielle had been living apart from her husband for three months, and felt as if a new life were beginning. "I'm woke up," she told herself. "I no longer am being controlled by him. I don't have to do things against my own will, and be intimidated."

Danielle was at a friend's house when her own face appeared on the local news. Federal agents were looking for her in connection with a major drug-conspiracy indictment. With the help of a friend, Danielle fled to Jackson, Mississippi. A relative who lived nearby took Danielle to church revivals and told her that God would protect her. Danielle chose to believe her.

Carl and Gleneisha stayed with Danielle's mother during the eight months that Danielle spent in Jackson. If she were arrested and they were in her custody, Danielle feared, they would be placed in foster care. Once, friends brought the children to visit. Danielle remembers Carl lying on her chest in his blue-and-white race-car pajamas—Gleneisha's were pink-and-yellow—and asking her if the tiny apartment she had rented was to be their new home.

Danielle told her son she had gotten into trouble; that fixing it might take a while, and they would have to live apart in the meantime. Carl ran to the bathroom and vomited.

The next day, the children went back to New Orleans. Five days later, police knocked on Danielle's door in Jackson.

"I'm so happy you came," she told the officers. "I'm tired. I'd like to get this over with."

After her arrest, Danielle said, investigators told her it was her husband, not her, they were after. If she told them everything she knew, she would go home.

Danielle did not tell the authorities everything she knew. Her lawyer, she said, told her not to worry—they "had nothing on her" and she was likely to be exonerated. Meanwhile, she said, she was hearing that her husband and his associates were more dangerous than she had realized, and she became afraid for herself and her children if she turned state's evidence.

When her trial came around, Danielle took the stand. She was the only one of nine co-defendants—including her husband—to do so. "This is my life," she told her lawyer. "I want them to know what I did." According to prosecutors, her husband had been the leader of a large and violent drug ring. According to Danielle, her own role in it was minor. She wanted to explain that, deal with the consequences, and move on with her new life.

Under mandatory sentencing, the only way to win a sentence reduction is to cooperate with prosecutors in building a case against someone else. The result is that low-level participants, who generally have little information on which to trade, often wind up serving much longer sentences than the "kingpins" for whom the laws were ostensibly intended. According to the U.S. Sentencing Commission, only 11 percent of those in federal prison on drug charges are high-level traffickers. "What passes for a drug king in ninety-nine percent of the cases is nothing more than a young man who can't even afford a lawyer when he's hauled into court. I've seen very few drug kings," one federal judge complained publicly.

What passes for a "drug queen" is even more questionable. Reporters from the *Minneapolis Star Tribune* analyzed some sixty thousand federal drug sentences, examined a hundred and eighty-eight court cases, and interviewed fifty-five women in prisons across the country. Many women, reporter Joe Rigert concluded, are "caught on the fringes of America's war on drugs" and wind up "serving longer prison sentences than the men who organize, lead and supply the organizations." Many are young, nonviolent first-time offenders whose drug-dealing boyfriends or husbands abused them. Many are "too loyal, too fearful or know too little to snitch on the boyfriends, husbands and other men who led them into the drug world." And many wind up with long sentences for minor roles in drug rings led by men.

In Danielle's case, a number of state witnesses received sentence reductions in exchange for their testimony. Today, they are free. "If they're drug dealers and I'm a drug dealer, what makes their life any more worth living than mine, if they say we both did the same thing?" Danielle was left to wonder.

Danielle keeps a "legal bin" in her cell where she stores some of her court documents. She reads and rereads them, underlining inconsistencies, looking for appeal grounds. Her clemency petition is on the desk of the United States Pardon Attorney, and has been for years. "If I didn't think I'd get out, what am I living for?" she asked. "Just my kids? That's the only thing, and I have to think I'm gonna get out, because I love them too much to just say I won't."

While she waits, Danielle places faith in a God-given justice that must inevitably supersede the convoluted laws of man. A decade into her sentence, she sees signs and portents everywhere. Why did her sister Adrian recently move to Stockton, California, just an hour from the prison? "Soon, it's just my thinking, she's going to come get me from here." Why did her two cellmates, as close to her as family, both leave the prison at the same time? "'Cause I'm probably about to leave." Danielle's voice took on a rhapsodic, singsong tone as she spoke of this sustaining faith in the prospect of her own liberation. "Every day I wake up and think, 'This might be my day.'"

Danielle's family shares her conviction that she will one day join them at their table. Adrian writes letters to presidents and attorneys general, and she organizes fund-raisers to finance an appeal. Danielle's mother, Barbara, sets aside her spare change for Danielle's legal fund.

Danielle believes this hope sustains her children as well, but it is also a source of tension and sorrow. Every year, she tells Carl and Gleneisha they will "claim" the coming year to be together as a family. Every time they join her in this ritual, they risk a corrosive disappointment.

"They say you never getting out," Danielle remembers Carl telling her angrily.

"They don't know me," Danielle answered. "They don't know the God I see. Everything happens for a reason."

"Well, what's the reason in this?" Carl asked her. "How do these people explain this, Ma? How do they explain giving you a life sentence? They don't want you ever to do anything else again in life, or to be with your kids?"

In prison, every form of communication, of connection, is rationed. Over the years, the rations have grown stricter. Danielle is permitted to keep twenty-five photographs in her cell. Phone calls are cut off after fifteen minutes. Danielle used to be allowed as many as she could afford; now she is restricted to twenty a month. If she runs out before the month is over, she writes her children frantic letters promising she has not forgotten them and will call again after the first of the month. Visiting, which used to run Thursday through Sunday, was recently cut to three days a week.

Despite these limitations, Danielle and her children describe themselves as close. Danielle encourages Carl to share his raps with her, no matter the language or the content—"I need to know what's inside of him, what he really feels." But she grills him also, the anxiety any mother of a teenager might feel heightened by her own experience, and the distance between them. "Does he work?" Danielle will ask her son, when he mentions a ride in a cousin's car. "How did he get a brand-new

Acura? Think. Think. You're out there. You know better than I do. You have to think about it."

Sometimes, Carl seeks a solace his mother is hard-pressed to provide. "Ma, I want to tell you something," he said when she called to wish him a happy seventeenth birthday. "Do you know I cried every day since you went into prison?"

"Every day?" Danielle asked him. She had not known.

"Don't tell Granny and them," Carl told his mother. "I don't tell everybody how I feel."

In photographs taken in the early years of Danielle's incarceration, Carl looks up at his mother. In recent photos, he looms over her. Carl often balks now as a visit approaches. "You don't think I'm tired of coming to the prison and seeing you in there?" he'll tell his mother over the phone. "I'm a big boy now, Ma. I got hair under my arms. I got a mustache. I practically grew up in that prison. I'm tired of coming there. I've been coming there too long."

The photographs Danielle's family sends her, taken on the outside, evoke mixed feelings for her. "Even with him getting older, and him growing up, I can still see the pain," Danielle said. "I get pictures and I tell people, 'My son is not happy.' They'll say, 'Well, he's smiling.' I say, 'Look at his eyes.' I can see straight through him. That's not the same son I remember."

Danielle's expressions of love for her children are frequent and extravagant within every available medium. Her fear is that no amount of love she can offer via telephone, letter, or weekend visit will be enough to convince her children they have not been abandoned.

"I always tell Carl, 'You can trust me,' " she said. "And he always tells me, 'I know I can trust you, Mom, but you're not here when I really need you.' "

. . .

It was raining hard on the February morning when I visited Carl at the pink, two-story wood-framed house in New Orleans where he lived with his biological father's parents. When he heard me pull up, Carl emerged in his slippers, carrying an umbrella, to escort me from the car.

The spacious four-bedroom home was a grandmother's house, redolent of potpourri and bright with fabric flowers. A needlepoint pillow on the sofa read, GOD CAN'T BE EVERY-WHERE, SO HE INVENTED GRANDMOTHERS. Family photographs covered every available surface. On the living room wall was a portrait of Danielle in a yellow off-the-shoulder gown, a white fur stole, and a double strand of pearls, sporting a 1980s asymmetrical hairdo. She was dressed for the prom. Carl's father was her date.

As soon as I arrived, Carl began sorting through a stack of photographs chronicling his visits to his mother: Danielle, Carl, and Gleneisha standing with their arms around each other before a Christmas tree piled with gifts, the industrial carpet and forced half-smiles the only clue that they were not at home. Gleneisha lying on a bench in the yard of the visiting area in a short plaid skirt and denim jacket, curly red ribbons in her carefully plaited hair. In the most recent photo, from a visit the previous November, Carl and Danielle stood against a fake blue-sky background with their shoulders pressed together. Danielle was in white, smiling; Carl, in black, looked solemn. He was nearly a head taller than his mother.

While Carl went through the photos, his grandfather, Tony Owens, shared his views on local and international politics. It was February 2004, and Tony, a retired structural engineer, had been watching the progress of the war in Iraq on the morning news. An Air Force veteran, he professed himself proud of his country's actions across the globe: "Any time you can stop a dictator from killing innocent people, it's worth every soldier's life, and all the time and money spent." But Danielle's case, he said, had shaken his faith in American ideals.

"You gotta have a case to coincide with the law," he said, stirring a pot of ribs on the stove in the open kitchen. "You can't just say, 'This guy's getting in trouble, we're gonna make an example of him.' That's what they did with Danielle. If you do that, then you're no better than a dictatorship where one man rules. Then other people look at you like they did in the Sixties, when Russia and China told America, 'Until you let a black man ride a bus in Mississippi, don't talk to us about human rights.'

"Me and my grandson, we're gonna get her out some kinda way," Tony said of Danielle, whom he still refers to as his daughter-in-law. "We don't know how and when, but we're working on it."

After Danielle was arrested, Danielle's mother Barbara sent Carl to stay with the Owenses, who live in a quiet neighborhood where Carl's family history was not well known. Danielle's case had been in the news, and the children in Barbara's neighborhood would tease him: "Your mama in jail. Your mama ain't never coming home." Gleneisha went to live with Danielle's sister Adrian.

Carl marks the year he turned twelve as a turning point, the year he put his childhood behind him. That was the year his mother told him the details of her sentence. "I was like, 'Damn, life's not really fair.' And at so young, I felt like I *had* to be serious," Carl said. Being serious meant rescuing his mother.

"Do you have some kind of legal help?" Carl asked Danielle more than once.

"Not that I know of," she answered.

So at twelve years old, Carl concluded that bringing his mother home was his responsibility. He knew his grandparents and his aunts and uncles loved Danielle, too, and would do what they could to help her, he said. "But it's just a different love. I feel like nobody is gonna strive as hard as I am. People love and care, but they wouldn't take it as far as I'm trying to take it. I feel like if I don't do it, it's not gonna get done."

Being serious has also meant keeping to himself. When he was younger, Carl would hide letters announcing events at school, because he didn't want anyone asking him why his mother wasn't there. "I like being quiet and writing raps," he said. "I don't like to talk too much, 'cause all the kids that I'm around—they live the natural life [with their parents], and by me growing up so different, we don't have too much to talk about."

At the time of my visit, Carl was getting ready for a meeting in New York with the rapper Ja Rule. After that, he planned to move to Chicago, where his manager and producer live. Things were happening, he told me repeatedly; this summer would be the one when everything changed.

After some prodding, Carl put in a CD of his music and cued it to the only song he deemed fit for my ears—a melodic rap ballad called "Positive + Positive = Positive."

> *For my kids with no parents at home*
> *My heart goes out to you . . .*
> *Nobody never said life's fair*
> *Money coming real soon, I can taste it in the air . . .*

A few bars into the next song—*If you a nasty broad, holla at me broad*—Carl jumped up and turned off the stereo.

"That's really what sells," he said sheepishly. "But I'd rather do ten positive songs, 'cause I have so much to say about that."

Carl sees Danielle once or twice a year, at Christmas and, when he can get there, on her birthday. The first time he visited, over a year had passed since her arrest. "When I first saw my mother," he said of that visit, "I was crying, but I wasn't hurt. I never really felt like that, so I was confused. Tears are coming out my eyes and I'm happy? My mother explained it to me— 'You're crying 'cause you're happy.' "

Friday visits were Carl's favorite. The prison held a "family day" in the yard, and he could beat his mother at basketball and show her his back flips. Sundays "hurt more than fire—knowing I had to leave at a certain time, and she's not coming with me." As the visiting hours drew to a close, Carl's neck would begin to twitch, or he would find himself falling asleep, as if his body wanted to spare him the imminent parting. Often, Gleneisha would have to physically lead her older brother from the visiting room.

Christmas at FCI Dublin was particularly grueling. Each year there was a tree with presents below it, but beneath the bright paper, the boxes were empty. Carl remembers lining up to sit on the lap of the jailhouse Santa, who would ask each child what he wanted for Christmas. Carl would repeat the same answer he'd heard the children in front of him offer—he wanted his mother home. "You shoulda already knew that," he would scoff as Santa handed him a candy cane, silently adding Santa Claus to the list of authorities who could no longer be trusted.

I asked Carl what kind of mother Danielle was able to be to him from prison. He was silent for a moment, trying to make sense of the question.

"She still the same," he answered, "except that she can't be there physically."

"She encourage me so much to keep going," he elaborated. "I love that about her. Even though she in a negative situation, she's just a positive person. She makes anything feel better when I talk to her."

Carl had recently turned eighteen, and he was anxious to describe the transformation that the birthday had brought with it. For years, he said, he had spent most of his time in his bedroom, sitting on a stool by the stereo, head toward the speaker, rapping and crying. He would smile for photographs, or to reassure his relatives, but rarely sincerely. Now, he said, he felt ready to leave that room and enter the world; to experience happiness and begin his real work.

Carl attributed this change to his deepening relationship with a complex God—one who could be counted on ultimately to provide justice, but also, in the interim, to make injustice tolerable. Ever since he came to understand Danielle's sentence, Carl said, he had been praying not only for his mother's liberation but also for his own; for God to lift the pain that kept him locked inside his room. Soon after his eighteenth birthday, that latter prayer was answered. He was watching BET when it occurred to him that he had allowed himself to become so absorbed in the videos that he forgot, for a moment, about the absence of his mother.

"God is real," he told me. "I know God so real, 'cause everything I be asking for, I get it. I used to ask Him to take it off my mind a little bit, and He took it off my mind a lot, where I could focus on what I had to do, and it didn't really hurt as bad. I don't cry no more. I just know what I gotta do."

Carl's voice took on the same rhapsodic tone his mother's

had when he spoke of his conviction that he would win her freedom. "Just keep rapping. That's the key. I know that's what's
going to bring her home. I been feeling strongly about it, but
now I'm feeling stronger than ever."

In letters, Danielle offers Carl encouragement and something more complicated.

"Did you get to see the Superbowl?" she asked in a letter that
Carl pulled from a bureau drawer so jammed full of years'
worth of communication that he had broken it trying to close it.
"I thought about you when I watched the 1/2 time show . . .
You performing on stage. Every time I see things like that you
come to my mind. Continue to pursue your dreams. You're
going to make it! I guess you can say that we're getting closer to
the day we are always talking about. I can hardly wait! Boy I
want to be home with you guys so bad! Your time is coming.
Mine too!"

Carl and Danielle are both waiting for the day Danielle turns
on the TV in the dayroom and sees her son on BET. He will be
wearing a FREE DANIELLE METZ T-shirt. She will be crying.
Millions of people will be watching. "Who is Danielle Metz?"
they will ask.

As soon as he is famous, Carl told me, "I'm gonna get my
mom. Fly out with lawyers. Let's go do it."

After that?

"Live. Just live. Smile, you know, and really mean it."

"Neisha groovin'," Carl said of his lively little sister, bemused
affection softening his drawl. "She ready for Hollywood. She
so full of life, I don't think it really get to her."

For years, Gleneisha was told that her mother was in the hospital. Rather than asking questions, she took it upon herself to

fill in the details. Her mother, she decided, was having a baby. That the baby never came was just one among many family mysteries. That story has long since crumbled, but Carl believes that his younger sister has not yet replaced it with a full understanding of the truth. When Carl brings up their mother's sentence, Gleneisha insists she never thinks about it, and turns away from him to giggle at her younger cousins' antics.

At thirteen, Gleneisha had the latent glamour, the anticipatory glow, of a pretty girl who was just on the brink of discovering her powers. I saw what Carl meant, but I wondered whether Gleneisha was in fact "groovin' " in exactly the way her brother believed—so caught up in the adventure of her own youth that she had not yet taken in the seriousness of her family situation. If she does not talk about it, it may be because she barely can.

"She tell me she gonna get out and stuff," Gleneisha said of her imprisoned mother, "but ain't nothing happening." There were so many tears behind her eyes that I changed the subject.

Gleneisha was a baby when her parents went to prison. Now, if she wants to know about what life was like when the family was together, she has to ask someone older to tell her a story. The trips to Toys "Я" Us are the stuff of family legend. Gleneisha can conjure the image of a baby doll, but even that may be a well-preserved anecdote rather than a firsthand memory.

Gleneisha is the only one in the family who has no plan of action; who is not saving her change or cultivating her talents in order to free her mother. Carl believes it hasn't hit her yet, but it may also be that she knows what he doesn't: this is the way things are; the way they always have been. The stories her mother tells her in the visiting room—we'll live together in a nice big house one day; we'll travel around the world—are no more or less real to her than the fairy tales of her infancy.

Gleneisha lives in Stockton, California, with her aunt Adrian and Adrian's four grandchildren, whom Adrian has cared for since their mother, Adrian's daughter, was killed by a boyfriend she was trying to leave. Adrian moved the kids from Georgia to Stockton so that Gleneisha could be closer to her mother as she entered her teenage years.

The house where Adrian and the children live in Stockton abuts an empty field. On the other side of the fence are train tracks, and beyond that the silos of an almond-processing plant. Inside, the curtains were drawn over heavily barred windows. Adrian stood at the dining table, her bifocals slipping off her nose as she rifled through a pile of bills. Her voice was hoarse from a cold and she was yelling to compensate.

Adrian works on commission selling home alarm systems. Before her daughter died and she took on her grandchildren, she made three or four thousand dollars a month and was living, she said, "almost the American dream." Now she is lucky to manage a thousand dollars a month in sales during the time the kids are in school. She gets $43 a month in Social Security for each grandchild; her daughter, who was twenty-five when she was murdered, had not worked long enough to earn full benefits. Adrian had to go to court to win the $324 in food stamps she receives each month to feed five children—she was originally denied because the value of her car, which she inherited from her daughter, put her over the resource limit. Her landlord, a pastor who lives next door, gives Adrian staples from the church food bank when she runs low at the end of the month. When she can, Danielle supplements the family income with money she earns at her prison job.

"I didn't really have the luxury of grieving," Adrian said of her daughter's death. "I still haven't grieved, because the kids were right there. Sometimes I feel sad, but I have to keep my composure because they're depending on me. I'm near the breaking point sometimes, but all I do is swallow it and keep going. My greatest prayer is that God would allow Danielle to come home. And I believe when that happens, she will be a big support for me with my grandchildren—that she will help take on the responsibility of caring for them."

One of the least-remarked effects of wholesale incarceration, the anthropologist Donald Braman has observed, is the way both families and communities are weakened when prisoners are forcibly prevented from participating in the reciprocal relationships that form the foundation of family life. "While incarceration forces offenders to answer to the state," he writes, "it also forces them to abrogate their familial and community responsibilities.

"While it is common for family members to help one another out in times of need," Braman notes, "the long-term, open-ended reciprocal relationships that family members have with one another can . . . spread the impact of incarceration so that it touches far more than those imprisoned. Were this something that few families faced, it might be overlooked. But our criminal justice system is pulling millions of families into its orbit, slowly draining them of emotional and material resources."

Several of Danielle's family members described the extended family as "shattered" by Danielle's sentence. Danielle's mother Barbara has eight children, seven of whom have not spent a Christmas with her since Barbara began spending hers with Danielle at FCI Dublin. Danielle has no means of returning to her sister the support she has received from her. She must watch her sixty-seven-year-old mother, who has spent the past thirty-seven years working the late shift at a bakery, postpone her retirement indefinitely so she can help support her grandchildren. She writes her children letter after letter pledging her support, but she will not watch over them as they grow into adulthood, nor will they care for her as she enters old age. The entire cycle of family life will be not just interrupted but obliterated, with even the prospect of restoration officially foreclosed. This is the meaning of triple life.

When Danielle tells her sister she can't stand it any longer, that she thinks of suicide, Adrian is compelled to offer a dreadful comparison. Look at my grandchildren, she tells the sister who is slated to die in prison: their mother is dead already. "Gleneisha still has you," Adrian exhorts Danielle. "Not really there, but you're alive. She can still talk with you. She can still visit. These kids don't have that. Even though you can't be with them physically, and a lot of times emotionally, just knowing that you're alive gives your children hope."

This also is a weight the children of prisoners carry: the burden of being their absent parents' reason for living. Gleneisha has concluded that it is her job to do well in school because it "sort of helps my mother out. It encourages her to go on." Last year, Gleneisha had all A's and B's, except for a C in science. This year, she plans to do better—no more C's—and try out for the track team, because her mother has asked her to get involved with sports.

At the same time, Gleneisha is discovering the limits of long-distance parental authority. When I asked her if she planned to obey her mother's edict that she "just talk" to boys, she made a face like smiling and eating a lemon at the same time, and declined to answer.

If Carl's role in the family is to be serious, gifted—the young messiah who will lead his family to freedom—Gleneisha's has been to remain locked in childhood, the "goofy" one whom no one has to worry about; who consents to believe that her mother is in the hospital, and walks out of the visiting room dry-eyed. But the family understands that Gleneisha can't maintain that stance forever, and her impending adolescence is cause for collective alarm.

Carl has taken Gleneisha's upcoming fourteenth birthday as a deadline to "make something happen where I could take it off her mind and she'll feel better, knowing that something is in progress." Danielle sees the curls pressed into Gleneisha's hair and wishes her daughter had stuck with the colored ribbons a little longer. During a recent visit, Danielle registered an objection to Gleneisha's tight-fitting dress. Gleneisha had dressed up for a Valentine's Day party earlier in the day. Danielle made her keep her jacket on.

"Some of the girls be wearing that stuff," Gleneisha complained later. "She don't really know how it is out here."

Perry Bernard used to be, by his own account, a pretty bad guy. As a young man, Perry used and sold drugs on the streets of New Orleans. There were times when he was certain he would be killed, and others when he feared he would kill someone else. At one point he was arrested thirty times in a single year.

Perry, forty, is Danielle Metz's older brother. When I met him, he was working in New Orleans as the assistant director of a local prisoner-reentry program. He was a small and compact man in black jeans, a tight-fitting black-and-yellow Polo Sport shirt open at the chest, and a gold chain around his neck. He had a couple of gold teeth, and a small scar along the left side of his nose.

A copy of the Urban Institute report on reentry—"From Prison to Home"—sat on his desk, near a mouse pad that had arrived courtesy of *Success* magazine. His office walls were covered with family photographs: his son at a seventh-grade dance; graduating from the eighth grade; his baby granddaughter; Danielle, against the brightly colored fake backdrops that visiting-room photographers make available to spare families the humiliation of posting images of prison interiors on their living room walls. In these photographs, Danielle is heavily made up, her hair carefully styled, an aging prom queen trapped inside a bubble.

In 1989, Perry was stopped by police with twenty-eight grams of cocaine in a satchel. As a habitual offender, he was sentenced to thirteen years in state prison. Perry was a year into his sentence when his dorm was selected to participate in a research project aimed at determining whether a form of "community building" developed by self-help guru M. Scott Peck could work in a prison setting. Perry and the men of Dorm 7 participated in weekly encounter groups that were a hybrid of 1960s-style consciousness raising and 1970s men's revival, complete with "deep sharing" and drum circles.

At first, Perry spent most of the time complaining. But after a few weeks, he stopped his griping and allowed himself to be drawn into the conversation. Eventually, he revealed to the group his own worst secret. Perry had been deep into the drug trade when his wife paged him one afternoon to tell him that their seven-year-old son was having a seizure and turning purple. At the hospital, doctors determined that the boy had ingested PCP. He spent a week in the hospital and only narrowly escaped brain damage. Perry believes a rival poisoned the boy;

that his son nearly died as a direct result of the life his father was living.

Until that day, Perry had been too ashamed to talk about the dangers to which his involvement in the drug trade had exposed his family. Talking publicly about—and taking responsibility for—what had happened was a turning point for Perry.

"I told people all of my life, everywhere I went, that I loved my child," Perry said. "But how can you truly love him if you're in the street? If I didn't change, it was a lie. And I didn't want that to be a lie."

Perry pledged to stay away from drugs in prison and finish his time as quietly as he could. "I wanted to get out there to raise my son, and do things with him, and teach him things," he said. "I knew if I had another chance, I would not come back to prison." At the banquet that marked the end of the community-building sessions, Perry won the award for perfect attendance, and he led the group in singing "Lean on Me," the class anthem. His son accompanied him to the front of the room to accept his award.

Because Perry showed evidence of rehabilitation—and because he had received a sentence which allowed for that possibility—he was granted the second chance he sought. A prison administrator took notice of Perry's calm demeanor and offered him a job as an orderly in the administration building. If he did well, Perry was told, he would be recommended for an early parole. He took the job, excelled at it, and was paroled after five years.

At his parole hearing, Perry recalled, the DA who had prosecuted him warned against his release, calling Perry a "menace" and reminding the parole board of his long criminal history.

Prison officials testified to his rehabilitation. The parole board weighed these opposing views and ruled in Perry's favor.

This kind of conversation—a dialogue, in essence, between representatives of one's past and present selves—will never be held on Danielle's behalf. Because judges have so little leeway under mandatory sentencing, the prosecutor becomes and remains the dominant voice in determining one's fate. Under mandatory sentencing, the person who meets you at your lowest moment—who knows you only as the sum of your offenses—becomes the dominant voice in the only official conversation that will ever be held about who you are and what you might become.

Perry remembers a prison officer warning him on his way out, "We have a bed for you." He has not used it. Keeping his place in his family, he said, has kept him out of prison. Perry left prison in time to raise his son and restore his relationship with his wife. Now he helps care for his baby granddaughter while his son and daughter-in-law work late shifts at a restaurant. When his mother's floor furnace goes out, Perry is the one she calls.

Perry remembers times when he would think about the things he had done and physically shake as the harm he had caused became real to him. He sees his work now as not just helping his clients find work or housing, but also leading them to that place of moral reckoning. He recalled a recent meeting with a twenty-one-year-old who had been picked up with cocaine. The man had a nine-month-old daughter. "Think about your baby," Perry told him. "You don't want people selling her drugs. You could sell drugs to another man, but you've got to realize that's somebody's child."

Prison worked for Perry. It incapacitated him until it rehabilitated him, then released him ready to take his place within his family and the larger society. When Perry was arrested fifteen years ago, the streets were made safer by his absence. Today, they are safer for his presence.

One of the justifications for the move to mandatory sentencing was that an offender who was punished harshly would serve as a powerful example to others. The judge who sentenced Danielle endorsed this vision, telling her and her husband, "I hope that by the sentence you receive, others who might be tempted to follow your path of crime will have second thoughts." The authors of the Continuing Criminal Enterprise statute expressed a similar goal—that the law and its enforcement would "serve as a strong deterrent to those who otherwise might wish to engage in the illicit traffic, while also providing a means for keeping those found guilty of violation out of circulation."

There is no question that Danielle Metz has successfully been kept out of circulation. But more than a decade after she was shipped off—and several decades into the mandatory sentencing craze—are the streets safer for her absence? Are her children, or her neighbors' children, more likely to grow up in neighborhoods free of drugs?

If the answer to these questions were yes, then the adults in Carl's life might have something to offer in response to his questions about the logic of his mother's sentence and the reality of his life. Had her example—and that of the thousands of other drug offenders locked away for long stretches in state and federal prisons—in fact proved an effective deterrent, then Carl might take comfort in the thought that the drug war to which his mother had fallen had made his own world safer.

The problem, however, is that there is little evidence that

long sentences curtail the availability of drugs. In fact, in the years since mandatory minimums were enacted, the drug trade has accelerated rather than diminished. According to government figures, there were 11.4 million illegal drug users in the country in 1992. In 2003—in spite of a near-doubling of the prison population—there were more than 19 million. In 2003, one in six American teenagers was approached by someone offering to sell drugs.

Louisiana currently has the highest incarceration rate in the nation, but that has not translated into safer streets for Carl. New Orleans's per-capita homicide rate was the highest in the nation in 2002 and in 2003. The state ranks sixth in the country for violent crime, and crack and powdered cocaine remain widely available, according to the Drug Enforcement Agency.

Ongoing research by criminologists Dina Rose and Todd Clear indicates that very high incarceration rates may actually make the neighborhoods most impacted by them *more* crime-ridden, by breaking up families, destabilizing communities, and damaging the credibility of the law and its enforcers. The result is that the children of incarcerated parents carry the double burden of both crime and punishment: they are left parentless—unprotected—in neighborhoods where they feel and are unsafe.

A major study by the RAND Corporation concluded that drug treatment is nearly eight times more effective than are mandatory minimums in reducing drug consumption. The million-plus dollars that the government will spend incarcerating Danielle Metz for life would buy a considerable amount of treatment. But the nation has yet to take on this kind of math.

Until we do, Carl is left to his own dizzying calculations: "People get life and they never come out. So you take one of her life sentences back and she still have two. You take another, she still have one. You take another one, she still have twenty years. So I was like, man. It really hit me."

Advocates have begun to call sentences like the one Danielle Metz is serving "death by incarceration." That is the vision I cannot shake: a middle-aged Carl picking up the phone to learn from a stranger that his mother's long confinement has finally ended. Will that be the moment he gives up hope, or will he have let go years earlier of the idea that if he just tries hard enough—earns enough money, garners enough glory, tells her story loudly enough—his mother will one day come home? I imagine him calling his own children, themselves long grown, and telling them he will not be able to keep the promise he has been making ever since they were old enough to ask why Grandma never leaves that building: that she will one day sit down to dinner at their table.

There is the beginning of a sentencing-reform trend afoot in this country, but it is driven less by principle than by fiscal desperation. With nationwide prison expenditures exceeding $50 billion per year, budget crises have inspired more than twenty-five states to reduce sentences, authorize early releases, and shift toward treatment for drug offenders. At least seven states have narrowed or abolished their mandatory sentencing laws. These changes, while welcome, have not been enough to counter the impact of decades of punitive legislation. During the year ending in June 2004, the nation's jails and prisons added nearly fifty thousand new inmates to their previous record totals. State prisons currently operate at an average of 16 percent above capacity, and federal prisons at 39 percent over.

Given the nature of her sentence, Danielle Metz is not likely to join the trickle of prisoners currently being let out the back door in order to cut costs. But even if she were—in two or three decades, say, when the nation's correctional system faces bankruptcy because of geriatric health-care costs—that would not make her sentence any easier to explain to her children. It will not be enough to tell Carl and Gleneisha, "We let your mother out because we got tired of paying for her prescriptions." When a prisoner wins early release because tax revenues are down, her child learns nothing of justice or of mercy. All she learns is, "Mom got lucky."

Where might Danielle Metz and her family be today had the response to her crime included opportunities to pursue her own rehabilitation: counseling to help her deal with the abuse she reported experiencing; vocational training to prepare her to support herself and her children legally; programs that would push her to reckon, as her brother did, with the harm to which she had contributed? How long would it have taken to rehabilitate Danielle; to make reasonably sure she stayed away from the drug trade from then on? These questions not only went unasked but were explicitly foreclosed by the laws under which her future, and her children's, were determined.

I asked Perry what he believed made his case different from Danielle's—why he was free at age thirty and she had no prospect of ever being so. He explained that he had been charged under state law and Danielle under federal; that she received a mandatory sentence and he an indeterminate one. Technical issues aside, he insisted, he would have made a better candidate for a life sentence than his younger sister, based on their respective criminal careers. Statistically speaking, her odds of doing well on the outside are greater: federal offenders with no prior arrest or conviction have a recidivism rate of less than 7 percent.

Like Danielle, Perry has placed his hope for remedy outside the judicial system. "I believe in God," he said. "I know what He's done for me. And I believe with all my heart and soul that the God I serve is a just God. He's going to make you pay for your wrongs, but He's going to make you pay a price consistent with the crime that you committed. So I believe strongly that somewhere down the line, a door is going to open for Danielle. I can't see God allowing her to die in prison."

The psychiatrist Robert Coles has written of the "moral jeopardy" faced by children who must struggle to survive in the face of danger and oppression, and of the remarkable ways in which some children respond by developing a sustaining moral purpose, rather than sinking into depravity in order to survive. For these children, Coles notes, conscience is not eroded by the struggle to get by; rather, it becomes part of their spiritual survival. At the same time, the pressures they face put them at constant risk of losing that sense of purpose and giving themselves over to rage or despair.

A child who loses a parent to illness or accident may lose his faith in God. A child who loses his parent to prison may lose his faith in the state. Carl's family has made sure that he has been well cared for, but the primal experience of being left parentless has created for him a kind of moral jeopardy to which several of his relatives alluded, even as they reminded me—as Carl himself did more than once—of what a good person he had grown up to be.

When Carl raps, Perry observed—the bitter songs that Carl would not play for me; that he told me he writes because they sell—"you can hear the anger. He doesn't realize that it's anger."

"Sometimes I can see it in his eyes," Perry said of his nephew—"he wants to fight the system for his mom. But you can't fight them by cursing at them and threatening them. You fight them by doing what's right, and making opportunities for yourself. And when you get these opportunities, you take advantage, and you remember that you got something to live for. You've got to live for Mama."

Venting his feelings through music, Perry believes, allows Carl to hold on from one day to the next. "But smart kids make bad decisions," Perry said. "If Danielle doesn't come home soon, Carl might make some bad decisions."

"As a nation," the psychologist Jerome Bruner has warned, "we could eventually be more deeply injured socially by mass imprisonment than by moderate crime. For imprisonment amplifies the alienation that so often fuels crime, particularly when imprisonment is so racially imbalanced."

The children of African American prisoners—whose parents are overrepresented at every step of the criminal justice process—face particular challenges as they develop their relationship with the state and the law. Blacks make up 12 percent of the general population but more than half of the prison population. They comprise 14 percent of the nation's illegal drug users—and use drugs at a rate similar to that of whites—but make up 74 percent of the nation's drug prisoners. At the federal level, mandatory minimums have exacerbated racial disparities in sentencing. Over the past two decades, the average sentence for whites has doubled; for blacks, it has tripled. Disparities have been documented even at the level of plea deals with prosecutors: whites who provide prosecutors with "substantial assistance" have their sentences reduced, on average, by twice as much as blacks who do the same.

The net result of these multiple disparities is that black children are nine times more likely than white to have an incarcerated parent. Nearly one in eight African American children has a parent behind bars today.

Racial disparities are far from invisible to children. Literature from the New York–based Osborne Association offers caregivers advice on how to answer children's most frequently asked visiting-room questions, including, "Why are there so many black people in prison?" Because prisons are frequently sited in mostly white rural counties, children are also forced to ponder the question of why so many of their black and brown parents' keepers are white—often while they themselves are being searched by white guards.

"The perception and reality of double standards," observes the legal scholar David Cole,

> contributes to the crime problem by eroding the legitimacy of the criminal law and undermining a cohesive sense of community. As any wise ruler knows (and many ineffective despots learn), the most effective way to govern is not through brute force or terror, but by fostering broad social acceptance for one's policies. Where a community accepts the social rules as legitimate, the rules will be largely self-enforcing. . . . The rules will be accepted, and community pressure to conform will be effective, only to the extent that "the community" believes that the rules are just and that the authority behind them is legitimate.

I asked Carl whether he had respect for the law.

"I respect them 'cause I know they could get away with stuff I can't," he said. "They can do anything they want."

. . .

IN BROOKLYN, DISTRICT ATTORNEY Charles J. Hynes greeted
me with a burst of prosecutorial bluster: "Are you one of those
finky liberals? Because I put lots of people in prison, young
lady!"

Hynes has been Kings County district attorney for more
than fifteen years, and he has developed the gruff and jocular air
of the grandfather at once admired and indulged. On the day I
met him, this image was enhanced by a three-piece suit with a
blue handkerchief folded neatly into the pocket and an American flag pin on the lapel.

If Hynes feels compelled to assert his law-and-order creden-
tials in dress as well as in demeanor, that may be because he is an
elected official who has developed and championed a constellation of programs that give virtually every illegal drug user in
Brooklyn the opportunity to stay out of jail or prison. Like increasing numbers of states and counties across the country,
Brooklyn has programs that divert low-level drug offenders
from jail to treatment. But Hynes has also pioneered the Drug
Treatment Alternative-to-Prison (DTAP) program, which
steers so-called predicate felons—those with serious priors,
who would otherwise be facing long prison terms under the
Rockefeller laws, New York's notoriously harsh mandatory
sentencing laws—away from prison and into drug treatment.

"We're the people who are generally saying, 'This person
needs to go to prison,' " observed Anne Swern, counsel to the
district attorney and one of the architects of DTAP. "Now
we're saying, 'No, this person doesn't need to go to prison. He
needs to be rehabilitated, because we think that's going to make
Brooklyn safer.' "

The DTAP model could not be more different from that of

mandatory sentencing, but the goal is identical: to rid the streets of drugs. The DA's office was motivated to start DTAP by the mounting evidence of its own failure to achieve this goal. New York State's prison population had doubled during the 1980s, and the proportion of prisoners who were there for drug felonies increased more than fourfold, but the crack and heroin trades were booming.

"We were incarcerating the same people over and over again, and even if they were incapacitated for that period of time—if their drug use got reduced or even eliminated in prison—they'd come back out and do the exact same thing," Swern said. "They'd continue to commit crimes, and it was bad for the community. We had to respect the community's desire not to have drugs on their street corner, or in the apartment down the hall."

Established in 1990, DTAP targets the hard cases—repeat felons with an average of five prior drug arrests and four years behind bars. Participants are offered a deferred sentence if they agree to spend fifteen to twenty-four months in a residential treatment program. If they succeed in treatment, the charges against them are dismissed. If they flee, a special warrant team goes after them and they face long prison sentences under the Rockefeller laws.

The National Center on Addiction and Substance Abuse at Columbia University spent five years evaluating DTAP. Participants, they found, were 87 percent less likely to return to prison than were drug offenders who simply did time. Ninety-two percent were employed after graduating from DTAP, compared with 26 percent before they entered. The DA's own analysis found that the cost savings in corrections, health care, public assistance, and recidivism, combined with the tax revenues generated by DTAP's more than seven hundred graduates, have totaled nearly 26 million dollars over the program's life span.

Eager not to be mistaken for finky liberals, Hynes and his prosecutors emphasize the role of the warrant team in making sure this savings is achieved at no cost to public safety: those who ditch treatment are back before a judge in an average of twelve days. The stick is there in the DTAP model, but it is brandished judiciously rather than wielded with abandon. The real public-safety value comes not from those who fail at treatment and are sentenced to prison, but from the majority who make it, and walk away from their encounter with the criminal justice system less likely to use or sell drugs—an outcome that prison alone rarely achieves.

"The next time a politician tells you that there's a jail solution to drugs, don't listen to them, because they're treating you like a child," Hynes said. "The more people you can divert, distract, take out of the criminal justice system, the better you are for it."

As soon as an individual is accepted into DTAP, members of the warrant team go out and interview his family members in order to get a sense of where he might go if he winds up absconding, and to enlist the family's support in keeping him from doing so. One of the things they hear most from children, said Brooklyn prosecutor Dave Heslin, is "Don't let Daddy come back if he's still using."

DTAP not only offers children much better odds than prison does of getting their parents back clean, and prepared to stay that way; it also allows them to witness and participate in a parent's transformation. Rather than being subject to the chaos and humiliation of a prison visit, children are able to spend time with their parents in a safe and orderly place where they and their parents are treated with respect. "For children, seeing is believing," said Swern. "They start to believe that maybe Daddy's gonna get better."

DTAP also reassures children, Swern believes, by modeling the kind of consistent "parenting" that children of drug abusers may lack at home. Drug addiction, she observed, often leads to "uneven parenting. Sometimes the parent's screaming at the kid when he did everything right and made his bed and did his homework. Then that kid could not go to school for three weeks, but if the father's on a binge, he's not going to be parenting the kid at all."

The traditional criminal justice system inadvertently mimics the drug-addicted parent. Because enforcement is spotty, children watch their parents "get away" with any number of illegal acts; then, when the hammer does fall, it does so with brutal force. DTAP models both consistent enforcement and reasonable consequences.

The DTAP model has been picked up by a handful of other prosecutors, and Hynes believes it will spread further. But he is also aware of the force of the tide he is trying to buck. On his wall is a blueprint for the Regina Drew House—named after his mother—an as-yet-unbuilt facility that would allow women to be diverted from prison and live under the same roof as their children while they received drug treatment and job training. Hynes believes such a facility would leave an intergenerational legacy. Many juvenile offenders have lost their own parents to prison, he observed; children who went with their mothers to the Regina Drew House would have a shot at avoiding that trajectory.

So far, however, the facility remains a sketch on the DA's office wall. "If this were a prison, it would already be called the Charles Hynes Correctional Facility," and it would be standing, Hynes grumbled, waving at the drawing. "They love to build prisons. But I can't get any money from the legislature to build this thing."

The Phoenix Career Academy is housed in a converted paint factory a fifteen-minute walk from the district attorney's office. The building is beautifully restored and literally transparent: Huge panels of glass fill the brick archways on the ground floor, the watchful eye of the community taking the place of locks and bars.

Phoenix Academy is home to 240 drug users, many of them referred by DTAP. It is a treatment facility and also a vocational institute: residents spend six hours a day studying carpentry, building maintenance, counseling, office skills, or culinary arts.

On the day I visited, Phoenix Academy was a hive of industry. In one room, a teacher was shouting instructions about pipes and plumbing as a cluster of students gazed attentively at a model of a toilet. In another, carpentry students were building a miniature house from the ground up. Counseling students sat in shirt and tie at long tables as an instructor paced among them, talking about stumbling blocks and personality types. The building also houses a small gym, a dining hall, a medical clinic, and a dental clinic. The services of this last facility are in such demand that a dental surgeon is in all day every Saturday just pulling teeth.

Like all "therapeutic communities"—the treatment model to which Phoenix Academy subscribes—the program is tightly structured. Residents must sign in and out of each floor and keep to a tight daily schedule; behavior is carefully monitored and small infractions vigorously policed. The result is that the facility evokes a boarding school, or a naval vessel—not luxurious, but very well kept.

The world outside is messier, rife with bullying bosses, disdainful bureaucrats, and smoothly persuasive drug peddlers. The homes to which many residents will return are riddled with sand traps as well: mistrustful wives and girlfriends; resentful teenagers; children who mock newly returned parents' authority and babies who cry when they try to pick them up. Any of these could easily become a "trigger" for a return to crime and drug use, and much of the work done at Phoenix Academy is aimed at preparing participants for the pitfalls that await them once they return home to their families.

"When our clients are addicted, there's a lot of shame and guilt and broken promises, which makes more shame and guilt, which translates into continued drug use," said Phoenix Career Academy Director Fred Cohen. Ten years earlier, Cohen himself was a DTAP client. Before that, he was a street addict and small-time dealer so desperate that, by his own account, he stole his mother's toaster.

His drug use caused his mother so much distress, Cohen recalled, that her blood pressure would rise dangerously. He responded to the suffering he was causing his family in a manner he has since come to see as entirely predictable: "When you hurt someone you love, it forces you to get higher, so you don't feel that pain."

A tall, thin black man with a pencil mustache, Cohen was—like everyone at Phoenix Academy—impeccably groomed and painstakingly polite. A round table in his office was draped with a red tablecloth and set with carafes of coffee and a plate of chocolate doughnuts. Cohen bobbed in his seat as he spoke, shaking his head and smiling wryly at the self he had, with the aid of DTAP, left behind. When he entered the program eleven years earlier, at the age of twenty-five, he had been using crack for a decade and was facing a four-and-a-half-to-twelve-year sentence as a repeat offender. That prospect, he said, is what kept him in treatment long enough to begin genuinely wanting to be there.

Phoenix Academy staff, Cohen said, are trained to treat clients' families as the "extended patient." They offer family counseling and weekend programs, where family members attend seminars aimed at helping them understand the phases of addiction and recovery. When clients begin going out on weekend visits with their families, Phoenix Academy staff are there to debrief them when they get back.

Because DTAP clients generally have years or decades of addiction and incarceration behind them, the families to which they return are often fragmented and fragile.

James, forty, had been at Phoenix Academy for six months. He told me his goal upon his release was to "be there" for his children; "to be the responsible father that I'm supposed to be." I asked him how many children he had. He paused for a moment and counted out loud.

James's five children range in age from seven to twenty, and they have three different mothers. "I know I don't know them," he said. "I've been in jail. It would be foolish of me to say I know them."

James's oldest daughter is away at college now. They speak on the phone sometimes, but when James tells her he loves her, she never reciprocates. "It's a hurting feeling," he said, "but it's my fault. I did that."

Alicia, twenty-one, had been at Phoenix Academy for seventeen months, and she was slated to leave as soon as she secured the secretarial job for which she had been training. She was ready, she said, for a house with a white picket fence, where her children could play in the yard. But she also had to deal with the fact that her two daughters were in the care of her aunt, who did not trust Alicia's recovery and was reluctant to let her see the children; that the first time she visited, her then two-year-old did not recognize her. "That's Mama," her older daughter instructed the younger—"Mama Alicia."

According to Cohen, it is crucial that clients face the damage they have done their families and begin working to repair it, while they are still in treatment rather than later, when an encounter with an angry spouse or disappointed child can be enough to send them running for the nearest street dealer. The program stresses learning parenting skills and rebuilding bonds, but also what Cohen called "reality therapy."

" 'You were away for ten years,' " Cohen might tell a client who returned from a home visit furious that his children were calling their mother's new boyfriend "Dad." " 'Your seat at the helm is taken. That is what is, and rightfully so.' Then we help him figure out where he fits in the picture."

3

VISITING

SUSANA DOES NOT REMEMBER ever seeing her father free. She recalls touching him only once, an embrace from which police forcibly removed her. He has never been able to feed or shelter his daughter, nor to protect her from the lifetime's worth of hurts she has accrued in her fifteen years. Yet he remains the most important person in her life, the one person she knows loves her—the only real parent she has.

Susana's dad is at San Quentin State Prison, serving twenty-one years to life under California's "Three Strikes" sentencing law. Having been caught with stolen property, and not for the first time, he has been determined by the court to be of no further use to society. But he matters to Susana. From the scraps of contact she has been granted over the years—a drawerful of letters, a few dozen collect calls, and intermittent visits—she has built herself a father.

The first time I met Susana, she was locked up in juvenile hall in San Jose, California, right next door to the county jail where she had come to know her father during sporadic visits over the course of nearly a decade. She was a pretty, broad-faced girl with wide-set brown eyes, a chipped front tooth, and long reddish-brown hair that draped over her oversized county-issue sweatshirt. In a glassed-in interview room with white cinder-block walls and a concrete floor, Susana spoke at length about the dad who spent most of her childhood in the place she referred to only as "next door."

"My dad's *handsome,* "she said, straightening in her chair. "I wish I had pictures of him. He has my face, with a mustache and thicker eyebrows, and then his hair is shaved in the back, shaved on the sides, and he slicks it back with gel."

Susana's father has told her stories about early days together, when he was free and she was small and he would pick her up and take her places; carry her in his arms. Susana can't recall a single image from that time. Her memories of her father start when she was five or six years old. Her grandmother would retrieve her from the foster home where she spent most of her childhood and take her downtown to see her dad.

"We had to wait in a waiting room for a really long time," Susana remembers, "and when we finally got in, he was behind glass and you had to talk on a phone." Susana's foster mother had discouraged her from mentioning or seeing her father or her mother—who was also in and out of jail—and so, with the natural narcissism of a small child, she assumed the conventions of the visiting room existed to obstruct her in particular: "I figured they were trying to keep us apart, and that's why there was glass and a telephone, and we couldn't touch each other."

Within a few years, Susana figured out where her father was, and why he was there. He, like her mother, was addicted to drugs—cocaine and later heroin—and stole in order to sustain his habit. As a result, he spent most of Susana's life in and out of jail ("mostly in"). Susana has moved from one place to another over the years, and her father has not always been able to reach her. When he does, he asks questions no one else does, such as "Have you done your homework?"

The man she has come to know in the visiting room is an affectionate, clownish dad, one who revels in teasing, and being teased by, his mischievous daughter; who expresses his love for her openly and likes to offer stern advice that Susana values but also mockingly dismisses.

"As the years went on, our relationship got closer and closer. He'd be trying to tell me what to do, and I'd say, 'OK, Dad, I'll do it,' but I'd be thinking to myself, 'What can *you* do about it?'

"His love for me helps me," Susana said, "and his support, the way he tells me, 'Don't end up like this, you shouldn't be in gangs, you should be going to school and getting an education.' That helps me in a lot of ways, but I ask myself sometimes, 'Why couldn't he do it for him?' "

When Susana was thirteen, her foster mother threw her out and she went to live with her grandmother. That was the year she saw her father for the first and last time without a wall of glass between them. His brother had died of cirrhosis of the liver, and he was permitted to attend the funeral. Susana and her boyfriend went out and bought him a suit for the funeral, new shoes, and a shaving kit. But he arrived at the funeral home shackled at the hands, feet, and waist, accompanied by guards and police. The gifts Susana had bought stayed in the bag, and her father stayed in his prison jumpsuit.

"When he came in the room, he didn't look at any of us," Susana recalled. "He just went straight to the coffin and he was praying there. Finally he looked at us, but he wouldn't look us in the eyes. One of my aunts asked, 'Can we hug him?' The police officer said, 'You know that's against procedure, but go ahead.' I got to hug him first, and I was hugging him for a while, and then he went on and hugged everyone else. Then he came to me and hugged me again, and that time I didn't want to let go. A police officer literally had to pull me off him. He actually restrained me, put my hands behind my back. After they took my dad, the police officer finally let go of me.

"I knew it was procedure and I should have gotten off of him when they told me to. But I just wanted to hold him, because I knew that would probably be the last time I'd ever hug him, kiss him, anything."

The first time Susana went to juvenile hall, she had been charged with auto theft and evading police after she borrowed a friend's car without permission, then crashed it into a pole trying to avoid the police. She was released to her aunt on house arrest, with an electronic monitoring bracelet around her ankle. Not long after, she said, she and her aunt got into an argument and her aunt locked her out, causing her to violate her house arrest. She'd been sent back to juvenile hall to await placement in a group home.

Susana is an athletic girl—loves swimming, boxing, lifting weights—with plans to finish high school, join the Navy, go to college, and become a professional bodybuilder, and her confinement was making her crazy with impatience and worry. She hated the idea of her father finding out where she was, but hated even more that she had no way of keeping in touch with him—incarcerated minors are not allowed to write to, or receive letters from, adult prisoners, even if those prisoners are their parents. That Father's Day was around the corner only made matters worse: Susana usually sends her father a card with a money order and handwritten verses from the Bible; he writes her back with his interpretation of the scriptures she's chosen. This year, their mutual incarceration would preclude this ritual.

Once she was released from juvenile hall, Susana would be transferred to a group home and would be permitted to correspond with her father, but the odds of someone taking her to see him were slim.

The last time Susana saw her father had been eight months earlier, the day after he was sentenced for his third strike. Susana went to visit him in the county jail, where he was awaiting transfer to state prison. *"Mija,"* he told her, "this might be the last time I'll see you in a while, but keep strong and don't let nothing get to you. Don't let this get to you, either."

Susana left the visiting room in tears and entered a hallway flanked by rows of cells. Often, when she would visit her father, other prisoners would whistle at her from their cells. This time, she heard someone counting quietly: "One, two, three. . . ." Then a chorus of male voices: "Don't cry, *mija*. We'll take care of your *papi* for you."

Susana knew right away her crazy father had somehow orchestrated the performance. She laughed so hard she found she was no longer crying. "I was like, oh my God, my dad is *too much.*" She told the story with a blush of pleasure at the quintessential adolescent experience of being embarrassed by her dad.

Susana has counted the years her father is likely to serve—eighteen at a minimum—over and over in her head, and she can tell you without hesitation how old they will both be when he gets out (thirty-three and sixty-two), but she's a little unclear about what the span of years will actually entail.

"I'll still be in college when he gets out, I think . . ." she speculated vaguely, counting out loud the years she'd spend in the

Navy, the years in school. She has agreed to wait until his release to get married—or marry on prison grounds, if he is allowed weekend "trailer visits" and she can borrow the chaplain—so he can be there to give her away. "He wants to be that person, you know? So I promised him."

Susana doesn't have too many other adults who want to be "that person" in her life. Like many children of incarcerated parents, Susana has bounced from one caregiver to another and been separated from her siblings. Her aunt and her grandmother won't take her calls now that she is locked up; she has no interest in maintaining a relationship with her former foster parents and no idea where her mother is. The last time Susana saw her mother was a couple of years ago, when she ran into her on a bus. Her mother didn't recognize her.

"I'm your daughter," Susana called out.

"Which one?" her mother asked.

In the face of this vacuum, the man Susana cannot, for the moment, write to, speak with, or touch—the man who will be behind bars until she is in well into adulthood—is the sustaining figure in Susana's life. She has no idea when she will see him next.

Prison visits matter. Children and parents will tell you again and again how important it is that they see each other, and research backs them up. Consistent, ongoing contact reduces the strain of separation, lowers recidivism, and is the single most important factor in determining whether a family will reunify after a prison term.

In a poem written at a prison-based summer camp for prisoners and their children, a young girl captured both her own sense of vulnerability in her father's absence, and the security she drew from the contact she was able to have with him.

> *911 emergency*
> *It's a bad man who's hurting me*
> *And my father here to rescue me*
> *Now it's OK he saved me*
>
> *I always know*
> *That my dad will love me so*
> *With that in mind*
> *I don't care about him serving time*

A much-cited 1972 study of California prisoners found that those who had regular visits were six times less likely to reenter prison during the first year out than those who had none. These findings, wrote researchers Norman Holt and Donald Miller, suggest that "it might be well to view the inmate's family as the prime treatment agent and family contacts as a major correctional technique." This report was commissioned by the California Department of Corrections, which recently responded to budget difficulties by cutting visiting days from three or four to two—driving some families to spend the night in their car outside prison gates to secure a place in line for scarce visiting slots.

Subsequent research has bolstered Holt and Miller's conclusions. In a 2000 review of the literature, Terry Kupers, M.D., found "little if any contrary argument and conflicting data to the general principle that the better the quality of visitation throughout a prisoner's incarceration, the better the effects on the prisoner, his or her post-release adjustment, the family of the prisoner and the community."

Nationwide, however, the trend has been to curtail rather than create opportunities for family contact. In 1978, according to a study by the National Council on Crime and Delinquency, 92 percent of incarcerated mothers received visits from their children. By 1999, fewer than half of parents in state prison had received even a single visit from their children. Another survey found that among those children who were able to visit their incarcerated parents, three-quarters did so less than once a month.

As increasing numbers of prison facilities are built in remote rural areas, more and more prisoners are held at prohibitive distances from their families. More than 60 percent of parents in prison are held more than one hundred miles from home. In California, more than 5,000 of the state's approximately 7,400 incarcerated mothers are held in two facilities in the remote rural town of Chowchilla, eight hours away from the urban centers of Northern and Southern California where the great majority of their children live. In New York state, the main institution for women lies about four hundred miles from New York City. For federal prisoners, who may be shipped anywhere in the country, distance is an even greater obstacle: nearly half the parents in federal institutions are held more than five hundred miles from home.

An early visit can reassure a child that his parent is not confined in the storybook dungeon of his imagination; that she is alive and has not abandoned him by choice. But new arrestees often must wait several days to be "processed" before they can receive visits in local jails.

These county jails generally allow only the kind of window

visits Susana described. The deprivation and humiliation a wall of glass evokes is visited on those on either side of the glass, each of whom will likely experience herself as walled off, walled in—jailed. Children will bang their fists or even heads against the glass in an effort to break through.

Denise Johnston—the director of the Center for Children of Incarcerated Parents in Pasadena, California—recalled a seven-year-old who was so confused by seeing her jailed mother behind glass that when her mother called the day after a visit, the little girl asked her, "Are you dead?" Another service provider described a toddler who sobbed so desperately after seeing his mother behind glass, and for so long, that he wound up in the emergency room.

For babies and small children, window visits are more than unsatisfying; they are largely incomprehensible. "Touch is more than just a nice thing for your relationship," said Dr. Barbara Howard, associate professor of pediatrics at the Johns Hopkins School of Medicine and co-director of the Center for Promotion of Child Development Through Primary Care. "It is basic to the nurturing process. If you're talking about children under a year of age, your main means of communication is touch. A baby looking through a plate of glass at his incarcerated mother would really be looking at his reflection in the window, not making a connection with the parent at all."

Once parents are released, Dr. Howard noted, "if they don't have a good relationship with the child, then their ability to take care of the child and have the child be responsive to them will be much diminished. If there were no bodily contact, I would expect no relationship at all with young children."

Melinda went three months without touching her children. Undoing the damage took longer. She was in the county jail for credit fraud at the time. The thought of her small boys sitting in plastic chairs, shoulder to shoulder with other visitors, gaping at her through the glass, was too much for her—and, she feared, for them—so she chose to forgo visits altogether. "Every time I want to hug you, I have to go to your picture," her six-year-old told her when she called home.

When Melinda was transferred to a special mother/child facility where she could be with her children, she couldn't wait to hold them. The reunion was not as she had imagined it. "When they came the first time, it was so sad," she recalled. "They just looked, and they smiled, but they were afraid to come touch me. I grabbed them and held them for a long time, but they were stiff, like I was a stranger."

Donna Willmott's daughter was four years old when Willmott went to prison for two years on conspiracy charges related to her involvement with the Puerto Rican independence movement. Now the family advocacy coordinator at Legal Services for Prisoners with Children in San Francisco, Willmott spent her first weeks behind bars in solitary confinement. During that time, she was permitted only window visits. Her husband came twice a week, but Willmott asked him not to bring their daughter.

"I was desperate to see her, but I didn't want to put her through that," Willmott said. "If you put a glass barrier between a child and a parent, it's crazy-making for the children. They feel they can't get to the person they love—there's this wall between them that they don't understand. It's almost like putting the parent in a box. The message children get is, 'Your mother is so bad you can't touch her. She's dangerous.'"

State and federal prisons generally offer contact visits, but those visits are rarely structured with a child's needs in mind.

Visitors often wait outside in line for hours, sometimes without access to bathrooms. Children may undergo a pat search or even a "diaper peek." They and their guardians must adhere to dress codes that vary from institution to institution and include vague prohibitions such as nothing that is "emotionally enticing to the inmate." Visitors who violate a dress code, often unwittingly, can be turned away.

Visitors must be approved before they are allowed to enter a prison, a process that can take several weeks. Some states require an original copy of a child's birth certificate, and a certified copy of a court order establishing a guardian's authority, before that guardian can bring a child to visit. New caregivers are unlikely to have these documents on hand, and obtaining them means paying money and taking time off from work. Children who lack these documents get turned away at the gate—as do those who are wearing the wrong clothes, have not been approved, or lack acceptable identification.

In their grandmother's living room in San Jose, California, sisters Kimara, Keneshia, and Kenyatta squabbled and giggled together until their grandmother gently steered the conversation to the topic of their incarcerated mother. "We were able to visit our mom only one time," thirteen-year-old Kimara volunteered. "The next time we went, they told us you have to have a birth certificate. Not the copy but the original. And so we didn't get to see her."

Kenyatta, nine, had been playing with the volume on her Walkman, retreating from the conversation. Now she took off her headphones. Being turned away, she said, "didn't feel good, because the first time we went to see her she was hugging us and kissing us and talking about how it felt in jail." Kenyatta made a choking sound, a tearless sob that quieted the room.

"You see?" said her grandmother. "Kids still hurt, for a long time."

Children who do manage to see their incarcerated parents must run a gauntlet of obstacles and humiliations in order to do so. They typically drive long distances, then stand in line to spend a few hours in overcrowded, noisy visiting rooms in which toys and even baby blankets may be forbidden. Food and drink are limited to the salty or sugary snacks available from vending machines.

"Visiting my mother in jail was no treat to me," said Lorraine, who remembers watching prison staff crumble to pieces a cake her grandmother had baked. "My stomach would hurt. I had to stand in long lines in the cold, only to get searched like a criminal. I hated that someone could tell me how long I could see my mother. Not being able to hug her was a horrible feeling. Every time I went up there, I left in tears."

Just as the child of an arrestee may perceive himself also to have been arrested, visiting children sample the menace of incarceration. Inside a juvenile-hall visiting room, I watched a little girl in overalls scamper across a scuffed linoleum floor. From time to time, she cast shy glances at a young woman who slouched in a too-small plastic chair, playing gin rummy with a tired-looking older woman who held a baby in her lap. A guard with a ring of keys at his belt joked to the little girl that he'd lock her up if she didn't settle down. She ran back to huddle beside the baby in her grandmother's lap.

"The heart of locking somebody up is the deprivation of love and touch," Denise Johnston observed. "The way you disempower people is to strip away all human contact." Intended for prisoners, this aspect of punishment falls heavily on children. In many facilities, physical contact—a small child's primary source of comfort and reassurance—is jealously rationed. Some facilities place an age limit on sitting on a parent's lap, so that a birthday celebration includes breaking the news that dad's lap is now off-limits. In some, a "brief embrace and kiss" at the beginning and end of a visit may be all that is permitted. Parents are required to enforce this regulation—which is to say, to push their children away.

The ritual humiliations that comprise most children's visiting experiences are justified in the name of security—necessary to guard against drugs in the diaper, or razor blades in a child's shoes. In fact, there is evidence that consistent visitation *enhances* security by motivating prisoners to follow the rules. Conditions that discourage visiting, it follows, might well pose a security threat.

A report to the Florida state legislature—which commissioned a study of prison security—contained this illuminating finding: while nearly half of all corrections officers believed that most contraband came from visitors, only 2.5 percent of contraband incidents statewide were in fact attributable to visitors.

"Security measures which are overzealously applied, result in only a small improvement in institutional safety and which extract a huge toll in disenfranchising families must be revisited and reevaluated," the report's authors concluded.

A prison visiting room is, despite everything, a repository of miracles. Inside these crowded, barren spaces, parents and children build a tent of intimacy that shelters and unites them. In the hours allotted, they struggle mightily to hold on to their connection and draw what they need from each other. When they succeed, they not only make a prison term more bearable for those on both sides of the wall; they allow families to sustain themselves, and pave the way for reunification.

Ida McCray did not see her children once during the first year and a half of her incarceration, because her mother did not have a car and was unable to bring them. "I experienced so much pain in not being able to see my children, it almost killed me," McCray said. "It feels like a piece of you has been torn off and you don't know where it is. I needed to see how my children looked. Were they OK? Were they cold? Not being able to see that made me feel less human. I felt less caring, because I couldn't care for who I really wanted to care for."

McCray went through the phone book and wrote letters to every church she could find until someone wrote back and volunteered to bring her children. When she first saw her kids in the visiting room, McCray recalled, she counted their fingers and toes as she had when they were born, to assure herself they were safe and intact. "Those visits we had were the most precious things I had to live for," she said. "It's like that first look they give you after they are born, except you get to see it twice. You think, 'This is it. This is enough.' My kids gave me a means and a reason to live and not be as awful as I could be."

McCray's son Jundid was three years old when his mother was arrested for her involvement in a sixteen-year-old airline hijacking. He was thirteen when she was released. In the grassy front yard of the San Pablo, California, home where he lived with his mother and grandmother, a sprinkler arced through the dusk as Jundid, then seventeen, tried to describe a decade of parenting measured in four-hour increments.

"We made the most of each visit that we had," said Jundid. "My mom was very special about trying to give time to each child. Like for my sister, she would sit there and braid her hair while she had her little private time to talk to her. I remember she used to teach me karate. I'd show her my muscles, even though I didn't have any. But just me being relaxed and having fun with my mother is what I remember most.

"I couldn't even begin to express to you in words," he continued solemnly, "how fulfilling that was to my soul to give my mother a hug. For her to give me a kiss. For me to sit on her lap. And for me to not do that—I would have felt very empty then, as a child, and maybe as well now."

If visiting a parent in prison is a difficult experience, young people will tell you, the alternative is worse. Will, eighteen, grew up in foster care while both of his parents were in and out of prison. He was granted a single visit with his incarcerated mother when he was ten years old, then did not see her again until he was a teenager.

"If there had been some time set up where I could talk to my mom consistently on a one-on-one basis, I think my life would be completely different," said Will, whose tendency to "blow up" took him through thirty foster homes and six group homes before he turned eighteen. "Just knowing I had a mother that cared. Even if it was fake, it would have helped to know that someone is there. You're livin' life solo, but there's a mother out there that you came from."

Phone contact could provide a partial answer to the challenges posed by prison visitation, but prison phone systems are structured in such a way as to make telephone contact prohibitively costly for families, and excruciatingly difficult for children.

Calls are typically limited to fifteen minutes, and several young people described the knot that formed in their stomachs as they tried to share a week's or month's worth of news with a parent while keeping one eye on the clock; the sense of loss and abandonment that was reawakened each time the phone cut off. Calling repeatedly is rarely an option, as families are charged a "connection charge" to initiate each fifteen-minute call.

Prisoners cannot take incoming calls and typically can place only collect calls. Recipients are charged exorbitant rates—as much as twenty times that of standard collect calls—under arrangements in which phone companies pay huge fees to prison systems in return for exclusive contracts. California nets more than $35 million each year in phone-company commissions—money that the state deposits in its general fund, creating what is essentially a special tax burden on the families of inmates. New York collects more than $20 million annually. These windfalls—as well as those the phone companies themselves stand to gain—are drawn directly from the pockets of prisoners' families. In Florida, the legislature found, families subsidized the Department of Corrections to the tune of nearly $50 million a year through collect calls, food purchased in the visiting room, and money sent to inmates' canteen funds.

Many families have their phones disconnected within the early months of an incarceration. Those who do manage to keep current with the phone bill must cut corners in already-tight budgets in order to do so. When, as is often the case, the person paying for a prisoner's collect calls is the same one who is caring for her children, the cost of these calls takes food from children's mouths.

Restrictions such as those on telephone calls are generally perceived, and justified, as simply part of the punishment incarceration comprises, part of the "price you pay" for breaking the law. But prisoners are for the most part *prevented* from paying this price themselves; it is family members who pick up the bill.

Elizabeth Gaynes, director of the New York prisoner support organization the Osborne Association, carries a telling souvenir: a key chain adorned with miniature handcuffs, given her by a telephone-company representative whom she encountered at an American Correctional Association convention.

"If you could make criminals pay for their own incarceration, wouldn't you want to do that?" the rep had asked, assuming Gaynes worked for a corrections department, and launching into his sales pitch. "Well, we have a collect-call system through which criminals support the cost of incarceration instead of taxpayers."

"A collect-call system?" Gaynes asked him. "Isn't that the families paying for the calls?"

"Families, criminals—it's the same thing," the vendor replied.

On a sweltering summer morning in Washington, D.C., nine-year-old Diamond sat in the silence of the basement of the Shiloh Baptist Church, squirming in his seat. As an image formed on the computer monitor before him, his eyes widened and the fidgeting ceased.

"Hi, Dad!" Diamond shouted, as if into a tin can; as if it were up to him to span the 360 miles that separated him from his incarcerated father, DeWayne Mixon. "Can you see me?"

Thanks to the magic of computer teleconferencing, Mixon—who was in the sixth year of a three-to-nine-year sentence for assault at the Corrections Corporation of America Northeast Ohio Correctional Center in Youngstown, Ohio—could, in fact, both see and hear his son. He was not, however, able to touch him, and it would likely be months before he could. With the exception of an extended visit earlier that summer, Mixon had not seen his son in person in over five years.

In 2001, the federal government closed Washington, D.C.'s decrepit Lorton Correctional Complex and began exporting its inhabitants. Today, nearly six thousand D.C. residents are in federal and private prisons across the country—some as far away as California. Children who were once able to visit their parents several times a month now see them only rarely—or not at all. A fifteen-minute phone call to the Washington, D.C., area cost a dollar from Lorton; now it can cost as much as $30.

Carol Fennelly spent the 1980s and most of the 1990s advocating for the homeless in Washington, D.C., living in and running that city's fourteen-thousand-bed Federal City Shelter. When D.C. started moving its prisoners out of state, Fennelly went with them. Starting out in Youngstown—a depressed former mill town that had come to depend on a constellation of private prisons for jobs and tax revenue—Fennelly began looking for ways to keep D.C.'s prisoners connected with home and family.

"Once a dad gets in prison, he's generally no longer considered a part of his family," Fennelly observed. "Nothing in our society encourages this man to stay involved with his children."

At the same time, she said, prison can offer a "redemptive moment in someone's life, when they have been taken out of the context where they were doing the things that got them there in the first place. A lot of times, because prisons are no longer focused on rehabilitation, that moment is lost. But if you can reach people when they want to do something in their lives—they want to be part of their families; they don't want to come back to this place—then that moment can become valuable, and it can lead to the redeeming of a life that might be lost."

Fennelly does not see teleconferencing as a substitute for hands-on contact—she also facilitates offline visits and summer camps where D.C. children spend several days with their incarcerated parents. But for many exiled parents, virtual contact with their kids may be the only kind they get.

In a forty-minute teleconferencing session with Diamond, Mixon made it clear that he worried about his fatherless son.

"Be careful out there," he lectured Diamond, who lived with his grandmother and three siblings in a D.C. housing project. "Now, you know right from wrong, don't you?"

"Yes."

"Don't be out there doing nonsense and acting crazy, you hear me?"

"Yes."

"'Cause you better than that, you hear me?"

"OK. . . . Daddy? Daddy?"

The connection had dropped, and not for the first time. Because the low-income neighborhood in which the church was located had neither cable-modem nor DSL access, Fennelly was using a standard telephone line. She did not have the bandwidth to run both sound and streaming video at once, so she alternated between the two, freezing the images in order for father and child to converse. Even so, the line got overloaded and the computer crashed regularly, requiring a several-minute pause as it restarted.

The disappointment on Diamond's face each time his father evaporated bespoke a problem that goes beyond bandwidth. The bits and pieces of their fathers that Fennelly is able to offer the children of D.C. prisoners only highlight the magnitude of what they have lost as prisoners have come to be seen as commodities that can be shipped from one place to another to meet market imperatives.

As the teleconference stuttered along, Diamond began to lose his focus. He scrunched up his nose, chewed on his shirt, peered into the microphone. Periodically, he looked to Fennelly, who was present, for guidance in talking to his distant dad.

"Diamond, what grade you going to be next year?" Mixon asked his son.

"Fifth." The image evaporated again. Diamond groaned in frustration and leaned in to restart the computer.

"You be good out there," Mixon told his son as the session drew to a close. "I love you, OK? Give Daddy a kiss on the cheek."

"How'm I supposed to do that?" Diamond asked.

In a telephone interview from the Northeast Ohio Correctional Center, Mixon, thirty-two, said teleconferencing offered him a chance to be a father, but also provided a painful reminder of the limitations of his role as a long-distance dad, and the risks Diamond faced as a result.

"It's killing me now," Mixon said. "I know that he definitely needs me out there. I just want to be careful what I say to him. Talk to him about doing good in school. Tell him to watch who he hangs around with, 'cause a lotta them young boys out there can be bad little role models. And I don't want him to follow in my footsteps. He listens to me, but being as I'm not out there, my hand is in the air. It's in the air."

With budgets tightening and prison populations ballooning, family connections increasingly fall victim to fiscal concerns. Hawai'i, for example, sends nearly half of its approximately

3,500 prisoners to private prisons on the mainland, where they are housed at roughly half what it would cost to keep them at home—and where visits are prohibitively expensive for family members. Arizona sends prisoners to Texas; Indiana to Kentucky; Wisconsin to Oklahoma. Once they are in the private prison system, inmates may be moved again and again if cheaper beds turn up in another state. Hawai'i transferred some of its mainland prisoners from Arizona to Mississippi—more than four thousand miles from home—in order to save nine dollars per inmate per day. After my visit to D.C., the Youngstown prison was closed, and Fennelly moved her teleconferencing program to a private prison in North Carolina, which holds about 1,400 men from D.C.

The cost to families of outsourcing prisoners is not factored into budget deliberations, but the bill comes due all the same. Hawai'i is finding that the recidivism rate is higher for prisoners who have been held thousands of miles from home than for those kept on the islands. Given the evidence that consistent visits prevent recidivism, it is likely the same holds true for other prisoners shipped out of state in the name of short-term savings.

As the distances between prisoners and their children increase, creative solutions such as Fennelly's abound. Several prisons operate family literacy programs, in which inmates tape-record stories to send to their distant children. Prisoners in Washington State learn how to send their children "paper bag hugs"—they draw and cut out brown-paper figures, which children are encouraged to wrap around themselves should they feel the need for a parent's embrace.

Each such program offers the children of incarcerated parents something that can best be described as better than nothing.

Each also brings into painful focus the magnitude of the problem it is intended to address.

THE TRIP ON A METRO NORTH commuter train from Grand Central Station in Manhattan to Ossining, New York, costs seven dollars and takes just under an hour. The route follows the Hudson River north through Westchester County, passing through affluent villages built into craggy hillsides, and offering expansive views of the wide, blue river.

On a Saturday morning in early fall, the train was nearly empty by the time it arrived in Ossining. Most of the locals had disembarked at towns along the way, and the remaining passengers piled into a handful of cabs that were waiting for the train at Ossining, to take the morning's visitors up the hill to Sing Sing Correctional Facility.

Trailers lined the drive to the entrance of the prison; correctional officers who live upstate sleep there between shifts. A skinny, striped gray cat skulked along a fence. From inside the prison, the sailboat-dotted Hudson gleamed blue through barred windows, filling the lobby with an intense, watery light. A flock of ducks floated over the prison and down to the river in a perfect V.

Constructed in 1825 and housing more than two thousand men, Sing Sing looms as an archetype of the American prison. The institution's renown is such that the state has placed a historical marker near the gate, where the curious are informed that the phrases "up the river" and "the big house" originated with this storied facility.

But if Sing Sing is archetypal, it is also atypical. Of the forty-one new prisons that the state of New York has constructed over the past two decades, forty have been sited upstate, where job-hungry rural communities compete for the privilege of hosting them, and prisoners' children are hard-pressed to reach them.

Two-thirds of the state's prisoners come from New York City, and most have family there. Sing Sing's proximity to these families makes it an ideal site for an ambitious effort to test the thesis that one can be an active, engaged parent from behind prison walls.

The woman behind this experiment is Elizabeth Gaynes. For the past two decades, she has been taking her own children, Ari and Emani Davis, from New York to Virginia to visit their imprisoned father. That experience has led Gaynes to see visits as more than a luxury or a special occasion; to believe that an incarcerated parent can remain a central figure in his children's lives.

"Look at the things that you do for your children," Gaynes suggested. "There's a certain amount of dressing them, shopping for them, taking them places and cooking for them. These are things that somebody else could do. What someone else can't do is tell them who they are. Give them their history; let them know their roots. Express a love and appreciation for them that knows no bounds. Children need to know that they are wanted; that there is somebody called a father or a mother who thinks they're the bee's knees. And you don't need to be living with them to do that."

In 1984, Gaynes's husband, Jomo Davis—from whom she had separated a year earlier—was in Virginia visiting his children from a previous marriage. A local drug dealer had stolen a chain from his son, and Davis and two acquaintances broke into the man's house in an effort to retrieve it, according to Gaynes. The man attacked Davis, stabbing him repeatedly with a knife.

One of Davis's acquaintances shot and killed the man. Davis was convicted of felony murder and sentenced to 107 years in prison.

Ari was two years old when Davis went to prison, and Emani six. Gaynes knew from the start that she would do what she could to keep her children's father in their lives. "I'm a daddy's girl," she said. "We intended these children. It never seriously occurred to me that if my children had a living parent, that person shouldn't be fully known to them."

Making this happen required a sustained act of will on the part of both parents, who entered into what Gaynes calls "a covenant, as important to us as marriage vows, about how we would raise our children." This covenant was painstakingly specific. Gaynes would bring the children to visit; accept collect phone calls (a commitment that she estimates has cost her more than $40,000 to date); and involve Davis in decisions about the children's lives. He would set an example for the children; accept responsibility for the life he had created for himself and his family; apologize for the harm he had done his own family and that of the man who was killed; and remember birthdays without prompting.

Emani remembers her mother's role in this covenant as something akin to benign enforcer: "Here was this little Jewish lady from the Bronx trying to raise these kids, and she wasn't going to have it fall apart. Her attitude was, 'You made these children with me and you're gonna raise them. Whatever it takes to do that from prison, that's what you're gonna do.'"

Several times a year, Gaynes would drive Emani and Ari the four hundred miles from New York to Virginia to visit their father. Gaynes remembers the children anxiously checking the speedometer as she drove, afraid they would be pulled over and lose their mother, too. She also remembers moments when a visit would crystallize; when the power of family was strong enough to blot out the context. In those moments, Gaynes would forget that the father of her children was wearing a powder-blue jumpsuit, that they were surrounded by strangers, that guards stood over him and would take him away in a matter of hours.

Emani, too, remembers moments of intimacy that she and her father were able to achieve even in the inhospitable environment of a traditional visiting room. "My father has high blood pressure, so I used to lick all the salt off the potato chips and peanuts from the vending machines, and I would give them to my father to eat," she recalled. "I loved that he ate from my mouth. It really speaks to the intense kind of connection that my father and I have been able to have."

"Many people think we're doing a service to children, when a parent is doing life, in having them sever contact," Emani continued. "But as children, we understand who we are as human beings by understanding who our parents are."

Emani remembers the moment she came to terms with both the limits and the power of a relationship maintained entirely through letters, phone calls, and visits. She was on a subway train and saw a black man with a mixed-race daughter of five or six years old—a pair that reminded her of herself and her father.

"You need to hold the pole," the man instructed the child, who was clutching her father's hand.

"Daddy, I don't need to hold the pole," the girl answered. "I'm holding your hand."

Emani found herself suddenly in tears. "My childhood died for me there," she explained. "I was clear that I was never going to get that time back. I was never going to be that six-year-old girl. But the beautiful thing was that my father was still my pillar. He was as strong to me as he had ever been."

In 1986, the Osborne Association launched the Family Works program, which operates children's centers at two New York men's prisons and offers parenting classes at three. It was the first such effort to address incarcerated fathers. Today, the children's centers host some six thousand visits a year, and about 150 fathers go through the parenting classes.

On the outside, Family Works runs a Family Resource Center in Brooklyn, where people with relatives in prison can come for support and referrals, and a hotline—staffed by ex-prisoners and relatives of prisoners—that family members can call for advice and assistance in navigating any of the state's seventy scattered prisons. Osborne also offers released prisoners services such as drug treatment and job placement, and offers visitation support and other services at the Albion Correctional Facility for women.

Family Works operates on a few basic premises: children love their parents, and parents love their children. People can be bad citizens but good parents. Incarcerated fathers can provide much of what children need from them. Relationships between fathers and the mothers of their children have a profound effect on kids. Contact between incarcerated fathers and their children can have a positive impact on both.

Weaving these premises into prison life is a complicated endeavor. By the time a child reaches the Children's Center at Sing Sing, she has passed through a lobby where a sign has warned her caretaker not to place her on the counter. She has taken off her shoes and passed through a metal detector. She has been assigned a row number and been admitted to a vast and bare visiting room, where a wall of windows offers a close-up view of coiled razor wire.

Along one side of the visiting room are rows of plastic chairs, in which couples are assigned to sit side-by-side. On the other side are tables, reserved for larger family groups. At the back are vending machines, beneath a sign which reads INMATE RESTRICTED AREA. For visitors who have yet to learn to read, the figure of a prisoner with a circle and a slash conveys the message: if dad wants a Snickers bar, you'll have to get it for him. Prisoners at Sing Sing, as elsewhere, are not allowed to use or handle money.

Within the Children's Center—a small, Plexiglas-enclosed enclave off to the side of the larger visiting room—all this evaporates. Inside the Center, fathers can hug and hold their children, read books to them, play computer games with them, help them to weave key chains out of colored string. Security dictates the transparent walls—correctional officers must be able to see in—but their effect is the opposite of the Plexiglas that separates parent and child in a traditional window visit: they foster intimacy rather than enforce distance. From inside the Center—especially if one sits at child-level, where shelves of books and toys obscure the view—the expanse of the visiting room disappears, creating a sense of shelter and privacy, a glass-enclosed island in an ocean in a bottle.

The toys that fill the Children's Center are not there simply to divert or entertain the children; they are there because Gaynes learned early on that small children do not connect with their parents via protracted conversation. Her own strongest childhood memories, she realized, consisted less of conversation—the only form of interaction permitted in many visiting rooms—than of shared activity: a trip to the fair, being pushed on a swing. A child who draws a picture with his father, or joins him in a computer game, gains access to the building blocks of a family history. A child who makes her dad a sandwich from plastic bread and cheese at a toy kitchen has constructed for herself the memory of a picnic.

The Children's Center gives men who have taken the Osborne parenting class a chance to practice what they have learned, and also works as a low-key recruiting office: when visitors sign in, they are asked whether they have taken the class and offered the opportunity to join. Inside the Children's Center, program staff—including several inmates—continue, in subtle ways, to educate the men about their children's needs and development. Often, staffers find themselves helping a father choose a toy or understand a game—many had little chance to play with toys when they were children themselves.

Researchers who evaluated Family Works found that prisoners reported that they and their children talked more and were more affectionate with each other, and that children's grades and behavior improved, once they began using the Children's Center. This last finding, the researchers noted, offers hope that the Center may help prevent children from "engaging in behaviors that, as they age, could escalate into more delinquent forms. As such, the Children's Center may be an important tool in reducing the inter-generational cycle of incarceration."

On a small table inside the Children's Center sits a stack of copies of the *Rainbow Gazette*, a thick quarterly magazine edited by inmate staff and written by prisoners and their visitors. Children who come to the Children's Center are invited to write for the *Rainbow Gazette*. In their submissions to the *Gazette*, visiting children offered their own assessments of the Center:

"I looked around and I got scared for a moment," one girl wrote of her first visit to Sing Sing, "but I was told that I was here for a good reason. I sat in the play room and two gentlemen help me feel comfortable and help me with the computers and games. It made me feel good about being here."

"Today was fun and interesting," a thirteen-year-old girl wrote, "because I got to make a butterfly and flower. I also had a great time by meeting new people and talking to them. The colors were kind of pretty. They were so beautiful. I felt good to come and see my daddy. I want to come every two weeks to children center."

"I love my father and I wish that he could come home," wrote a six-year-old (with caregiver assistance). "On Father's Day I am going to get a nice card for him. He is nice to me and he tickles me a lot when I come to visit him."

The hope that drives the Children's Center is that butterflies and tickles—not just bars and razor wire—will lodge in the children's memories of time spent with their fathers. On the day I visited, Mariano, who had been at Sing Sing three years, was familiarizing himself with a Barbie computer game his daughter Marie Isabel favored. A wiggly six-year-old with a wide grin and four missing teeth, Marie Isabel kept her arms wrapped around her father's waist as he spoke.

Before he was transferred to Sing Sing, Mariano had been at a facility that had no children's center. Once, in the visiting room there, Marie Isabel tripped and fell in front of him. He had to leave her on the ground; getting out of his seat to pick her up would violate the rules. The hardest part was explaining to his then-three-year-old daughter that her father would get in trouble if he reached for her.

Marie Isabel was clearly getting restless as her father and I spoke. Her wriggling escalated until, with the gleeful imperiousness of a newly crowned princess, she succeeded in leading him away. They left the Children's Center to get their photograph taken together beneath a banner that read, in ornate hand-painted script, THINKING OF YOU ALWAYS.

At eleven a.m., the Children's Center emptied abruptly. Women and children returned to their assigned tables in the main visiting room, while the men stood beside them—arms at their sides or clasped behind their backs—for "count."

Samuel—a forty-three-year-old black man with long, graying dreadlocks—is one of the inmates who staff the Children's Center. At count time, he told me, he sometimes looks around and does a silent accounting of his own. For every child in the room, there is likely another child who has been hurt by a prisoner's actions. For every family striving to connect inside Sing Sing, another has been ruptured by a crime. Samuel looks around the room and sees harm multiplying outward—ghost victims everywhere, not least his own.

Samuel sat in a small, toy-filled office in the back of the Children's Center, his hands folded in his lap as he carefully chose his words. He was a few years out of high school, working in a watch-repair shop and expecting his first child, when he agreed to act as a lookout in a robbery. The victim, who turned out to be an off-duty housing officer, pulled out a gun and started shooting. Samuel's accomplice fired back and killed the man. Samuel, who was seriously wounded, was convicted of felony murder and sentenced to eighteen years to life.

"For me, remorse is an action word," he said. "If I'm going to say that I'm sorry, then my actions have to coincide with that. If someone really wants to express remorse, then they want to rehabilitate themselves."

Samuel paused to accept a game of Candyland from a little girl in pigtails. "For the most part, incarcerated men need to work on themselves, to make themselves better people," he continued. "Children hear what you say, but they more so watch what you do. It is this example they begin to shape their lives by."

Samuel's daughter was six months old when he went to prison. Now she is twenty-two. In the interim, Samuel has acquired a bachelor's degree from Nyack College and a certificate in ministry and human services from the New York Theological Seminary, and he has taken parenting and Aggression Replacement Training. He's had one "ticket" in twenty-two years, for wearing a uniform with tapered pants (he'd brought them with him from another institution, where customizing was permitted). He studies books with titles such as *Boon Doggle: A Book of Lanyard and Lacing,* and he can rattle off—and execute—elaborate ribbon-braiding techniques such as the Chinese Staircase and the Twisted Cobra. He recently turned down an opportunity to be transferred to a medium-security facility so he could continue his work at the Children's Center.

Lately, Samuel doesn't see his daughter as often as he used to: she's in college, working nights, and she likes to spend her free time with her friends. Samuel doesn't ask for more; if he were twenty-two and free, Sing Sing would likely not be where he'd choose to spend his weekends, either. But because he has managed to make himself an example to his daughter, he's granted himself a bit of paternal license. When he does see her, he warns her about bad company; instructs her to stick with school and stay away from drugs.

Samuel interrupted his narrative again, to issue colored string to a four-year-old with golden curls piled atop her head.

The girl's father, who sat at a nearby computer with his older son, did not take his eyes off his daughter as she ventured back with the string.

"It's our hope that by the time a child leaves out that door, that child is now filled with so much love from their father that it'll sustain them until the next time they come back," Samuel said. "That's what we try to do inside here."

On a Thursday evening, I sat in on a new class—Alternatives to Domestic Violence, initiated at the request of men in the parenting class—and listened as one participant described his drug dealing as something he had been compelled to pursue in order to feed his family. Had we been in the better-established parenting class, Elizabeth Gaynes told me later, that analysis would not have passed unchallenged; the other men would have dismantled the man's self-justifications before the teacher even had a chance.

Gaynes's aversion to excuses comes not from a law-and-order disposition but from an evolving understanding that children benefit when incarcerated parents take responsibility for both their actions and their absence.

Her own children, Gaynes noticed, would ask their father again and again to explain the events that had led him to prison. For a while, she wondered how they could keep forgetting. Eventually, she came to see that as they matured, they were able to understand different aspects of the story, and they needed it explained to them in ways that kept pace with their capacity to comprehend.

"I had to push a little bit at one point, because Jomo was embarrassed about what he had done," Gaynes recalled. "It's not a great feeling to have to tell a nine-year-old that you made a huge mistake; you've made a mess of your life, and everybody else is paying for it."

As Emani remembers it, her father got the message: when she would feel sorry for herself at spending Father's Day in prison, he would remind her that they were lucky; another child was spending Father's Day alone because of what he had done.

"Most of what passes for work in this field rips people off by romanticizing or demonizing them," Gaynes observed. "Both fail to acknowledge the power people have to transform their lives, and both underestimate the extent to which we are the source of what happens in our lives. Transformation is a function of the degree to which our participants see that they have the power to choose, in every moment, how they will meet their circumstances, even though they cannot choose their circumstances, and can only rarely change them. Accountability is not blame or credit, but it is seeing oneself as the cause, rather than the effect, of one's life and circumstances. It is a powerful place to stand, especially for parents."

In a letter to the *Rainbow Gazette*, a correspondent tried to convey his evolving understanding of his own responsibility:

Dearest Family Members,

It has taken me years to recognize that there are people who suffer as a result of my being away. I was so busy focusing on "the system" as my personal nemesis that I failed to see I was not a victim. One of the saddest days of my life was when my little girl asked me "when are you coming home" (she is five) and I had to explain to her why I could not "come home" . . .

I realize that to facilitate change, love and righteousness, one must learn by example. I am used to being

treated in a "rough manner," but it is love and kindness
that catches me off guard.

In the sixteen-week parenting class he teaches at Sing Sing,
Dr. Carl Mazza, a Lehman College sociology professor, spends
much of his time trying to get his students to the "powerful
place" Gaynes described; to chip away at their defenses and re-
place them with a sense of agency. He uses psychology and
child development theory—Maslow, Erikson, Freud—to ease
his students toward a painful but crucial understanding of how
children experience a parent's incarceration.

At the beginning, he said, his students tend to be "well-
defended. They want to pretend that their coming to prison really did not have an effect on their children; that their kids are
OK, their kids understand. Some of them will actually say, 'My
kids are better off without me.' "

Mazza encourages his students to empathize with the anxiety
and discomfort their children will experience when they visit a
prison, but also assures them that even a difficult visit is preferable to the alternative: "When she doesn't have contact with
you, she interprets that as, 'Daddy doesn't love me anymore. I
was bad, and Daddy doesn't want to be with me.' Visiting may
be scary for a kid, but ultimately it's healthier."

On the Thursday night I sat in on his class, Mazza was talking about anomie, which he defined for the men as "the state of
not belonging, particularly when you're surrounded by other
people." Most of the men were taking notes. Their questions
were urgent and thoughtful, and regularly drowned out by the
sound of a train passing by; the tracks literally run through the
prison grounds. Mazza paced and gesticulated like Robin
Williams in *The Dead Poets Society*, sweat stains blossoming on

his purple-checked shirt as he struggled to match the intensity of his interlocutors.

"You mentioned a child's need for safety when his parent is incarcerated," a student raised his hand to ask. "Did you mean physically or psychologically?"

"Mostly psychologically," Mazza answered. "All of the child's energy goes towards checking twenty times that Mommy's still in the kitchen. He's got no time for anything else, because all his energy is absorbed in trying to protect himself. He might have a hard time going to school, because he's so worried about what's going to happen at home."

"I have a five-year-old daughter," another man offered. "Her mother cannot leave the house. My daughter throws fits. She tells her mother, 'Daddy never came home.'"

Mazza suggested that the man be as consistent as possible, but sparing with his promises. "If you say you'll call on Thursday, and the prison is on lockdown on Thursday, that reinforces your daughter's lack of security. She doesn't know what lockdown is. She only knows that you said you'd call and you didn't."

A white man in his sixties, with thick plastic-framed glasses and almost no hair, raised his hand. "Isn't love a crucial part of a child feeling safe?" he asked in a heavy European accent. "When my son was eight or nine, he would grab me by my arm in the visiting room and say, 'Daddy, let's go home. I need you.' I would say, 'Son, I can't come home now.' He would say, 'Why? You don't love me anymore?'"

Samuel, a parenting-class graduate, remembers sitting in the classroom and finally comprehending why, after he was first locked up, his daughter would flinch when he tried to pick her up. Only when he was introduced to attachment theory did his hurt feelings give way to an understanding of his daughter's perspective.

In a 2002 interview with the Osborne Association newsletter, Samuel's daughter credited his participation in the parenting class with improving their time together. "I felt a change," she said. "He turned into a better listener, responding in a more understanding way. I could tell him my problems without his getting upset, and that was a comfort to me."

In 2003, the U.S. Supreme Court upheld a Michigan policy that placed strict limits on prison visits. "The very object of imprisonment is confinement," explained Justice Anthony M. Kennedy, writing for the majority. "Many of the liberties and privileges enjoyed by other citizens must be surrendered by the prisoner."

Long before the Supreme Court made it explicit, visitation policy was guided by the construction of family contact as a privilege that is granted or denied inmates, rather than a right that accrues to children. In fact, the two are inextricable: to assert that prisoners have no intrinsic right to visitation is also, necessarily, to assert that children have no right to contact with their parents.

Discouraging visitation also reduces the odds that a prison term will serve a useful function. Prison may be intended to isolate, but it is also, at least ostensibly, intended to rehabilitate—and there is tremendous evidence that it is connection that rehabilitates. Restricting access to family only ups the odds of failure once a parent gets out.

"More than half the guys in here literally don't know where the visiting room is," observed Gregory, a Sing Sing inmate and Osborne Association staffer. "They have never seen it. It makes a series of changes on you when you're here ten or twelve years, you never get a hug; the only people you talk to are other prisoners and guards. You shrink to deal with what your world is. And it's difficult to imagine how that's going to be effective when you're called on to make this big transition from here back to New York."

4

GRANDPARENTS

WHEN THERESA "ROXANNE" CRUZ went to prison, her children lost not just a mother but also a grandmother. Roxanne's mother, Theresa Azhocar—the "weekend grandma" Roxanne's children had known and adored all their lives—had been affectionate to the point of indulgence. She had money for Disneyland and the energy to enjoy it. When her grandkids would visit for the weekend, she would take them into the garden of her home in Chula Vista, California, just south of San Diego, and teach them to plant flowers. Then she'd line them up in a row; bathe them and wash their hair; give them her husband's white T-shirts for nightgowns; and snuggle with them on the sofa to watch *The Nutcracker* until bedtime.

"My God," their grandfather used to tease, "we have all these channels and all we watch is the Disney Channel."

In January of 1991, Roxanne was sentenced to twenty-five years to life for conspiracy to commit murder (the sentence was later revised on appeal to seven years to life). Three days later, her father, Theresa's husband of twenty-seven years, died of a heart attack. In the course of a week, Theresa Azhocar became a single parent to four young children, including an infant with medical problems.

The cohort Theresa had joined so abruptly was large and growing. In a trend that is fueled by both addiction and incarceration, 4.4 million children now live in grandparent-headed households. Half of all children with incarcerated mothers, and a sixth of the children of incarcerated fathers, are cared for by grandparents.

When Roxanne went to prison, Theresa was transformed from a doting weekend grandma to a harried caretaker who had no time for the Disney Channel, much less Disneyland. Theresa, then forty-eight, worked up to sixty hours a week as a naval electrician, then came home to mountains of laundry, grieving children, and unpaid bills from her daughter's lawyer. If someone left the milk out, she might fly off the handle.

By the time I visited, Roxanne's three older children—Andrea, Antoinette, and Carlitos—had grown up. Adriana, the youngest, was the only one living with her grandmother. She was thirteen and at school much of the day, but the house was full of children all the same. Theresa now cared for a rotating crew of grandchildren and great-grandchildren while their parents worked. On a spring morning, three long-haired girls in flowered cotton dresses played on a swing set in the backyard under the supervision of Theresa's seventy-seven-year-old mother, Felicitas. A yellow parakeet sang in a cage in the dining room; outside, two more cages held baby parakeets and a gray rabbit that Theresa was keeping for a vacationing daughter. The creak of the screen door was constant as children ran in and out from the yard to the kitchen and back again.

Theresa sat at the kitchen table as Antoinette's son Alfonso—a three-year-old with sun-streaked brown hair and the brown saucer eyes of an *anime* character—snuggled blissfully into his great-grandmother's arms and went to sleep. Theresa was beautiful at sixty-one, in a red-and-black print dress that reached to her ankles, with the same brown-gold hair as her grandson's, cut into soft layers around her face.

The inevitable chaos that comes with a house full of kids—a child dribbling a giant silver exercise ball through the living room; another climbing onto the kitchen counter to investigate a chicken salad—did not appear to faze her. When friends tell her she's crazy to be caring for yet another generation of children, she doesn't reference duty or necessity. "You'd be surprised how much I get out of it," she tells them instead.

At lunchtime, one of the girls objected to the chicken salad and was given a bowl of homemade pasta salad instead. Another required a ham-and-cheese sandwich, apple juice, and chocolate milk, which Theresa mixed from an industrial-sized tin of Nestlé's Quik. After lunch, the children ran outside to play. Theresa's face, which animation had lifted in the presence of the children, fell a bit, settling into its true age as she began to talk about Roxanne.

According to family accounts, Roxanne had left an abusive relationship but was being hounded and threatened by her ex at the time of her crime. She had been prescribed Xanax for panic attacks and, according to Theresa, became addicted; in the month before the crime, she took as many as three hundred pills.

When her ex sued for custody of Carlitos, the son they had together, Roxanne's panic intensified. On June 15, 1989—the night before a scheduled custody hearing—Roxanne was outside in a parked car as acquaintances went to confront her ex-boyfriend. One of the men shot him in the legs. Theresa maintains that Roxanne had no idea the man intended to shoot her ex; that she had fallen asleep in the car and woke up to the sound of gunshots.

Four days later, Roxanne had taken four-year-old Carlitos to McDonald's for a Happy Meal when police surrounded their car. They arrested Roxanne and took Carlitos to the home of a paternal aunt. Carlitos was later placed in the custody of his father.

Initially, Roxanne was charged with assault. It was a year before she went to trial. By then, the man who did the shooting had been convicted of attempted murder and sentenced to thirty years to life. Roxanne's own charge had been revised to conspiracy to commit murder.

Roxanne was out on bail during her trial and had moved in with her mother and her children. Theresa said that Roxanne, who became pregnant with Adriana while awaiting trial, stopped using drugs during that time and returned to her former self—baking cupcakes, taking the girls to play basketball, bringing them to church.

Theresa and Roxanne were home with baby Adriana when Roxanne's jury came back with a verdict. As soon as they got the call, they raced to the courthouse. Theresa dropped Roxanne and the baby off and went to look for parking. When she got inside, she found the judge's secretary in the hallway holding Adriana. Theresa entered the courtroom in time to hear the world "guilty," and see her daughter taken away.

Theresa remembers screaming and crying in the car on the way home—the baby, in the back seat, slept through it—then trying to pull herself together in time for the older children's arrival from school. She had just gotten home when they burst through the door, competing to see who could get inside first to give their mother the valentines they had made for her that day.

Andrea, the oldest, was the first to notice that her grandmother's eyes were red. "Where's my mom at?" she shouted.

"She's not here right now," Theresa said, the fear in Andrea's face compelling her to blunt the truth. "She'll be back in a little bit." The girls began to wail.

Andrea was nine years old when her mother went to prison. Antoinette was eight, and Carlitos—who remained with his father—was five. Four-month-old Adriana had been born prematurely when Roxanne's placenta ruptured during her trial, and she suffered from digestive and breathing difficulties that required constant monitoring.

In the midst of the maelstorm that had hit her family, Theresa's own sorrow and anger remained largely submerged. She had no more time, or space, to grieve her husband than she did her daughter. Only last year—fourteen years after his death—did she finally put a headstone on his grave.

Theresa was born in Mexico and raised in the United States. Her mother had always told her, "It's God and the United States—believe that. This is the best country in the world." She used to get a lump in her throat when she heard the Pledge of Allegiance. Now she winces when her grandchildren and great-grandchildren recite it. When Los Angeles residents rioted in the wake of the Rodney King verdicts in 1993, Theresa was appalled to find herself thrilled by the violence, as if the rage she could not afford to express had found a physical manifestation. "I wish they would come downtown and start with the courts," she told a co-worker bitterly.

"I could say that I was grieving at that time," Theresa said of the years after her daughter was sentenced. "I realize that now. I was inside myself. It was like my whole system was poisoned by the anger that I had in me."

Once, she overheard a co-worker talking about an upcoming jury-duty assignment.

"You know how to say 'guilty,' don't you?" joked another colleague.

"It was like they had lit a fire on me," Theresa remembers. "I told him, 'Yes, and when you say "guilty," remember that next time it could be you or your kids.'"

Theresa went to bed many nights to the sound of her grand-children crying in their beds. Long after they fell asleep, Theresa would lie awake, struggling with the guilt that was more powerful even than her anger.

"Sometimes I think that the family of a person who commits a crime is worse off than if the person had died," Theresa said. "You wonder, 'How can my kid have done this? How could I have stopped my kid from doing this?'" She would finally fall asleep, only to wake up an hour later with the same questions pressing in on her.

Sleeplessness is commonplace among grandparent care-givers, as is depression. Their worries are endless: that they will die and leave their grandchildren parentless; that they will not be able to manage, as they grow older and slower, to keep the children safe and fed; that they will lose this generation to the same forces, or failures, that overtook the last; that their chil-dren will never come back and retrieve the grandkids; that they will.

Whether or not she had slept, Theresa left the house at six each morning to get to work by seven. Antoinette and Andrea remember being rushed out the door some days with mismatched shoes—two lefts on one girl, two rights on the other. In addition to childcare, food, and clothing for the kids, Theresa was paying two lawyers—one for her daughter's appeal and one to represent Theresa in a custody battle with Carlitos's father (the two were ultimately awarded joint custody, and Carlitos spent weekends at Theresa's house). Because of the inflated cost of collect calls from prison, her phone bill averaged $150 a month. She mortgaged her house to the limit; spent her retirement savings; and ran up more than $60,000 in credit-card debt, which she was still working to pay down when I met her.

The only support for which Theresa was eligible was $663 a month as a child-only grant from Temporary Assistance to Needy Families (TANF). Had the children been in foster care, given Adriana's special needs, the payments would likely have totaled several thousand dollars a month. But Theresa—like many grandparents faced with the same choice—was not willing to place her grandchildren in the custody of the state, with all the attendant risks and intrusions, in return for a monthly stipend. In 1997, only about 200,000 of the 1.8 million children then living with relatives received foster care payments. Many did not receive other services—such as food stamps or Medicaid—for which they were eligible if they were low-income. Nationwide, of those children being cared for by relatives in 1999, only about a quarter received financial support in the form of either foster care or TANF payments.

Grandparents who do choose to have their grandchildren placed with them as foster children live in fear of losing them if social workers should deem the grandparent too old, ill, or otherwise unfit. The children they care for are hardly immune to this threat. Lorraine was raised from infancy by her grandmother while her mother was in and out of jail and prison.

When Lorraine was eleven years old, her grandmother had a stroke and became less able to supervise her. When Lorraine hit adolescence and began getting into trouble, she remembers a social worker telling her, "You are walking on eggshells. If you don't do well in school, I'm going to pull you out of the house."

Márta, sixteen, was at home with her two-year-old brother and nine-year-old sister on a Friday afternoon while her grandmother was at work and her mother was in prison. A social worker dropped by and, finding Márta alone with the younger children, took them away to the shelter. It wasn't "healthy," the worker told Márta, for the children to be under the supervision of a teenager during the after-school hours. A childcare subsidy for the family was not available. Shelter care, at $5,000 a month, was.

Nearly two-thirds of children being raised by single grandmothers live in poverty. The multiple expenses associated with maintaining contact with an incarcerated family member—phone charges, travel to visit and sometimes overnight lodging, overpriced vending-machine meals in the visiting room, money for commissary—comprise a significant drain on already-scant resources. These costs—above and beyond the cost of feeding, clothing, and housing prisoners' children—have led the anthropologist Donald Braman to conclude that "incarceration acts like a hidden tax, one that is visited disproportionately on poor and minority families; and while its costs are most directly felt by the adults closest to the incarcerated family member, the full effect is eventually felt by the next generation as well."

Grandparents often take pride in having "rescued" their grandchildren from foster care, and emphasize that there was never any question of whether they would do so. "Our children are luckier than most," I heard one California grandmother tell a group of others. "They're not in a foster home. They get to know that we've loved them since they were born."

All the same, the disparity between the support relative caregivers receive and that a stranger might is a source of bitterness as well as hardship. "I've seen grandmothers mortgage their houses to the gills in order to provide for the child," said Susan Burton, a former prisoner who founded and runs a network of homes for reentering prisoners in Southern California. "I've seen them lose their homes. Go into bad credit to supply the needs of the child. Then you see the amount of money that would go into foster care for that same child. It says that the state is promoting the separation of families—that children's needs are more apt to get met if they are taken from their family."

Antoinette is a mother herself now—single, working, tired—and is beginning to understand what her grandmother was up against. As a motherless child, she took everything personally.

"When you see a lady yelling and screaming all day, and how tired she is, you think, 'Well, she's tired of me!'" Antoinette said. "I felt like I made her life harder than it should've been."

When her mother went to prison, Antoinette felt that her whole life had been transformed overnight. She stopped going to school and was medicated for depression. Once, Antoinette threw a penny into a wishing well at a shopping mall. She and her grandmother looked at each other without speaking and both burst into tears. Sometimes Antoinette would wake up with her pillow soaked from crying in her sleep.

When Roxanne went to prison, the hallmarks of her children's daily life went with her. Roxanne had always made a production out of holidays—assembling elaborate Easter baskets topped with inflated bunnies; recruiting a male relative to play Santa Claus at Christmas. Theresa dreaded the holidays—the demands of daily life were more than enough for her. The girls hated them, too—the bulky knit hats and sweaters their grandmother put under the tree were painfully out of style. "You know what? I'm not good enough," Theresa would say when she saw the disappointment on their faces.

Sports fell by the wayside; there was no one to take the kids when their grandmother was at work. When a classmate invited Antoinette to the prom, she felt compelled to turn him down; there was "no energy" in her household for shopping and primping. When there was an event at school—an open house, or parent-teacher night—the girls would make up excuses not to go.

When other kids went to slumber parties, Andrea and Antoinette were not allowed to go. Theresa had good reason to be protective—she worked full-time and found it difficult to provide the supervision she felt the children needed, and she had already lost one daughter. But instead of making the girls feel safe, these restrictions heightened the social alienation that came with having a mother in prison.

For a while, the children felt their mother's power and presence in their daily lives, even from a distance; they felt her, as Antoinette put it, "standing over what happens in the home." When they complained to her about not being allowed to go places with their friends or encouraged to play sports, Roxanne would talk to her mother and things would get better. As the years passed, that power ebbed. "I'm tired," Theresa would tell Roxanne when she lobbied for the children. "If you were here, you'd do it."

Roxanne had always been Antoinette's confidante—a young

mother who was like a best friend. After Roxanne went to prison, the simplest conversation turned into a minefield. "She would ask me questions—'What did you do today? Did you play basketball?'—but once her questions were up, we were quiet on the phone," Antoinette remembers. "How do you ask someone who's sitting in a jail cell how they're doing? I felt bad for her to know what I'm doing in life. I feel bad to tell her that I'm eating tamales for Christmas. When I'm sad, I don't want her to know about that either, 'cause she cries every night. It's been fourteen years and she's still crying."

Talking to her grandmother—or her great-grandmother, who retired from her job and moved in to help care for the children—offered little solace. They seemed old-fashioned to Antoinette, out of touch with the crises and opportunities she faced as a young woman. Adapting to their ways entailed constant concessions. "After my mother left, there was no taking naps in the day," she recalled. "When my great-grandmother made my bed, I wasn't to touch it, until it was dark. That's the way they lived back in the day. And here I am in the 1990s and I can't even take a nap when I come home from school."

Her friendships grew strained as well, as Antoinette struggled to keep her mother's status secret.

"Tell your mom to drop us off at Rollerskate Land," her friends would say.

"How do I turn around and tell them that I don't have my mom anymore?" Antoinette would wonder.

Eventually, she told her best friend where her mother was, then a few others. It wasn't long before the whole school knew.

"Who did your mom kill?" classmates would ask her mockingly.

"I felt that people thought of me like that," Antoinette remembers—"that they thought of my grandma and my uncles and my whole family like we were jail people."

Antoinette constantly felt—in a phrase she used repeatedly to describe her life growing up—"out of the circle."

The "circle" was the world where "everybody's normal," Antoinette explained. "Even to this day, I feel like I'm not. I've never lived a normal life. My life is different than yours, yours, yours, yours, yours. Everybody. I'm different."

Most weekends, Theresa loaded the children into the car and drove the two and a half hours to the California Institute for Women. She'd wait to be let in for three or four hours in the baking sun, watching the children's clothes and faces get progressively grimier as they played in the dirt. She was not allowed to bring a baby carrier for Adriana, or even a blanket. Inside the visiting room, the baby, who had grown accustomed to her grandmother's care, would cry when her mother tried to hold her. Roxanne would cry with her.

"I used to get out of there just wanting to wreck my car" from rage, Theresa remembers. But she had to drive carefully. Her car was full of children.

Eventually, Roxanne received clearance for extended visits in the Family Living Unit (FLU), an apartment on prison grounds where Theresa and the children could spend three or four days with her. Inside the FLU, Roxanne baked cookies with her children, combed their hair, tucked them into bed. If Easter was coming, they'd color eggs and hide them. If it was anywhere near someone's birthday, Roxanne would bake a cake. Photographs taken during FLU visits show a tight cluster of children with their mother at the center. Roxanne is youthful and beaming, looking like a sister to her daughters. They all wear their long, dark hair the same way—swept up in the front and loose at the sides.

For Adriana, now thirteen, who had no memory of Roxanne outside of prison, the FLU visits offered the only chance she'd get at the kind of intimate, hands-on mothering her sisters remembered. At home, Adriana, whose Halloween costumes were store-bought, would stare enviously at old photographs of her sisters standing beside their mother in black cat costumes Roxanne had sewn by hand. Inside the FLU, Roxanne would put an oversized white T-shirt on her youngest daughter and use makeup to paint whiskers on Adriana's upturned face.

For Andrea, the FLU visits offered a respite from social isolation. "I have a mom, too," she could tell herself, as well as her friends. "She's there. She does things."

Theresa remembers all four kids piling into Roxanne's double bed during these visits, vying to be near her, competing for the chance to speak with her alone. The older girls would barrage their mother with questions about boys, sex, puberty—things they wouldn't dream of discussing with their old-fashioned grandmother. The trips were costly and time-consuming for Theresa, who had to miss work and bring in all the food and supplies, but they left her with a sense of relief all the same, a feeling that she and her daughter were partners in raising the children, and that Roxanne was carrying some of the weight.

Five years after Roxanne went to prison, the Department of Corrections imposed a new regulation: prisoners serving life sentences would no longer be eligible for FLU visits. "That was when I began to have real trouble with the older girls," Theresa remembers. Antoinette and Andrea were just entering the fraught territory of adolescence when they were told they could no longer spend more than a few hours with their mother. "You're too old," they would scold their grandmother, dismissing her efforts to help them navigate this passage. "You don't understand." Theresa could not argue with them. She'd always been good with small children, but teenagers—especially those as angry and alienated as her grandchildren were becoming—were a different matter.

It is not uncommon for grandparent placements to fall apart during the teenage years, as grandparents' health begins to falter and their charges' behavior grows more challenging. The Azhocar family held together, but it was not easy.

"To be honest, I started not caring anymore," said Antoinette, who was twelve years old when the FLU visits ended. She quickly became, to use her phrase, "very bad." Now, when her grandmother told her she could not go somewhere, she went anyway, slamming the door as she left.

Antoinette was sitting on her grandmother's sofa as we spoke, and she began to cry. Her children, Alex and Alfonso, who had been playing nearby, came close and hovered, patting her gently, Alex bearing drawings and treasures from school. Andrea's son Ruben brought his aunt a paper towel to blot her tears.

"When my mother was sentenced, I felt that I was sentenced," Antoinette continued. "She was sentenced to prison—to be away from her kids and her family. I was sentenced, as a child, to be without my mother."

Over time, this feeling of being punished calcified into a sense of destiny. "I felt that I was one of those children that was put on this earth to live without a mother, and that's the way my life was meant to be," she said. "You know when someone be-

comes a movie star, it's like they were meant to be a movie star?
I felt like I was meant to grow up without parents."

Now, at twenty-three, Antoinette feels frozen. Even if her
mother were to walk in the door tomorrow, Antoinette believes,
she would not be able to escape her motherless destiny; to get
her childhood back. But she does not feel ready to let go of it,
either.

"I feel like I've grown old, but my mind is left back in second
grade," she said. "Like when she comes home, I want to start all
new again. I want to be a child again when she comes home."

In the meantime, Antoinette is a mother. It is a role that con-
sumes her, into which she invests not only her will to protect her
children from what she experienced, but also her wish to be par-
ented herself. "Sometimes I look at my kids and I say, 'You
know what? I wanna make up with my kids all the time my
mother and I didn't have.' I don't want them ever to feel neglected, or lonely, or scared," she said.

But the insecurity Antoinette felt growing up has seeped into
her adulthood. Her dreams are suffused with anxiety about her
ability to protect both herself and her children. In some of the
dreams, she "does something bad" and her boys are taken from
her. In others, she herself is endangered, and must save herself
against great odds for the sake of the children: her car goes over
a cliff and she jumps out midair, clinging to the bushes as the car
plummets; she is lost at sea and must swim and swim to reach the
shore.

In each of these dreams, she thinks only of her children, even
as her own life is at stake. Sometimes she wonders why her
mother could not be that single-minded.

"I don't want to say it, but she took my childhood away,"

Antoinette said. "I feel that she could have done things to prevent herself from leaving us. Stayed away from that man, you know? When I was little, I always said, 'Wasn't I important? Wasn't I more to her than anything?' I think of my kids now—they're more to me than anything. I would jump off a bridge in a second right now, for them to live a beautiful life. Why didn't she do that for me?"

On April 30, 1998, Theresa got a call from her daughter's appellate attorney. Roxanne's conviction had been overturned after a federal judge found multiple problems with the original trial.

The state of California appealed this decision, but the judge agreed to release Roxanne on bail pending the appeal. Two months after Theresa got the call, Roxanne left CIW and came home to her family.

Theresa had bought tickets for Disneyland and Sea World, but no one wanted to leave the house. The children kept their mother up until two in the morning, talking and talking. Theresa remembers looking at her grandchildren's faces and seeing the years fall away, as if the children had reverted to the age they were when their mother went to prison.

Roxanne finally got the kids to bed, then crept into her mother's room to go to sleep herself. Theresa remembers waking up over and over again in the night to look at her daughter, straining to make out her features in the dark.

Roxanne had been home less than a week when her lawyer called again. The state had successfully appealed the ruling that had released her on bail.

"You mean I'm going to have to turn myself in?" Roxanne asked. The children, who were within earshot, began to scream. Eighteen days after she walked out the prison gates, Roxanne

walked back in. A circuit court later reinstated her original conviction and left her to complete her indefinite sentence.

After Roxanne went back to prison, Theresa remembers, "It
was like somebody died in our house." Meals were eaten in silence. For Adriana, Roxanne's respite from prison had represented not a return to the familiar but something entirely new.
For eighteen days, Adriana had been granted a taste of daily life
in the presence of a mother; had gone to school with ribbons in
her hair. When Roxanne went back to prison, the bows came
out, and Adriana reverted to the life she had always known.

"What was mom like?" Adriana grew up asking her older
sisters. "What did she do with you guys?" She has an album in
which she keeps letters and a few photographs. There is a baby
picture of her, in her mother's arms at an FLU visit. Her most
recent photograph of her mother is on a 1998 California ID
card, for which Roxanne applied during her eighteen days of
freedom. The ID came in the mail after she returned to prison,
and Adriana made off with it. In the picture, Roxanne is young,
pretty, and solemn. When Adriana showed me the ID, it had
just expired.

Once, when Adriana was five or six years old, Theresa saw
her wishing on a star and asked her what she had wished for.

"For my mommy to kiss me at night before I go to bed,"
Adriana answered.

"Adriana, I kiss you all the time," Theresa said.

"But you're only a grandma," the little girl said. "You're not
a mommy."

When she was small, Adriana would wander around the
prison grounds during the FLU visits staring at the fence or the
sky. "I'm thinking of a way to get you out of here," she would
tell her mother. Sometimes, she fantasized about stealing a cor-

rectional officer's gun and shooting her way out, but she settled instead for cajoling her mother's keepers: "Can my mommy come home now?"

Lately, Adriana told me, she and her mother were "not getting along," and so she had stopped visiting. The visiting room, she added, "stinks like bad breath." Theresa told me later that Adriana had come to feel, and to resent, that her mother was closer to her older children, because she had lived with them.

"She loves you just the same," Theresa tells her granddaughter.

"But she raised them. She didn't raise me," Adriana answers.

Roxanne's children have struggled with the question of whether their mother's indefinite absence has been more or less painful than her death might have been. As it is, the wound caused by Roxanne's absence is reopened every two weeks in the visiting room; every time the phone rings and a disembodied voice says, "This is a call from an inmate at a correctional facility . . ."; every time the parole board meets and tells Roxanne to try again the next time.

In 1996, the California legislature passed Assembly Bill 231, also known as the Theresa Cruz Act, which instructed the Board of Prison Terms to consider a history of domestic violence in making parole decisions. In May 1996, Roxanne was turned down for parole, as she would be at each subsequent hearing.

Theresa has boxes upon boxes of paper attesting to her daughter's rehabilitation behind prison walls—dozens of certificates of appreciation, achievement, accomplishment, and completion. Roxanne has been trained in Data Processing, Cobol, Advanced Cobol, Unix, Lotus 1-2-3, Equipment Utilization, and Survival Skills. She's got a Life Plan for Recovery; has Broken the Barriers; been a Special Blessing; and bestowed upon others the Ability to Dream. She's acquired her High School Equivalency Degree and her General Educational Development certificate; attained a Certificate of Completion in Responsibility of Self-Determination; and made it through the Twelve Steps over and over.

A prison chaplain for whom she worked as a clerk declared Roxanne "cooperative and willing to take direction. . . . She has been concerned as long as I have known her with a continuing bonding with her children."

A drug-treatment instructor asserted that she had "transformed her life into one that is of service, caring, and hard work. I am certain she will continue in recovery and continue to help other women after she is released back into the community. She is a leader of women and can be a great asset to the recovering community in our society."

A parole officer who worked with Roxanne at an in-custody drug-treatment program asserted that "it is my professional opinion that Theresa Roxanne Cruz is a well-respected lady today, who has taken responsibility for her actions and who has great insight regarding her past criminal behavior. . . . She will be an asset to our community. My family could feel safe with her as a neighbor. . . . My opinion is that taxpayer money is being wasted by denying this inmate parole."

"Ms. Cruz will be a valuable, productive, responsible and respectful asset to the Community upon her release."

"The positive impact she has had on the CIW Community will benefit society as inmates are released back into their communities."

Her "commitment to continue to affect change in other women after her release will be a valuable asset to our society upon her release."

When I visited the Azhocar household in the spring of 2004, Roxanne had another parole hearing coming up, but her family wasn't talking much about it. Roxanne had been turned down for parole seven times already. Hope in the Azhocar household had become a controlled substance—as potent in its dangers as in its healing powers.

Roxanne's children have stopped asking when she will come home. Now it is her grandchildren who ask questions: "Why does Grandma Roxanne have to stay here?" "How come we have to drive so far?" "Why is this her home?"

At sixty-one, Theresa has nineteen grandchildren and seven great-grandchildren. "My daughter's incarceration has affected five generations," she said. "My mother, me—it completely turned my life around—my daughter, her children, and their children, who now, which is sad, go to prison to visit their grandma. There has to be a better way, and not just for the person who's incarcerated."

Each of Theresa's adult children and grandchildren has a key to her house, and weekday mornings find a stream of parents bustling through on their way to work. By the time Antoinette arrived at 7:45, Theresa's great-nephew Jordan and granddaughter Emily were already in residence. At eight, Andrea and her son Ruben stopped by for raisin bran and oatmeal, respectively, on the way to Ruben's school, which was down the street. Felicitas came into the kitchen in a floral housedress and leopard-print slippers to make a cup of coffee. Ten minutes later, Andrea grabbed Ruben and Jordan, whom she would also drop off at school, and was out the door.

At 8:45, Theresa made herself a piece of toast. The doorbell rang. Four-year-old Bunny—another granddaughter—had arrived to play with Emily. "You want some breakfast?" Theresa asked Bunny. Emily began to fuss for her gymnastics outfit, which she had left at home. Alfonso started shouting. Theresa's toast got cold.

The Disney Channel reigns once again in the Azhocar household, and sometimes Theresa even finds time to sit down for a few minutes and watch. Alfonso might drape a blanket over her legs, take her hand and kiss it. Sometimes Theresa looks at her younger grandchildren and great-grandchildren and wonders at the expression she sees on their faces—an unfettered happiness that was absent from the house during the years when she was raising Roxanne's children.

Theresa is more indulgent with the current crop of grandchildren and great-grandchildren than she was with the ones she raised single-handedly. "Look how she takes them to McDonald's all the time. She takes them to Sea World," Antoinette said with a touch of petulance. "I don't understand why she didn't do it with us."

Part of the reason is surely pragmatic: Theresa was working more than full-time when Antoinette was small; now she has retired. But caring for this latest generation has also given Theresa the opportunity to revert to the role of grandmother rather than surrogate mother. The children who fill Theresa's house and yard these days are not likely to shout at her, "You're not my mother!" They know their mothers will be coming for them at the end of the day.

In October of 2004, six months after my visit, Theresa went into the hospital for what she thought would be a gallbladder operation. After the surgery, doctors told her she had Stage IV liver cancer.

Five days later, Roxanne went before the parole board for the eighth time. Her parole was denied.

Theresa was in and out of the hospital in the weeks following her surgery, suffering from jaundice and dehydration as the cancer advanced. The children were scattered to an assortment of other relatives' homes. Everyone was missing work. The Azhocar house, Antoinette told me, had grown oddly quiet; most of the lights were kept off.

Adriana wrote an open letter on behalf of her grandmother:

> She is a rose, she is a flower that blooms, she is the one that has the voice to make many people's flowers bloom. She is everyone's best friend, a mother and my grandmother. . . . After her husband's death, her life was committed to raising her grandchildren, Andrea, Antoinette, Carlitos and Adriana. . . . All her giving was volunteered and out of her heart. . . .
>
> Please, we need all the help we can get. HELP SAVE HER LIFE!

Neither Antoinette nor Andrea could bring themselves to break the news to Roxanne, so Andrea's husband did it. As soon as he said the word "cancer," the phone line went dead. After that, Roxanne called several times a day, worried about Theresa. Antoinette's phone bill reached $600. She could not afford to pay it, but neither could she bring herself to tell her grief-stricken mother not to call.

"I feel helpless," Antoinette said. "I don't know who to talk to, or what to do."

Near midnight on December 7, 2004—six weeks after she was diagnosed—Theresa died at home, where she had returned to receive hospice care. When she first learned of her illness, she had begun the process of adopting Adriana—she had held off over the years out of respect for Roxanne—so that Adriana would be eligible for survivor benefits under social security, but Theresa died before the paperwork could be processed. She had also hoped to make a final visit to the prison, to say good-bye to her daughter, but she became too ill to be transported before she could complete the arrangements.

Roxanne—who had not been able to attend her father's funeral fourteen years earlier—requested a family emergency leave to pay her last respects to her mother, but was denied. As a lifer, she was considered a flight risk.

When Andrea and Antoinette were girls, Andrea used to drive Antoinette crazy with her worries. "An, what are we gonna do if Grandma dies?" Andrea would ask her younger sister. "Who are we gonna live with?"

"Stop saying that!" Antoinette would order. "She's not gonna die." Now it is the twice-orphaned Adriana to whom she must offer some kind of reassurance.

The same week that Theresa died, her mother, Felicitas, had a heart attack and went into the hospital. Andrea and Antoinette have been caring for Adriana, taking turns picking her up from school and driving her to sports practice. "I know this is going to affect Adriana a lot, her whole entire life, but we're just trying to keep her spirits up," Antoinette said. "We don't want her to fall down."

"I don't want her to not want to go to school, be depressed—how I was when my mom left," Antoinette said. "My grandmother *is* her mom—that's all she knows."

. . .

IN LITTLE ROCK, ARKANSAS, Dee Ann Newell has turned the master bedroom of the house where she grew up into a grandmother's parlor, with a shiny, waxed wood floor; floral-print sofa and stately stuffed chairs; an oak armoire and a gleaming upright piano. The walls are a faint, dusky pink with cream trim, and the street outside is shady and hushed.

The space bespeaks rest, and the women who visit it are tired. Some grew up in sharecropping families and spent their own childhood years working in the fields. Many now work more than one job. All are caring for their grandchildren and worrying about their incarcerated children. They meet in this room each Thursday to talk about parts of their lives that many feel compelled to keep secret at work and at church. Their grandchildren meet simultaneously in Newell's old bedroom, which has become a children's center.

The house is the headquarters of Arkansas Voices for the Children Left Behind, a coalition that Newell founded in 1994, then incorporated in 2001 as a direct service and advocacy organization focusing on the families of prisoners. Arkansas Voices runs a mentoring program; hosts support groups; and staffs a "warm line," which anyone with a relative in prison can call for advice or referrals. The organization is also developing a statewide grandmother's lobby to advocate on behalf of incarcerated parents and their children.

Newell is the chairman of the board. She also runs the Family Matters Program at the Centers for Youth and Families, the largest children's mental health center in the state. A federally funded demonstration project, Family Matters offers case management to twenty-seven families affected by parental incarceration. The Family Matters clientele reflects the group that is, nationwide, taking on the lion's share of responsibility for the children left parentless by incarceration: elderly African American women, poor and in ill health. The average household income of Family Matters clients is $7,200 a year.

Through Family Matters, grandparents and children attend support groups and receive counseling. Family advocates meet with caregivers and children two or three times a week, in their homes and at school. They help grandparents establish guardianship, obtain public benefits, enroll their grandchildren in school, and prepare for their children's return. They also meet monthly with incarcerated parents and arrange special visits.

Family Matters organizes its services around what grandparents say they most need. Food comes up frequently, as does gas to get to prison. Some grandmothers want to know how to get medical care for a child when the only document they have establishing guardianship is a note from that child's mother, written on her way out the door. Some want information on how to file for bankruptcy. Some seek help finding new homes for their grandchildren as their own health fails.

Newell is "near sixty," with chin-length red hair and watery blue eyes. She brings to her work a personal connection: When she was nine years old, her father, who had manic depressive disorder, was taken screaming from the house in a straitjacket in the middle of the night. Newell remembers the psychiatric hospital where he spent the following year as "like a castle with turrets, and bars on the windows." For several months after her father was taken, Newell refused to go to school.

"I don't use this as any sort of therapeutic thing for myself," she said of her current work, "but I do know that some of my experiences make these kids extraordinarily special for me."

Sometimes, when she spoke about "these kids," or "my grandmothers," her voice quavered and it seemed as if she were having a hard time catching her breath. When she revealed a particularly egregious aspect of the way the grandmothers were mistreated or maligned, her voice dropped to a stage whisper. She had occasion to take this tone frequently.

Paula Pumphrey, the director of Arkansas Voices, ran the state's parole and probation department when Bill Clinton was governor. The intimacy with which she and Newell spoke of their clients, and the level of detail, evoked gossip, except that it was infused with the opposite of malice. Get these two started on the subject of The State v. Grandma, however, and they get each other into a lather fairly quickly. It's not hard to see why.

A grandmother calls the child welfare department seeking kinship foster-care payments on behalf of her grandchildren. She is told that she will first have to place the children in the custody of strangers while the department does an investigation to determine whether she and her home meet state standards. This information tends to register as what Newell called a "veiled threat, if not a direct threat: we're gonna take your kids and you won't have any assurance that you'll get them back." Few grandparents pursue this avenue of support any further. Out of the approximately three thousand Arkansas families receiving foster care payments, only about two hundred are kinship families.

A woman is caring for her incarcerated sister's children. She seeks TANF payments on the children's behalf—which in Arkansas amount to $81 a month for the first child and $42 for each subsequent child—and is told she is not eligible. Newell schools the woman in the eligibility requirements and coaches her to return to the welfare office. On her third visit, a worker concedes that she is in fact eligible, but warns her that if she seeks benefits, her sister will be required to pay the state back upon her release.

A grandmother is caring for her incarcerated daughter's four children. The father of one of the children has been paying the state $25 a week in child support, which the state has been keeping in the mother's absence. The mother has been in prison for ten years, and the pot has grown to $15,000, none of which the child has seen. Pumphrey and the grandmother pay multiple visits to the child support office. After months of wrangling, it is determined that the grandmother is entitled to the money on behalf of the child. However, the state first reimburses itself for TANF she has received over the years on behalf of *all four* children, leaving something under $3,000. Finally, the grandmother receives what money is left—at which point her TANF payments are cut off because the $3,000 pushes her assets over the eligibility limit. This is a family whose children have been known to call Pumphrey themselves to tell her they are hungry.

Why would institutions that ostensibly exist to help and protect children go so far out of their way to make things harder for these already-overburdened old women, not to mention the children who rely on them? Newell has given this question thought, and has spent enough time at conferences and convenings at the Capitol that she's been able to pick up on the prevailing attitude toward grandparent caregivers, which might best be summarized thus: they've already screwed up one generation. Why should we help them screw up the next?

This is the kind of talk that makes Newell's voice fall to a hiss. Arkansas is home to nearly thirty-seven thousand grandparent-headed households. Newell estimates that a parent is incarcerated in about one-third of these families. "We are standing on the backs of these grandmothers," said Newell. Were they to withdraw their unpaid services, she pointed out, it would "break the bank of the state."

"You want to say, 'Well, would you like to come meet the women I know who have done everything they know how to do but have six children in a basement?'" Newell said. "What is it we're gonna tell them they need to be doing that they're not doing? They're trying to survive. They're trying to keep those kids safe. They can't."

In her 1974 account of kinship networks in a poor black community, the anthropologist Carol B. Stack outlined the complex informal rules governing intergenerational rights over, and responsibilities to, children. "This system of rights and duties should not be confused with the official, written statutory law of the state. . . ." she cautioned. "Community members clearly operate within two different systems: the folk system and the legal system of the courts and welfare offices." What is wounding when the legal system fails to recognize the folk system is not just the denial of much-needed support but the message that grandparent-headed families are somehow illegitimate.

The questions that drive "eligibility"—whose child is this, anyway?—bear little relationship to the reality of grandparents' lives: they are caring for their grandchildren while their children are gone. When grandparents describe the struggles they face trying to enroll their grandchildren in school, get medical care for them, or seek government assistance—the shame and fear they face in their dealings with public institutions—one is reminded of the experience of undocumented immigrants.

The grandmothers will tell you that Newell and her colleagues were not only the first to offer help; they were and remain the only ones who didn't make them feel ashamed for needing it. Marilyn, an Arkansas grandmother, wept as she described applying for TANF on behalf of her granddaughter after her daughter was arrested. A worker told her she was not eligible; her daughter would have to come down and sign the forms. When she explained that her daughter was in prison, she said, "It was like they weren't interested [in helping]. Like it's bad. That's how you feel."

Newell and Pumphrey have been ruthless in their efforts to communicate a different message. They rallied a crowd of grandmothers and had them pull their grandkids in red wagons to the steps of the Capitol, and managed in 2003 to get legislation passed guaranteeing funding for services to children of prisoners and their families. Now they are working on a campaign to establish a guardianship subsidy for relatives, so they can receive support without subjecting their grandchildren to the vicissitudes of the foster care system.

The two women are ruthless, also, in the bare-knuckled advocacy they practice on behalf of individual grandmothers. Arkansas, Newell observed, is a good-ol'-boy state, and she is something of a good ol' boy herself. She grew up in Little Rock in a prominent family; her husband was Clinton's legal counsel when he was governor. During my time in Little Rock, we did not enter a restaurant without someone influential rising from his seat and greeting her by name. Pumphrey, also, is well connected. Newell recalled standing with her on the steps of the Capitol and watching one legislator after another stop to pay their respects.

Pumphrey, Newell, and their staff work every connection they can to help grandmothers navigate state and local bureaucracies that seem bent on putting them through the twelve trials of Hercules before they are deemed worthy of a few dollars or a Medicaid card; to stop them from being evicted, losing their food stamps, or getting turned away at the emergency room. Their success rate is high, and Newell speaks with rightful pride of their ability to wrangle child care vouchers or a payment plan on a delinquent electric bill. Listening to them describe a day's work, however, one gets the sense that they are struggling to contain a brush fire that is constantly replenished at a source they cannot access.

On a summer afternoon, a leisurely caravan of older sedans made its way out of Little Rock, heading through maple and pine woods, dogwood and pecan, to Ferncliff, Arkansas. The cars were full of grandmothers, many of them with younger children in tow, on the way to the final evening of a weeklong summer camp sponsored by Family Matters. The site—Camp Ferncliff—is owned and operated by the Presbyterian Church; Newell went to camp there as a child. The camp offers the children a chance to spend time in the company of others who share their secret, and so be relieved of it. For grandparents, it provides an entire week of respite.

In the back seat of Pumphrey's Lincoln Town Car, Jerry sat with his NBA baseball cap on his lap. He was thin as a stalk in jeans, a woven leather belt, and a striped short-sleeved shirt. His hair was gray and his basset-hound eyes were set in a web of fine lines.

Jerry works as a school custodian and collects cans for gas money. Three years ago, he got a call from his daughter's boyfriend asking him to come pick up his then-nine-year-old granddaughter, Taylor, whose mother had just been arrested for "bothering people's stuff."

Jerry drove right over. Taylor was waiting, her clothes balled up in a plastic bag. He and his second wife have been caring for her ever since.

In his back pocket, Jerry carried a letter from his daughter, who was about to be released. "I'm praying that my daughter comes in and does well with Taylor," he said. "Taylor's come a long way since she's been with us. . . . She's stable, and I don't want her to lose any of that."

Jerry spoke of his granddaughter with a tenderness infused with anxiety. "She wants to be grown; next minute she's back combing those baby dolls' hair." Lately he's found himself lecturing her a little more than usual. He's worried that her school attendance will slip once her mother comes home; that she'll stop going to church.

As we pulled into camp, Taylor spotted her grandfather and leapt off a picnic table to chase after the slowing car.

"You like my necklace?" she asked eagerly. "I made it out of glass." Jerry kissed her on the forehead. She was a beautiful, lanky girl—close to her grandfather in height—with smooth, dark skin and hair that showed the wages of a week at the lake.

"I guess I can do that tomorrow," Jerry said under his breath when he caught sight of his granddaughter's unkempt hair— "get an appointment to get her wig twisted for Sunday."

Children were clustered around picnic tables beside a murky green lake. Many had damp hair. On the porch of the main building, several of the younger children stood together, singing, "Hello Mudda, Hello Fadda, here I am in Camp Granada." A group of mallards tentatively picked their way among the tables.

Down by the lake, three men began drumming. Slowly, the children drifted into the circle and joined in before-dinner song.

Taylor had left a space beside her and waved her grandfather over.

After a meal of barbecued beef and pork sandwiches, a dreadlocked young man in a purple and green dashiki paced around the fire pit, telling folk tales and leading songs in English and Swahili. At least one couple had formed during the week; they sat shoulder to shoulder at the story circle, holding hands when they thought no one was looking. Brenda—who was there to see her eight-year-old grandson Patrick—sat on a log and called out answers to the storyteller's questions as enthusiastically as the children. ("What do American children call the yam?" "Sweet potato!").

Brenda has cared for Patrick since his father, Brenda's son, went to prison eight years ago. At first, Brenda took in both Patrick and his then-fifteen-year-old mother. Then the young woman moved out, taking Patrick's welfare benefits with her but leaving him behind, Brenda said. Brenda hasn't made an issue of it for fear of losing Patrick.

Patrick is doing well; he's an honor student and "grandmom baby" who has won trophies for being "most coachable." But Brenda is excruciatingly aware of his vulnerability. When Patrick's father—also named Patrick—was six years old, Brenda spent seven months in prison. Her husband had just died, and her twelve-year-old daughter was dying also, from non-Hodgkin's lymphoma. Brenda took an unpaid leave from her job to care for her daughter and ran out of money. Close to losing her house, she tried selling drugs.

After Brenda returned from prison, she said, Patrick Sr. remained resentful and got involved with a gang. He has since written a song about his time without his mother, called "Continuing Tears."

When Brenda was an infant, her mother left her with a paternal relative and never came back for her. When her husband and daughter died, she had little family support; when she went to prison, her children had none. She found an extended family later, she said—for herself and for her grandson—in the Family Matters group, where she became a peer leader. When Brenda's legs went bad—her doctor has told her she needs both knees replaced—and she had to stop working and lost her home, another Family Matters grandmother took her and Patrick in for six months while Brenda waited for her disability application to be approved.

"We're kind of like a family," Brenda said. "We give each other a chance to vent; to talk to an adult, when you may not have seen one since the last week! You can talk about stuff and nobody is going to look down on you, because they are going through the same thing. If you have a child that acts up at school, you can talk with your sisters about it, and get feedback from somebody who is living it with you. That helps a lot, because they understand."

After the story circle, I asked Brenda how she thought the children understood the focus of the camp. She called her grandson over and asked him, "Do you know why you're here?"

"Because my dad's in jail," he said, then ran off to rejoin his friends.

The story circle dissolved into dancing; then the crowd drifted away. The children would spend one more night here. Some would go directly to the men's prison to visit their fathers the next day; others would go home with their grandparents.

As we pulled out, one of the grandmothers began reading a storybook to her two sleepy younger grandchildren in the back seat. An ambulance drove by, sirens blaring. "It's gonna get you!" one boy told the other.

"These grandparents make enormous sacrifices," Newell said, "but when you pin them down, they say, 'This is the way I wanted to do it, and I will take what comes in order to keep my family together.' What more could we ask, in terms of family values, than that?"

5

FOSTER CARE

CHRISTINE STOOD IN THE window and watched two police cars pull up outside her apartment complex. She was seven years old. She knew what was coming.

The police put Christine's mother in the back of one car. Christine and her four-year-old brother rode in the other. After that, the two were sent to separate foster homes. By the time Christine saw her brother again, several years had passed and he had been adopted. He had a new name. He didn't remember her.

What was Christine to think as she rode away in the police car on that day when everything ended? Only what children are already inclined to think when misfortune strikes their family: that she was to blame; that her actions had somehow caused her family's suffering.

Nothing in Christine's subsequent experience disabused her of this notion. Jail, Christine understood, was her mother's punishment for using drugs. Her own, for crimes unnamed, was having her brother taken from her, being sent to live with strangers, and being raped in foster care. Christine was ensconced in juvenile hall by the time she was eleven, for stealing a bike and, in her words, being "really, really bad. They didn't know what to do after that, because nobody wanted me."

After juvenile hall came a receiving home, then another foster home, a second rape, a pregnancy. At thirteen, Christine gave a child up for adoption. When I met her, she was twenty-one and living in a transitional shelter for homeless young adults. "I lost a lot of trust in foster care," she told me flatly.

As the writer Nina Bernstein has observed, "The stronger the desire to discipline society—and growing inequality demands stricter social discipline—the stronger the appeal of schemes that promise to rescue poor children by removing them from their failing families." It should not then be surprising that the foster care population has grown at a rate that mirrors—if not quite matches—that of the prison system, doubling over the past two punitive decades to well over half a million at last count.

The criminal justice and child welfare systems are deeply intertwined: two ballooning bureaucracies that feed and fuel each other. The growth of both depends on the same willed misapprehension: that we can make things harder for parents without also making them worse for children.

At any given moment, 10 percent of the children of women prisoners and 2 percent of the children of incarcerated men, are in foster care. One study of children in long-term foster care done by the Center for Children of Incarcerated Parents found that as many as 90 percent of them had at least one parent who had been arrested or incarcerated, and 40 percent had two.

But aren't these kids better off without their convict parents? This is the question I hear most frequently when I talk or write about the children of prisoners. The assertion that children are "better off" without drug-using or otherwise lawbreaking parents is one that is generally made in absolute terms. Children do not have the luxury of such abstraction. Viewed from the vantage point of a child, the question is always relative: when we remove her parents, what do we offer by way of substitute? The answer is rarely encouraging.

Like the prison system, the child welfare system has been crippled by its own growth. The result is that the bureaucracies to which foster children are consigned simply do not have the resources to sustain them. Any criminal justice policy that adds to the pressures on families, and thus to the number of children in need of care, also exacerbates the looming crisis in foster care.

The ills of our foster care system, well documented elsewhere, are too voluminous to detail here. But a few things are worth remembering when we make the decision that a child is "better off" in substitute care than with a parent who has broken the law.

Children in foster care are extremely vulnerable. All fifty states have failed a federal foster care review designed to measure their capacity to protect children from abuse and neglect and find them permanent homes. According to Richard Gelles—professor of social work at the University of Pennsylvania and an expert on foster care—"no one is able to identify a child welfare agency in the United States that actually works. . . . There are none. There are no best practices."

Most children will fare better in foster care than did Christine. But Christine's experience, while extreme, is far from unprecedented. Children are significantly more likely to be abused and neglected in foster homes than are their peers in the general population.

They are also increasingly likely to land in institutions. As the number of children entering foster care has grown, the number of families willing to take a child home has dropped. The result is that children wind up in group homes, residential treatment centers, or other institutions. The longer a child stays in this kind of care, the more likely she is to develop emotional and behavior problems—problems that up the odds she will continue to be institutionalized.

Children of incarcerated parents may be at particular risk for this sort of escalating placement—a Sacramento, California, study found that 90 percent of the children in that county's most costly child welfare placements, such as residential treatment centers, had an incarcerated parent.

Those young people who are placed in family foster homes often careen from one to the next, a scenario custom-made to exacerbate the "attachment problems" to which children of prisoners are already vulnerable. In California, researchers have determined that children who experience five or more placements are six times more likely than those who stay in one place to wind up with mood, behavior, anxiety, and adjustment disorders. Nearly a third of the state's foster youth will experience five or more placements during their time in care.

Danny Rifkin, who runs a summer camp for the children of incarcerated parents in Northern California, recalled a child who was left behind when camp ended and no one came to pick her up. It turned out that the child welfare department had terminated her foster care placement and moved her to a group home while she was at camp—but no one appeared to have told the group home where they might find her.

Those who grow up in foster care and "emancipate"—or leave the system—at eighteen show few signs of having been made better off by their experience in the hands of the state. Nearly half of all eighteen-year-olds leaving the foster care system do so without a high school diploma; fewer than 40 percent are able to find and keep a job. In California, 65 percent transition directly into homelessness.

Foster care itself is one of the best predictors there is that a child will wind up behind bars. A University of Chicago study of more than seven hundred teenagers in foster care found that 61 percent of boys and 41 percent of girls had been arrested by the age of seventeen. One in five women prisoners, and nearly as many men, lived in a foster or group home as a child. These numbers ought to give pause to those who insist that the children of offenders must be raised apart from their families lest they follow in their parents' footsteps.

When I speak with young people who have found themselves in foster care when their parents are imprisoned, this is what I find them most eager to convey: that though their parents may be less than perfect, though they may be angry at their parents, though they may feel abandoned and betrayed, their love and need for their parents—and their terror and sorrow when their parents are taken from them—are of the same magnitude and quality as any other child's.

In a writing workshop run by San Francisco's Pacific News Service, a juvenile detainee offered this account:

> *You don't know what it feels like to come up in the world with parents that can't stay out of jail.*
> *You don't know what it's like to have your sisters and brothers took from you and placed in a group home.*
> *You don't know what it's like to have no family to be by your side when you need them in a time of hurt.*

You don't know what it's like to be me and never will, so I'll
    tell you . . .
It feels like a forever going rollercoaster ride through fire and
    water that ends when you fall.

Criminality does not negate or erase parenthood. Arrest and incarceration too often do. Increasingly, for those families caught in the crushing nexus of the criminal justice and child welfare systems, that erasure is both explicit and irremediable.

Tougher sentencing laws have conspired with a new emphasis in child welfare on speedy termination of parental rights, welfare reform, and a shift in enforcement of child support laws to put tremendous pressure on already-vulnerable families. The net result is that single mothers who serve time on even minor charges are discovering that the penalty for their crime includes forfeiture of their children. For children—who may have a hard time understanding that their mother has disappeared not by choice but by decree of the court—this loss is likely to be experienced as a profound abandonment in a life already marked by instability.

The federal Adoption and Safe Families Act (ASFA), passed in 1997, has hit people who are or have been incarcerated hard. ASFA mandates that the states begin proceedings to terminate parental rights once a child has been in foster care for fifteen out of the past twenty-two months—six months if the child is under the age of three. The law also promises the states bonuses of four thousand to ten thousand dollars for each adoption over pre-ASFA levels. ASFA was intended to address a real problem: children spending years or decades bouncing from one foster home to another while their parents blow chance after chance to get their lives together. But, as with any pendulum swing, ASFA has had some overly extreme consequences, sweeping some families into its net before parents have had the fair shot that they—and, more important, their children—deserve at preserving family bonds.

Across the country, those who work with and advocate for incarcerated women say they have seen a particularly steep increase in terminations of rights among prisoners. Philip Genty, a clinical professor of law and the director of the Prisoners and Families Clinic at Columbia University Law School, works with prisoners in New York–area facilities, where he and his students lead family law workshops, and he has written widely on termination of parental rights. He has found that, in the years since ASFA was enacted, appellate cases involving terminations among incarcerated parents have gone up 250 percent.

Women prisoners facing termination proceedings were once the exception, said Genty; now, among those whose children are in foster care, they have become the rule. "It is a very rare situation where a woman prisoner with a child in foster care has not been confronted with this," Genty said.

Many prisoners do stints even for minor infractions that exceed ASFA's six- and fifteen-month time limits. In New York state, more than 90 percent of women convicted of felonies, including low-level nonviolent crimes, will serve at least eighteen months—three months more than the longer of the ASFA time limits. Nationwide, the average term being served by parents in state prison is eighty months.

Social workers, Genty explained, "feel that ASFA puts pressure on them to move children out of the system quickly, even when they think there may be a decent relationship between parent and child. They don't have the ability to wait for the parent to get out of prison."

As early as 1944, the Supreme Court recognized that parents have a "fundamental liberty interest" in the custody and care of their children. In a series of subsequent cases, the courts have gone on to establish that incarceration itself is not sufficient evidence of a parent's inability to care for her children to warrant the permanent revocation of her right to do so. One court noted, "While 'use a gun, go to prison' may well be an appropriate legal maxim, 'go to prison, lose your child' is not." Nevertheless, thirty-four states now have statutes in place that explicitly cite parental incarceration as a criterion for termination of parental rights. In Georgia, for example, "imprisonment that has a demonstrable negative effect on the quality of the parent/child relationship"—which is to say, imprisonment—is identified as a factor favoring termination. Several states also identify parental incarceration as an "aggravating circumstance" that relieves the state of the obligation to work to reunify a family.

Technically, social services departments are required to help provide the resources a parent needs before determining that she is incapable of raising her children. But imprisoned parents are not necessarily top priority for overburdened workers, who may not even have met clients who are locked away in distant facilities.

Ben De Haan, who has headed both the child welfare and correctional systems in Oregon, put it bluntly: "I was a child protection worker—when someone was in prison, you write 'em off. That's the standard drill; that's what they teach you. Throw in ASFA and you're adding even more pressure."

Under a New York statute, a parent who does not visit or otherwise communicate with a child is construed to have abandoned him. According to the statute, "in the absence of evidence to the contrary, such ability to visit and communicate shall be presumed." This presumption may be ill-founded when it comes to incarcerated parents. Nationwide, 75 percent of foster care administrators say they do not consider proximity to the jail when placing the child of a parent who has been arrested.

Women whose children are in foster care often do not inform their caseworker when they are arrested, because they believe to do so would make their situation worse, not knowing that their silence can be construed as "abandonment." If a social worker does not locate and arrange visits with an incarcerated parent, an abandonment finding may be issued and termination proceedings launched.

Staying in contact with one's child is crucial to defending oneself against termination of parental rights. But prisoners face tremendous obstacles to maintaining relationships with children in foster care—and with the social workers who act as gatekeepers to those children. Prisons are often sited hundreds of miles from prisoners' home counties, and foster parents or social workers are often unwilling or unable to make the trek. As a result, only about 13 percent of prisoners' children in long-term foster care visit their incarcerated mothers, and less than 5 percent visit incarcerated fathers. Prisoners cannot receive phone calls and usually can only place collect calls. Transfers from one facility to another are common and unannounced, so social workers who do make the effort may have a hard time even locating an incarcerated parent. Incarcerated parents who have child welfare cases before the family courts often do not receive court notices in time to appear, or do not know how to get permission and transportation to attend.

When the Child Welfare League of America surveyed state

child welfare systems nationwide, only five were able even to offer estimates of how many of the children in their care had an incarcerated parent (these estimates ranged between 10 and 30 percent). Only six states had a policy in place to address the needs of children of incarcerated parents, and only two provided their staff any training specific to these children.

"We have a crisis in our child welfare system," asserted Arlene Lee, director of the Federal Resource Center for Children of Prisoners at the Child Welfare League of America. "Social workers are overwhelmed, overworked, and leaving in droves. When that happens, the cases that are hardest to deal with don't get dealt with, and trying to maintain a family bond when a parent is in prison is a challenge even for the best of them."

"Every time my social worker would come over, I asked to set up a date to go see my mom," recalled Randall, whose mother served time for auto theft. "He would always say, 'We're trying, we're trying.'" Arranging a visit took two years.

Researchers from the Vera Institute of Justice found that more than half of New York foster children whose mothers were incarcerated had their "permanency planning" goal changed to adoption rather than reunification. Among those incarcerated parents whose children were ultimately made available for adoption, more than half had lost their parental rights due to "technical abandonment."

The net result, said Philip Genty, is that "the mood in prison is one of despair. Essentially, what incarcerated parents are being told is that no matter what they do—how hard they work at overcoming the issues that put their children in foster care and brought them to prison—they cannot avoid having their parental rights terminated."

Pam Martinez—who spent seven years at the California Institute for Women at Corona for stealing a toolbox—has witnessed this despair firsthand. Martinez was working in the prison law library when ASFA hit. The result, she said, was "heart-wrenching and pathetic."

"This mother will come in really naive and say, 'Oh, the baby's with a nice family. There's going to be pictures, and they're going to bring the baby to visit,'" Martinez said. "I watched one after another lose her child."

"This will be known as the great baby-snatching era," predicted Martinez, who said many of the women who sought her advice in the law library did not understand the significance of the legal documents they were receiving in the mail. The final custody hearing—in which parental rights are formally terminated—is "the most pathetic," Martinez said. Many women "don't believe that it's really going to happen. They don't know, when they go out for that hearing, that they have no more say in that child's life, and they will probably never see the child again."

Even with papers in hand, said Martinez, many women continued to believe they would be reunited with their children. "They would come in and ask, 'What's going to happen next? Can they really take my child?' I had to tell them the heartbreaking news all the time."

"The ones that do understand it get out and come right back, forever," Martinez added. "They're back and back and back and back."

Martinez's own parental rights were terminated in 1989, after she served eight months for shoplifting a pair of socks. She has not seen her son, now seventeen, since.

When Martinez lost her parental rights, her situation was less common than it is today. Since ASFA, she said, she has seen dozens of her fellow prisoners go through the same experience.

"If there was a chance that you could do well and succeed after prison," she said, "it's gone. You feel like you're not worthy to participate in society, because you have failed as a mother—as a human being."

Even those inmates who manage to get out of prison with a little sand left in the ASFA hourglass face a daunting obstacle course if their children are in foster care. First, the social services department will hand them a reunification plan that requires, for example, that they complete a drug-treatment program, attend a parenting class, and provide a stable residence for their children. Since anyone with a felony drug conviction is ineligible for benefits, including housing, under welfare reform laws in many states, this last may prove particularly challenging. A criminal record also makes finding a job difficult, so market-rate housing is likely out of the question.

Former prisoners who do manage to obtain legal work may find their wages swallowed up by child support enforcement laws enacted over the last decade, ostensibly as a means of corralling so-called deadbeat dads. Designated "non-custodial parents" during their time behind bars, prisoners can be held liable not only for court-ordered payments to the other parent, but also for welfare or foster care payments received on behalf of their children during their absence. With interest and penalties for nonpayment accruing throughout their sentences, prisoners may wind up with bills they cannot possibly hope to pay: incarcerated parents owe, on average, more than $20,000 in child support debt when they walk out the gates. Should they subsequently manage to find legal work, their wages can be garnished by more than half. Failure to pay can mean more prison time, and *less* opportunity to contribute to one's family.

Denise Johnston of the Center for Children of Incarcerated Parents recalled working with a former prisoner who had, since her release, worked her way up from minimum wage to eight dollars an hour, and retrieved her children from foster care. Then the state caught up with her and began garnishing her wages by 50 percent. At four dollars an hour, she could no longer cover rent, food, and child care. "She was basically saying that she was going to go back to what she used to do," Johnston said. "I had nothing to tell her. There was nothing she could do."

Faced with these barriers, many former prisoners fail to meet the multiple requirements for retrieving their children, and termination proceedings begin.

"Half the women in here have lost children," said Ida Mc-Cray, standing outside a county jail women's unit. McCray, a former prisoner, founded and runs the nonprofit agency Families With a Future, which facilitates contact between prisoners and their children. "Momentary arrests, where she's out in two days, mean a woman could lose her kids. She gets arrested for petty theft. There's nobody to take the kids. Child Protective Services gets involved. They take the kids to the nearest emergency shelter. Now they've opened a case. When that person gets out in two days or two weeks, she can't meet the requirements to get her kids back." In various surveys, half or more of child welfare supervisors have confirmed that even in cases where an arrested parent is released within a few days and there is no indication of abuse or neglect, they will not automatically return a child to his parent's care.

With black families grossly overrepresented in both the child welfare and the prison system, McCray suggested, the intersection of tougher sentencing and child welfare laws has set in motion "the greatest separation of families since slavery."

For many women, losing the right to care for their children triggers a powerful despair—at their own failures, their children's resultant suffering, and the seeming omnipotence of institutions that many find incomprehensible, if not hostile. They treat this despair not with Prozac or Zoloft but with methamphetamine, heroin, crack cocaine—taking themselves one step further from the rehabilitation that is ostensibly the motive for incarcerating drug addicts.

Maintaining family contact is one of the most effective means of achieving successful reentry into society. When you eliminate that prospect, Philip Genty observed, "it removes one of the most effective tools towards rehabilitation."

In the 1997 John Woo film *Face/Off,* Nicolas Cage's FBI agent, confronting an intransigent witness, brandishes the worst threat of all: "I'll send you to jail, and your kid will go to foster care." Intentionally or not, this threat has become part of the arsenal, part of the equation of crime and punishment.

The central issue, however, is not whether ASFA is hard on incarcerated parents but whether it is good for kids. The law was intended to stem the out-of-control growth of the foster care system by providing "permanency" for children, but that system shows little sign of shrinkage. The average time spent in foster care is exactly the same today—thirty-three months—as it was pre-ASFA. But the number of children made legal orphans each year—their ties to their parents severed but no new parents identified—went from just under six thousand in 1997 to more than twenty-four thousand in 1999. Seven years after

ASFA passed, there were some 129,000 children designated as "waiting" for an adoptive home—which is to say, entirely parentless in the eyes of the law.

The federal Department of Health and Human Services has taken on this problem by partnering with the Advertising Council to publicize the availability of these children, using the welcoming slogan, "You don't have to be perfect to be a parent." Apparently, this standard applies only to adoptive parents; less-than-perfect biological parents need not apply.

Elizabeth—an energetic brunette who resembles the *Norma Rae*-era Sally Field—is still trying to absorb the judge's decree, handed down a year earlier, that she is no longer mother to now-seven-year-old Anthony.

Anthony was four years old the day his mother made the mistake that would separate them forever. Elizabeth had filled her cart with eighty dollars' worth of groceries and was standing in line waiting to pay for them. On impulse, she picked up a Bic lighter and slipped it into her pocket. In a lifetime that had already given her plenty to regret, Elizabeth would come to regret this action more than any she had ever taken. It would trigger a chain of events that left her unlikely ever to see her child again.

Elizabeth, thirty-nine, was not simply a shoplifter; she was also a drug offender, with a lengthy history of using and selling methamphetamine. It is a history she said drew to a close within the last few years, as, in fits and starts, she managed to get herself into a rehab program, secure permanent housing, stop using drugs, and stabilize her life. But Elizabeth didn't do these things quickly or consistently enough; didn't do them on the timetable handed to her by the court that claimed jurisdiction over her son in the wake of her shoplifting arrest. As a result, she saw her parental rights permanently terminated and her child placed for adoption.

"It's a nightmare going through my head over and over," Elizabeth said. "In the last two years, I have turned my whole life around. I haven't had any police contact. I have a car, a job, I maintain my home. My life has been good from when I started my [rehab] program, but as far as the system is concerned, it was too little, too late."

Elizabeth's "nightmare" began two days after her release from jail following her shoplifting arrest. She had spent thirty days behind bars, during which time her sister cared for her son. The day after her release, Elizabeth did not make it to a drug-rehab program where her sister had secured a bed for her because, she said, she had to attend a court hearing that day. She failed, however, to communicate this to her sister, who assumed Elizabeth simply hadn't bothered to show up and responded by delivering Anthony to the local police station and declaring him "abandoned." The police handed Anthony over to social services, which opened a file and placed him in foster care, first with Elizabeth's sister and later with strangers.

Elizabeth was presented with a reunification plan that required her to enter drug treatment, secure housing, attend a parenting class, and get therapy. According to Elizabeth, the drug-treatment programs she contacted either had long waiting lists or couldn't reach her when they did have an opening because she didn't have a stable place to live; obtaining housing was difficult in a market where prices had gone through the roof; and once she got around to seeking therapy, the department would no longer pay for it because her reunification services had been cut off. Armed with evidence of Elizabeth's failures, the court terminated her rights and declared Anthony available for adoption.

From Elizabeth's perspective, when she turned to social services for help, she came up against an impenetrable bureaucracy that failed adequately to communicate its requirements, then penalized her when she could not meet them. From the department's perspective—spelled out in reports her social worker submitted to the court—Elizabeth continued to live a life of instability and probable drug use despite the fact that she had been offered both help and a clear warning of what would happen if she did not change her ways.

Lynn Vogelstein, a New York attorney who has represented prisoners in custody proceedings, said this kind of perception gap is far from unusual. Often, she said, caseworkers first meet a client at her very lowest point, so they may not be receptive to evidence of transformation. By the time Vogelstein meets them, often months later, "a lot of my clients are doing great things, but have been unable to communicate that to the agency."

Elizabeth did not claim to have been an ideal mother. "Part of the problem with substance abuse is you don't think you're doing anything wrong," she explained. Only once she got into a rehab program did she realize that the parenting standards she had set for herself were far too low.

"I thought I was doing a good job by just providing a roof over the head, paying the utilities," she said. "But I wasn't there mentally and emotionally, putting his needs first."

Elizabeth even came to understand her sister's decision to

turn Anthony over to the police. "She knew it wasn't fair the way I was raising him," Elizabeth said. "And I know she meant it in my best interest for somebody to intervene. Somebody had to do it. She just didn't know the system—the way it worked."

Elizabeth often wonders how Anthony understands her disappearance from his life. "He'd just turned four when all this happened," she said, "and what he understood as far as why he wasn't in mother's care was, 'Mom had a drug problem and she had no place for you to live.' So he always thought if Mom got a house and went to this [rehab] program, that he'd come back home. Now he's seven, and Mom did all these things, and he's still not home. You've got to wonder where his little mind takes him. He's still my child, and there's always going to be that question in his mind: 'How come I'm not with Mama?'"

Ahmad spent much of his childhood pondering this very question. He was born while his mother was in a California state prison and was cared for by relatives and foster parents in San Francisco, but retained a close relationship with his mother, who was released from prison when he was still a baby. He remembers himself as a mischievous child who spent a lot of time loose in the streets, getting into trouble. So when he was brought to court for what turned out to be a termination hearing, he assumed he was there through some fault of his own.

"Mommy, I'm sorry, I won't be bad again," wailed the five-year-old Ahmad as the bailiff carried him away from her after the judge announced his ruling.

"I knew from her expression, her tears, begging the judge, what had happened," Ahmad said. "I was reaching out to her, trying to have that last hug, and they picked me up and took me away."

Ahmad went on to be adopted by a single father. He was denied further contact with any of his relatives, including his mother and sister, ostensibly to spare him confusion. Even his family photographs were taken from him.

This stratagem failed to relieve Ahmad of his confusion. "All my life I thought something was wrong with me," he said. "Was I that bad a child? Was I that much of a problem that people didn't want to take care of me?"

Ahmad was sixteen and living in South Carolina with his adoptive father and brother when he came home from school to find a message from his mother, who had somehow tracked him down. Ahmad's father broke the news gently, assuming Ahmad would be resentful that his mother had turned up after such a long absence. Instead, Ahmad packed his bags and got on a Greyhound bus for San Francisco.

Ahmad had lost more than a mother when his legal connection to his family was severed. In San Francisco, he reconnected with his grandmother and sister, met a whole crop of cousins, held a nephew he had not known existed.

"My whole impression growing up was that my family were drug dealers, in and out of jail, but it wasn't like that," Ahmad said. "My sister was this working mom. My mom had gotten over her past and cleaned herself up."

Ahmad moved in with his mother and enrolled in high school in San Francisco. He and his mother talked and talked. He grilled her about her childhood and the years they had spent apart. Whenever she hesitated, Ahmad insisted. "I have to know what you dealt with," he told her, "to know what I'm dealing with."

Ahmad discovered that his mother was intelligent and curious—"She probably would have been a psychologist, if drugs had not prohibited her." He learned that she had read to him in utero. Her love for him, she told Ahmad, had kept her alive as she finished her prison term.

"I started thinking, 'Maybe my mama cares,'" Ahmad said.

"Kids own the right to have a relationship with their parents," asserted Ellen Barry, founding director of Legal Services for Prisoners with Children, "even if they're not the best parents. The child has a right to be angry, to ask the parent to explain her behavior. That's his choice, not the society's choice. Society does have an obligation to keep children safe, but that's very different from terminating parental rights."

In fact, Barry pointed out, termination is a concept most children can't begin to grasp. "It makes no sense to them that the court could come in and, with a wave of the hand, decide that the mother who gave birth to them is no longer their mother. Whether she's able to take care of them at this moment is a separate question."

Reconnecting with his mother allowed Ahmad to let go of the idea that what had happened in his family had somehow been his fault. His mother's addiction, he came to understand, was "something she had to battle her way through herself, and I couldn't change it."

Ahmad understands now that his mother had a problem; that "something wasn't right" when he was small. But he wonders why the state's response to that problem was permanently to sever his bond with his entire family, rather than to help his mother shoulder her responsibilities to him so he could remain part of that family.

"There was so much emphasis on me, supposedly, that they forgot about her," he said. "They wanted to protect little Ahmad. Why didn't they care about his mother? There are mothers out there that are abusive to their kids, so the system has to step in and do something about that. That's understood. But when there's a mother struggling with an addiction, struggling with herself, but is not abusive towards her kids, then the system has to help better that situation. What would have helped me most is compassion for my mom."

Ahmad's early losses predated ASFA, but the insights he has gained from them are more than relevant in an era of accelerated and widespread termination of parental rights.

"Me and my mom, today, we have a good relationship," Ahmad said. "We argue a lot over little petty things, but we love each other. I never stopped loving her for my whole life."

WHAT IF ONE CAR HAD PULLED up outside Christine's apartment, rather than two? What if those responsible for addressing Ahmad's mother's drug problem had taken his connection to her into account? What if there were a place where mothers and children could go together; where the mothers could get the help they needed, and the children the care they required from parents rather than from strangers?

In California, a small group of women prisoners and their children are now offered exactly this opportunity. Family Foundations is an in-custody program operated by the California Department of Corrections at two sites—one in Santa Fe Springs, outside Los Angeles, and another in San Diego. Both facilities were designed and constructed specifically to house women prisoners together with their children. Women who have been convicted of nonviolent and nonserious offenses are eligible for the program, where they serve one-year sentences together with up to two children. Some women at Family Foundations enter together with their children six and under (if the child is already in foster care, they must first receive permission from the juvenile court). Many enter pregnant and deliver while they are there. After the year is up, they can choose to enter a six-month residential aftercare program, followed by six months of outpatient care.

The legislatively mandated program has been up and running since 1999. Eighty-one percent of the program's 220 graduates have successfully completed their parole, compared to about half of the women paroled from typical California prisons.

"When people are in crisis, it's one of the best opportunities to change," observed Arlene Lee of the Federal Resource Center for Children of Prisoners. "If you can intervene during the crisis of arrest and incarceration, and help someone identify ways to change, it's a tremendous opportunity." In traditional prisons—where inmates are separated from their children and opportunities for rehabilitation are scarce—this "crisis opportunity" is routinely squandered. Family Foundations represents an effort to milk it for all it is worth.

Vera Institute of Justice researchers who studied nearly 15,000 families with children in foster care in New York found that one-third of the mothers had criminal records. They also found indications that the cycle of incarceration and foster care runs in both directions: mothers' arrest rates rose sharply in the year their children were placed in foster care, and remained high after that. This trend was so marked that the researchers concluded that "family preservation efforts may function as a crime reduction tool. Successful efforts to avert placement not only keep families together and children out of foster care, but can also prevent the increase in maternal criminal activity that can take place following a child's removal."

In the case of Family Foundations, it is the Department of Corrections—rather than the child welfare department—that has taken on this challenge, the same one encapsulated in Ahmad's question: "What about the mothers?" If the program works in the long run, it may not only keep some children out of foster care at the time of arrest but also stem the "downward spiral" that makes many more children vulnerable to removal at some point in their lives. Several women I met at Family Foundations told me they were certain that, had they not been sent to the program, their own "downward spiral" would have continued and their children been taken from them at some point later on. Many also said they believe that would have been the right thing; that their children did not "deserve" the consequences of a mother's addiction.

In the nineteenth century, babies born in prison often stayed there until the end of their mothers' sentences. Few special provisions were made for these tiny prisoners, and the results were predictable. Before New York opened its first specialized prison nursery, nearly every baby born at Sing Sing died before making it to freedom. One visiting journalist reported that one child who did survive imprisonment "had been kept so long incarcerated, that on going out of the prison it called a horse a cat."

Today, there are prison nurseries in eleven states. What makes Family Foundations unusual is that it is not housed within a traditional prison facility, and every effort is made to buffer the children from the correctional aspect of the program. Prisoners brought in from county jails are slipped in a back door. Their handcuffs are removed and they are given a change of clothes before the children can see them. Inside Family Foundations, the women wear street clothes. There are no bars or guns, and while the women are prohibited from leaving, the doors are unlocked.

The program is also structured so that mothers and children walk out those doors together at the end of a year. In most prison nurseries, a woman can keep her baby for a fixed time—ranging from one to eighteen months—but if her sentence lasts longer than that, the baby leaves without her. Other programs aimed at keeping imprisoned mothers with their kids kick in toward the end of her sentence, when she may be transferred to a mother-child facility. Family Foundations prevents separation at both ends.

The women at Family Foundations are state prisoners, bound by the rules and regulations of the California Department of Corrections, but the goal is to make sure the children barely notice. This aim is reflected in every aspect of the facility design. From the outside, the low-lying beige building that houses the Santa Fe Springs facility could easily be mistaken for a Department of Motor Vehicles office. There is little on the inside, either, that evokes a correctional facility.

In the nursery—a room full of cribs, each with its own Mickey Mouse mobile—music played quietly as several women walked around carrying babies, rocking infants, or leading toddlers by the hand. In the living room, filled with soft couches and overstuffed chairs, a visiting facilitator conducted a spirited discussion on guilt, anger, and redemption. Next door, pre-school-aged children were making baskets and zealously washing their hands—the day's health lesson had highlighted the perils of germs. In the cafeteria, stocked with high chairs, a "baby food menu" listed the day's offerings for the toothless set: mashed carrots, mashed potatoes, apple sauce, crushed hard-boiled egg. The well-appointed playground—alive with children blowing bubbles, swinging, zipping around on trikes and scooters—was visible through a wall of floor-to-ceiling windows along the main hallway, so that it was impossible to get from one room to another without being reminded, by the sight of children playing, of the purpose of the place.

The women at Family Foundations spend each minute of the day working on two closely intertwined endeavors: caring for their children and rebuilding themselves. From morning until night, they attend classes and groups on substance abuse and recovery, relapse prevention, domestic violence, child development, health, anger management, journal writing, cooking, computers and GED (General Educational Development) prep. They prepare the meals and clean the facility. A therapist is on site to provide individual and group counseling. And the women take care of children, their own and each other's.

Sharrell Blakeley, the energetic former social worker who oversaw the development of the program from the ground up, said her goal was "to blend policy issues between the child welfare and criminal justice departments, because social services doesn't think about incarcerated parents, and corrections doesn't think about children."

"We live not by our words but by our deeds," Blakeley observed. "Here, the child gets to see the mother in action, changing her behavior. She's looking at them. She's listening to them. She has assumed the loving, nurturing role. They fight—they have normal mother-child issues—but they work through them. And they have playful, joyous interactions as well."

Jaime sat at a cafeteria table inside Family Foundations and gingerly spooned soup into her swollen mouth. She had just returned from the dentist, where two teeth—decayed from years of methamphetamine use—had been pulled. The hot soup hurt, but Jaime went out of her way to mention how much she appreciated it all the same, because she had helped to prepare it, and because she had the opportunity to eat it in the company of her six-month-old son Xavier, who burbled cheerfully at her side.

A slight brunette with henna-streaked hair and an elfin face, Jaime radiated a hippie calm in the hectic cafeteria. Jaime, who grew up on Kauai, had come to the program via the streets of Hollywood, where she had spent the previous decade supporting herself—and her meth habit—first by modeling and then by selling her stained-glass creations in Melrose Avenue boutiques.

Before Family Foundations came a detour through the psychiatric ward of the Los Angeles County Jail, where, Jaime said, she was constantly medicated because she was "crying, freaking out, very depressed" over being separated from her infant son. Xavier had been three months old when Jaime was arrested on a two-year-old warrant for skipping out of a residential drug-treatment program. She had left him with friends and did not even know where he was from day to day. "When you're in jail, you're helpless," she said. For a mother, "that's the worst thing on earth."

At Family Foundations, the goal is not simply to punish drug users for breaking the law, but to strengthen them, as individuals and as mothers, by pushing them to face both the causes and the consequences of their actions. According to Sharrell Blakeley, one of the challenges is breaking down the self-centered worldview that often accompanies drug addiction. "When you're a drug abuser, you're the most narcissistic creature that walks," she said, recalling an outing to an amusement park where staff had to instruct residents not to get on the rides without their children. Both the prison and child welfare systems, by forcibly separating parents and children, do little to challenge—and may actually foster—the narcissism to which Blakeley refers. Family Foundations, on the other hand, simply does not leave room for women to turn away from the needs of their children.

"What's good about this situation," said Jaime, "is that everything is about the children. It's not about us trying to survive out there, meeting life on life's terms and then finding time for them. Everything is about them."

Shakeh, twenty-seven, said she barely knew her three-year-old son before he was returned to her custody at Family Foundations. "The first day he got here, he cried for six hours straight," she recalled. "I thought he hated me. I was like, 'Here you go, take him! And send me back to jail.' But I got to know him, and as time went by I fell in love with him, and that gave me a reason to stay clean.

"The more you put in time with him, the more experiences you have, then you become a mother," she said. "You become a mother because you're fulfilling your child's needs."

The women at Family Foundations told stories that varied in the details but struck common themes. Many had been in and out of jail and prison for years, had been separated from one child after another, and were all too aware of the harm they had caused their children. One woman used to get high in the bathroom while her little girl cried and begged for her to come out. "Just a minute," she would call to her daughter, while silently praying to choke on the pipe and die. In group and individual therapy, the women at Family Foundations are encouraged to face up to this kind of damage, but also to move beyond it, rather than staying mired in shame and guilt and turning to drugs to assuage those emotions.

Nationwide, between 6 and 10 percent of women enter prison pregnant. Taloma, twenty-seven, was in the county jail in Los Angeles when she delivered her now-eight-month-old daughter. After she went into labor, she was handcuffed and placed in a police car, which transported her to the hospital (an ambulance had taken too long to arrive). After she gave birth, she was allowed to spend three days in the hospital with her newborn daughter, but she was kept shackled to the bed the whole time.

Taloma had been through this before, with her older daughter, now seven, who also was born while Taloma was in jail. The next time Taloma saw that daughter, six months had passed, and a wall of glass separated them.

This time around, things were different. Soon after her daughter was born, Taloma was transferred to Family Foundations and her baby was returned to her. At Family Foundations, Taloma said, she was learning that to love her children, she needed also to value herself. "What made me relapse before was loneliness, lack of confidence—going job-hunting and I just can't find one—failure and guilt. I always felt self-pity— 'I'm a failure, I'm a failure.' And really, I'm not, you know. I'm a very strong woman, very intelligent, and I know I have talent. I do hair, make music. I have good friends that can see me through and support me. I had to come here to realize that I am not a failure."

The women I met at Family Foundations were hardly archvillains. They were shoplifters and check forgers, battered women, single mothers trying to support their children on minimum-wage jobs. They were women who felt cornered and helpless and had turned to drugs to relieve that feeling when they found themselves unable to overcome the circumstances that inspired it. "Up against the wall" was a phrase more than one woman used to describe the way she felt when she committed the acts that led to her arrest.

The use of drugs and alcohol to suppress or assuage trauma is so widespread as to be, if not universal, at least highly predictable. One study of combat veterans with severe post-traumatic stress disorder found that 85 percent developed serious drug or alcohol problems after their return from war. Some research suggests that this response is virtually instinctive; the body itself responds to trauma by altering its regulation of endogenous opioids, natural substances which have the same pain-muting effect as the synthesized variety.

Inside a prison that holds women or girls, the connection between trauma and drug use is impossible to miss. Nearly 50 percent of incarcerated girls meet the criteria for post-traumatic stress disorder, as do as many as one-third of jailed women. More than three-quarters of the women behind bars have been physically or sexually abused. Eighty percent of women in state prisons have substance-abuse problems. That women are often retraumatized in jail and prison—by strip searches, body-cavity searches, and sometimes sexual abuse—only decreases the already-slim odds that incarceration will cure them of their inclination to use drugs.

Rebecca Patch, the Family Foundations social worker, conducts intake interviews with each prisoner. Nearly all, Patch said, have experienced some form of trauma, from child abuse to domestic violence to rape. Many have never had an opportunity to talk about those experiences before, turning instead to drugs for solace or oblivion. At Family Foundations, this opportunity is woven throughout the day. When they are not with their children, the women are with each other, engaged in a process of reflection and self-examination that flows from formal to informal but never seems to stop.

The benefits to the women of being with their children at Family Foundations are clear. But what about the children? Their mothers have been restored to them, but has the price—their own freedom—been too high?

Program director Angela Knox, who has also run a drug-treatment program inside a California women's prison, said any potential harm is mitigated by the child-friendly atmosphere of the facility. "I've worked in an institution, and I know what that feeling is," she said. "This doesn't have that feel at all, so the children don't really think they're locked up. Sometimes, I don't think the residents think they're locked up."

Most of the women at Family Foundations echoed Knox's view. But some expressed concerns about keeping children behind bars, no matter how prettily painted. A few of the older children attend a nearby school during the day; some go on weekend visits with grandparents or fathers; the entire facility takes occasional outings to nearby lakes or amusement parks; and in the latter part of their sentences, residents are allowed brief passes to leave the facility. Nevertheless, the fact remains that the children spend most of their time in a building that they, like their mothers, cannot leave at will.

"The kids are incarcerated, too," worried April, twenty-three, who was sentenced for credit-card fraud. April had her eighteen-month-old son with her and would soon deliver a new baby at Family Foundations, but was glad that her two older children were with their grandmother rather than inside the program.

"A six-year-old will wanna go to the park when it's a sunny day," she said. "They'll wanna go to Chuck E. Cheese's. There's a lot of things where you gotta tell them 'no,' and how do you explain that to them? How do you say, 'Well, we're in prison?' "

On weekday mornings, April's son attends an Early Head Start program next door to Family Foundations. On weekends, she said, "when we pass by the door that we leave out of to go to school, and he knows he can't leave out it, he gets real upset."

Like April, Melinda was at Family Foundations because she committed credit fraud. Her two boys are five and six—old enough to speak for themselves—and will tell you they love it at Family Foundations: they've made new best friends, there are plenty of toys, and their mom is with them every day. At lunchtime in the cafeteria, as they waited for their chicken nuggets to arrive, the two boys—impeccably dressed in matching gray T-shirts, Tommy Hilfiger overalls, and pristine Nikes—entertained each other by stuffing their hands into the bibs of their overalls and announcing, "I have no hands!" Asked if he ever gets bored and wants to leave, six-year-old Kenji was unequivocal: "Never ever ever. I have my toys. I like to play with my friends."

Even so, Melinda feels terrible about the situation in which she has placed her children. Every week, she said, they ask her, "Mommy, can we go to Legoland? Mommy, can we go to Raging Waters?"—places Melinda enjoyed taking her kids in her previous life.

"When Mommy gets out of here, I'll take you wherever you want to go," she tells the boys, then hustles them outside to play in the yard.

"But it hurts me every time they ask," Melinda said.

Family Foundations has done everything possible to make the facility appealing to children; to gloss over the fact that the place is a prison. That women like April and Melinda must choose between abandoning their children and bringing them to prison is less a flaw in the program design than a statement about the limits of the world we've prescribed for children whose parents have broken the law. These limits in turn reflect the boundaries of our penal imagination—that the only response we can dream up to fraud, forgery, shoplifting, or drug use is to lock someone's mother away.

"Parental love cannot be synthesized," Jonathan Kozol has written. "Even the most earnest and methodical foster care demonstrates the limits of synthetic tenderness and surrogate emotion. So it seems of keen importance to consider any ways, and *every* way, by which a family, splintered, jolted and imperiled though it be . . . may nonetheless be given every possible incentive to stay together."

Kozol was writing of homeless families pressed and often fragmented by the impenetrable constellation of bureaucracies that were avowedly designed to aid them but more often functioned to undermine them. He might also have been writing of those under the sway of the criminal justice system, except that these families—splintered, jolted, imperiled already—are split to pieces by explicit state action rather than malign neglect.

Those residents who ventured a critique of Family Foundations were always quick to qualify it: of course, they said, it was preferable to the alternative. By "the alternative," they meant the status quo: mothers sequestered; children scattered.

The California prison system is home to about 7,400 mothers of nearly 18,000 children, most under the age of ten. As many as 2,700 of these children are in foster care. Several hundred more children are born each year while their mothers are inside California prisons, and separated from them within days. The majority of California's women prisoners are nonviolent offenders with drug problems—the population for which Family Foundations was designed. The two Family Foundations sites have room for seventy women and ninety children.

Family Foundations is terrifically well thought out, a more-than-humane institution, given the context in which it operates: one in which prison, and the resultant family fragmentation, is the default response to drug use. But because the program offers no challenge to this framework, the fact remains that in order to reap its benefits, children are required to forfeit the same thing any prisoner does: their right to be part of the larger world. In this sense, Family Foundations serves an important symbolic function. It makes literal what is emotionally true across the board: whatever sentence we pass upon a parent, her children will serve with her.

Looking around this self-contained and highly self-conscious community—at women with each other's children on their hips, keeping stray fingers out of doors, offering each other advice and the occasional admonition—one catches sight not just of another model for corrections but also of another way of raising children. In this alternate universe, poor mothers are not forced to rear their children in isolation, bearing sole responsibility for meeting those children's every physical and emotional need. Instead, they can raise their families in a supportive, sustaining community, where whatever personal or parental shortcomings they might have are answered with assistance and instruction rather than blame alone.

I felt, at Family Foundations, that I had wandered into that "village" in which Hillary Clinton famously instructed us to raise our children; the only problem was that it happened to be behind bars. If parents could access just a portion of the resources available to the women and children at Family Foundations without getting arrested, what impact might that have on the seemingly unstoppable metastasis of the foster care and criminal justice systems?

In 1999, I interviewed and surveyed more than 140 young people who had grown up in foster care, seeking their ideas for reforming that system. My question, they told me, was off the mark. They didn't want a better foster home. They wanted to be with their families.

Foster children whose parents have broken the law offer no exception. "Being in the group homes and foster homes, knowing that my mom was in jail and then in prison, was hard for me," said Curtis, twenty. "Going from here to there, you don't know these people; you don't know if they're using you just for the money, or if they really want you to be there, or even if they care about you. I don't care how bad whatever we was going through [at home], I just wanted to be with my mom."

When I asked the same 140 foster youth what might have kept their families together, their response was equally consistent: help with a parent's drug problem.

"My father was into drugs instead of me," one teenager wrote. "That's why I'm in the system."

"If there wasn't drugs," wrote another, "I probably would not know what a system is."

One young woman had gone through more than forty different placements—foster homes, shelters, group homes, and juvenile halls. At twenty-one—struggling to support herself and make her way through community college without having graduated from high school—she had some questions about the money, likely hundreds of thousands of dollars, spent to keep her in one institution after another while her mother's drug problem went untreated in and out of jail.

"They could have put that money into my mom," she said. "They could have put it into my grandmother, so she could have kept me with her. They could have put that money into my education. I could have gone to a nice boarding school for what it cost to throw me in all those places!

"If you take all these poor kids' parents that are breaking the law and you institutionalize them, what do you think these kids are going to do?" she asked. "They're gonna go to foster care, and you're gonna have a whole generation of institutionalized parents and kids who are gonna breed more institutionalized parents and kids."

6

REENTRY

PHILLIP GAINES WAS ON the phone with his mother when the call-waiting sounded.

"Have you seen President Clinton's press conference?" his mother's attorney asked him. "Your mom's getting out."

Dorothy Gaines was in the Federal Correctional Institute in Tallahassee, Florida, six years into a nineteen-year term for conspiracy to distribute crack cocaine. Phillip was 250 miles away in Mobile, Alabama, where he lived with his sisters Chara and Natasha and Natasha's husband and three children. Clinton had included Dorothy in a group of prisoners—most, like her, women doing long sentences on shaky drug-conspiracy convictions—to whom he had granted clemency as his second term came to a close.

"When the news came in that she was on her way home, I can't even explain how it felt," Phillip told me three years later, as we sat on the glass-enclosed sun porch of the Gaines's home in Mobile. "I can see myself now, jumping around. It's exciting just to think back on it."

Rain lashed the windows as Phillip sat in a T-shirt in the cold, smoking a cigarette that was not permitted inside the house.

Phillip was nineteen by then, a burly young man with a green scorpion tattooed on his neck. Scattered gold teeth brightened a sweet, rare smile that emerged only when he reminisced about the past—the years before his mother was arrested, and that shining moment right after she was freed and before their new reality coalesced.

Dorothy's clemency was announced on the morning of December 22, 2000. Natasha and her husband picked her up, meeting her at the gate as dozens of other inmates waved and shouted. She was home by nine that night. On the ride home, Dorothy borrowed Natasha's cell phone and called her younger children.

"Mama, hang up the phone," Phillip told her. "I talked to you enough on the phone. I want to see you face to face."

Phillip remembers rubbing his eyes as Dorothy emerged from the car, unsure it was really his mother stepping onto the curb. Chara rushed to embrace her. Phillip hung back, taking his time. He had stopped visiting his mother because the departures were too painful, and had not seen her in over a year. "Are my eyes playing tricks on me?" he wondered. "Is that my mom?"

Three years later, Phillip was still asking that question. Dorothy's homecoming has been more difficult than anyone expected, for her and for her children—especially Phillip, her youngest. Phillip had cherished the memory of the mother Dorothy was before prison: a hardworking nurse technician who always provided what her children needed; who was there in the stands at each of his football games; who went to church each Sunday, then came home and spent the afternoon cooking. The woman who returned to him was homeless, jobless, and—

as her efforts to reestablish herself were repeatedly stymied—increasingly defeated.

For her part, Dorothy had left behind a nine-year-old son who was a Boy Scout, an honor-roll student, a mama's boy who clung to her like a barnacle and lived to make her proud. She came home to a sullen, embittered teenager who flouted her authority; who had flunked the eighth grade three years in a row.

In 2004, nearly 650,000 Americans were released from prison. Seven million more left local jails. Most faced tremendous obstacles, both practical and emotional, as they tried to rebuild lives and families disrupted by their forced absence.

"People think that you can just come out and jump back in; that life has left a space open for you," Natasha told me. "There is not a space open for my mother. There is not a place for her."

Children experience a reentry process of their own when parents come home from prison—one less remarked, but no less difficult, than that their parents face. Anger they may have suppressed during brief and precious visits or phone calls boils to the surface. Children who have grown into adolescents chafe under the authority of parents eager to reestablish themselves at the helm of the family, and struggle with the changes prison has wrought in now-unfamiliar mothers and fathers. The realization that things will never be as they were—that lost time cannot be made up—can be overwhelming.

A few weeks after Dorothy came home from prison, Phillip tried to hang himself from a tree outside his sister's home. The attempt was symbolic—he fashioned a noose and placed it around his neck but kept his feet on the ground, tilted his head at an ugly angle, and waited for his mother to rescue him. When

Dorothy caught sight of him, she rushed outside and took the rope from around her son's neck. Three years later, both of them were still waiting to be rescued from what Dorothy called "a prison after prison."

Phillip staged the suicide attempt for attention, he told me, struggling to describe the lack he felt almost as acutely in his mother's presence as he had in her absence.

"I know I can't be nine again, but I wanted my mom," he said, the corners of his mouth turning down. "She was there physically, but mentally she wasn't. She's been out for three years, but it's like she's still incarcerated. Her mind is somewhere else, like she's still confined."

"A single traumatic event can occur almost anywhere," the psychologist Judith Herman has written. "Prolonged, repeated trauma, by contrast, occurs only in circumstances of captivity." One of the most intractable aftereffects of this kind of prolonged trauma, according to Herman, is helplessness, or learned passivity.

Herman quotes a Latin American dissident who returned home to his family after many years' imprisonment:

Once we got out, we were suddenly confronted with all these problems. . . . Ridiculous problems—doorknobs, for instance. I had no reflex any longer to reach for the knobs of doors. I hadn't had to—hadn't been allowed to—for over 13 years. I'd come to a closed door and find myself momentarily stymied—I couldn't remember what to do next. Or how to make a dark room light. How to work, pay bills, shop, visit friends, answer questions. My daughter tells me to do this or that, and one problem I can handle, two I can handle, but when the third request comes I can hear her voice but my head is lost in the clouds.

There was a haunted quality about the Gaines household when I visited—a brittle silence punctuated by arguments that were always about something other than they purported to be. Phillip slept late, sometimes into the afternoon. Chara—who had recently moved into her own apartment—dropped her two-year-old son off at preschool, then sat and watched cartoons on her mother's sofa. Dorothy, too, found it difficult some days to make herself leave the house.

Craig Haney, a psychologist, has written about "prisonization"—the psychological process of adapting to life in an institution where one is neither expected nor permitted to make decisions; where trust is a liability and intimacy a danger. Walking out the gates does not automatically reverse this process.

"Before she went to prison, my mom could go to the store, pick up a pack of hamburger meat, and just—without our consent—come home and cook it," Phillip said, his voice clouded with resentment and confusion. "Now she'll go to the store and she don't know what to cook. She'll bring groceries back and say, 'I hope y'all like this. I hope y'all like that.' It's a small thing, but it puts a hole in my heart. Just makes it so heavy."

When his mother was gone, Phillip said, he felt "confined within myself. Now she's back, but I'm still in that box. No matter what I do, it's just not right, 'cause I don't feel right with myself no more."

To say that Dorothy's sentence came as a surprise to her family is more than an understatement. None of the Gaines children had ever known their mother, who supported them by working long shifts at the hospital, to go anywhere near drugs. When she learned that her boyfriend was using, she hustled him off to rehab, then ended the relationship when the treatment didn't stick.

Almost a year passed before she and he were both arrested, accused of playing roles in a local drug ring. He testified that Dorothy had known nothing of any drug-selling enterprise. The state of Alabama determined that the evidence against her was too thin to prosecute, but federal prosecutors stepped in and went after her anyway. Dorothy maintained that she had no knowledge of any drug conspiracy, and so was unable to offer testimony in exchange for a deal. She was convicted in federal court solely on the word of witnesses who received sentence reductions in return for their testimony.

Dorothy's former boyfriend told the judge that he had heard his co-defendants—who were all kept in the same jail cell—"trying to get their stories straight" regarding Dorothy's supposed involvement. Ultimately, they testified that she had kept crack at her house and delivered it when told. No drugs or drug paraphernalia were found in her home or her possession. U.S. District Judge Alex Howard declared at sentencing that Dorothy "was not one of the leaders or organizers of the conspiracy." Then he sentenced her to nineteen years and seven months in prison, as dictated by federal mandatory sentencing laws.

Under the conspiracy provisions that were tacked on to the mandatory sentencing laws of the 1980s, this kind of scenario is all too common. People who don't sell drugs—who merely have the bad fortune, or judgment, to be associated with those who do—can wind up being held responsible for large quantities of drugs they may never have seen, much less sold. For a woman whose husband or boyfriend is involved in the drug trade, "conspiracy" may consist simply of having drugs in the house; driving him to the bank, where he deposits ill-gotten gains; or taking phone messages from drug associates. In some cases, prosecutors have not even been required to prove that a "conspirator" knew she was committing any of these acts; a finding that she should have known what her man was up to has been sufficient to secure a conviction. If the same standard were applied to crimes that did not involve drugs, we might see wives whose husbands were implicated in the corporate scandals of recent years doing time for conspiring with caterers to host suspect dinner parties.

Phillip remembers clowning around with Chara in the back of the courtroom during his mother's trial—play-fighting, or ducking under the benches. He was too young to understand most of the proceedings, but his mother's face when the judge read her sentence—235 months—told him all he needed to know. As marshals escorted Dorothy from the courtroom, Phillip charged to the front of the room and flung himself at the judge, clinging to his leg. "My father died when I was two years old," he shouted. "My mama's all I got. Don't take her away!"

"Get back, son," Phillip remembers the district attorney instructing him. "Do you want to get locked up?" It took several marshals—one in tears—to pull Phillip away.

Phillip was vomiting as Natasha led him from the courtroom. "Where's my mom going?" he asked the nineteen-year-old college freshman who had just become his sole caregiver. "What's all them months the judge said? How many years she got?"

At first, Natasha declined to help her younger brother with

the math, believing the full weight of Dorothy's sentence would be too much for him to handle. But she did sit him down and try to explain his immediate situation. "You and your sister are going to be staying with me for a while," Natasha told Phillip. "Mom's not going to be here."

"As soon as she told me that," Phillip remembers, "my mind went all the way up. I'm still sitting here listening to her, but my mind's in another place."

For Phillip, the sharpest disappointment has been coming to believe this condition may be chronic. Motherlessness, he has learned, is not something that can be remedied simply by returning the mother. It has become etched on his face, a part of his character. He is plagued by a feeling he described as "a separation—not just separated from my mom, but my mind, mentally, separated from me."

During her years in prison, Dorothy fought hard for her freedom. She wrote so many letters—to lawyers, advocacy groups, reporters—that prison staff joked that she'd used more stamps than anyone in the history of the institution. Phillip, too, battled his despair by fighting for his mother. He and Chara stood on the corner with a sign with Dorothy's picture on it, collecting signatures on a handwritten petition for her release. Phillip wrote letters—to the judge, the president, anyone he could think of—declaring his mother's innocence and pleading for her return.

"Dear Judge," he wrote shortly after his mother was sentenced,

> I need my mom. Would you help my mom? I have no dad
> and my grandmom have cancer I don't have innyone to
> take care of me and my sisters and my niece and nephew

and my birthday's coming up in October the 25 and I need my mom to be here on the 25 and for the rest of my life. I will cut your grass and wash your car everyday just don't send my mom off. Please Please Please don't!!!

Phillip included his phone number in case the judge decided to take him up on his offer. When the phone didn't ring, Phillip moved on. "Dear President Clinton," he wrote in March of 1995. "I hope you can free my mom. I need her. Because I am just a little boy! I am ten year old. I need my mom very much. Please get her out I need her."

Before her arrest, Dorothy and her kids had kept busy together. Dorothy was on the PTA, chaperoned field trips, sent Chara and Phillip to Girl and Boy Scouts, attended their sporting events. Natasha was nineteen when she became a parent to two bereft preteens in addition to her own two small children (Natasha married and had a third child while Dorothy was in prison). Scout meetings and football games soon fell by the wayside. Phillip stopped going to school and landed in juvenile hall for truancy and shoplifting. His goal, he told Dorothy, was to be locked up like her. He was proud of his mother's fortitude behind bars; of the stoic way she "handled" her sentence. If she could do it, he could too.

Some young people cut themselves as a way of making their emotional pain literal, and thus somehow manageable. Phillip took comfort in making his psychological prison—"that box"—physically manifest. Inside a cell, the rage that dogged him lifted, but this incongruous peace came at a price. As with his mother's, Phillip's "reentry" process is now stymied by practical as well as psychological barriers: he is entering his adult life with a criminal record and minimal education.

"I'm nineteen and I stopped school in the ninth grade," he said. "Now my mom's out, but I lost more than she lost."

I first met Dorothy Gaines in the summer of 2001, in the lobby of the Embassy Suites Hotel in South San Francisco. She had been out of prison just seven months and was still something of a celebrity; an advocacy group had flown her out from Mobile to speak against the drug war. She was self-possessed, almost stately, in a purple silk blouse, her braids pulled back in a neat bun.

The euphoria of her freedom had not left her, but she was already beginning to comprehend the obstacles she would face in reestablishing herself and her family. Before her arrest, Dorothy had lived in a HUD development where, for the first time in her life, she'd had the space to cultivate a garden. She was such a model tenant that her landlords used her image in public-relations campaigns. As soon as she got out of prison, she had reapplied for public housing but been denied because of her drug conviction (unlike a pardon, clemency leaves one's criminal record intact, and Dorothy left prison with five years' probation). She was staying with Phillip, Chara, Natasha, and Natasha's family—eight people crammed into a three-bedroom apartment with a single bathroom. Dorothy shared a double bed with Chara, who was pregnant, and Natasha's two daughters. In prison, Dorothy used to rise at four in the morning to have some privacy in the shower. Now she found herself reverting to that habit.

Even so, Dorothy seemed possessed of a formidable energy. She was exploring a new identity as an activist, and she pledged not to forget "the ones I left behind." She had marched Phillip and Chara down to school and gotten them reenrolled; had taken one look at Phillip, with his sagging pants and untended Afro, and told him, "The hair is coming off and the pants are coming up."

"They knew then that Mama's back in town," she told me proudly.

Above the mantel in Dorothy's home in Mobile there is an 8"-by-10" photograph of her standing alone in the prison yard. She is dressed in white, her long hair blowing into her face, staring fiercely into the camera like an avenging angel. This is the woman I felt I was meeting in San Francisco—a warrior, unstoppable, who had freed herself through the power of her own voice and faith.

More than two years passed before I spoke with Dorothy again. The voice on the phone was unrecognizable. "It's a suffering time," she told me flatly. "So many doors close in your face."

Dorothy's path had not been easy before she went to prison—she was a single mother of three who'd had her first child as a teenager—but she had managed to assemble a life that worked for her and her family. She had acquired a skill that allowed her to feed her children, and she had made the most of what government support was available in order to provide them a decent home. With a felony conviction, all of that was foreclosed to her. Not a single piece of her prior life was within her reach, much less as she left it.

After the first few months, she told me, the speaking engagements had dwindled. The week before we spoke, Dorothy had been laid off from the only job she had managed to secure since her release—a receptionist position in the insurance office where Natasha worked. Chara had undergone minor surgery the day before and needed antibiotics, but Dorothy did not have the money to fill her prescription.

"Right now I'm just at the end," she said. "I don't know where to turn."

A few weeks later, I visited the Gaines family in Mobile, where they lived in a four-bedroom brick house in a quiet subdivision. An anonymous supporter had rented the house for Dorothy when she had proven unable to find work or housing. It was a comfortable home for her and her family, but the subsidy had run its course, and she would soon have to leave if she couldn't find some way to come up with the rent herself. She did not know where she would go. Her faith in herself had been replaced by talk of winning the lottery.

"God didn't bring me out of prison to be like this," she said—"begging and borrowing. No."

We reminisced briefly about our earlier meeting. "I wish I was still the same way now that I felt then," Dorothy said. "I pray for that energetic spirit I had before. It's like a prison after prison out here."

I asked her whether she were referring to a psychological prison.

"No, it's real," she answered. "So many doors closed, and so many obstacles in your way."

As criminal penalties have escalated in recent decades, so have the civil consequences of a criminal conviction. Under the 1996 federal welfare reform law, anyone with a felony drug conviction is barred for life from receiving TANF or food stamps, unless their state has opted out of the ban. Drug offenders comprise one-third of all released prisoners. Ironically, their access to drug treatment may be limited by the TANF ban, as many treatment programs rely on clients' welfare checks to help pay their overhead.

It is worth noting that families affected by the welfare ban lose only the mother's share of benefits; they may remain eligible for the "child-only" portion of the grant. As Senator Phil Gramm, the sponsor of the provision, explained, "What an individual does does not affect the eligibility of that individual's children or other family members." Gramm's locution reveals a central misconception underpinning our policy of post-prison punishment: that parents and children do not eat from the same pot; that the doors we close to "an individual" do not also slam shut on her children.

Public housing is closed to most people with felony convictions, and family members who allow a released prisoner to stay even briefly may face eviction themselves. If grandma has your kids and is living in the projects, you can't come home to your family without putting the roof over their heads at risk. In 1998, Congress cut off financial aid to students who have been convicted of drug possession or sale. Another federal law requires states to suspend the driver's licenses of those who have broken the drug laws or lose federal highway funds. Immigrants may be released from prison only to find themselves deported if they have been convicted of any one of a growing list of crimes. The number of deportations attributed to criminal conviction has nearly tripled over the past ten years, reaching more than seventy-seven thousand at last count.

More than 47 million Americans, or a fourth of the adult population, have criminal records. Thirteen million, or 6 percent of the population, have felony convictions. The array of restrictions and barriers this group of people faces amounts to the establishment of a criminal caste, subject to all the obligations of citizenship, but denied fundamental rights and opportunities.

Many returning prisoners confront even greater barriers than has Dorothy, and with even less support. The majority of those who enter prison do so with a drug problem, but only one in ten receives any treatment behind bars, down from one in four in 1991. Educational and vocational programs—which, like drug treatment, have been shown to reduce recidivism—have faced cuts as well, and most prisoners walk out the door having participated in neither.

Those leaving prison often lack access to fundamental resources. In California, for example, there are two hundred shelter beds available for more than ten thousand homeless parolees. There are four mental health clinics for approximately 18,000 mentally ill parolees, and 750 treatment beds for about 85,000 released drug abusers. The California prison system has a recidivism rate of nearly 80 percent.

Taken together, the restrictions imposed on those who have done time represent a highly successful effort to codify and institutionalize widely held attitudes toward those who have broken the law. The historian and criminologist Howard Zehr has written about the abiding stigma that accompanies a criminal record:

In the popular view, guilt is not merely a description of behavior but a statement of a moral quality. Guilt says something about the quality of the person who did this and has a "sticky," indelible quality. Guilt adheres to a person more or less permanently, with few known solvents. A person found guilty of theft becomes a thief, an offender. A person who spends time in prison becomes an ex-prisoner, an ex-offender, an ex-con. This becomes part of his or her identity and is difficult to remove.

Stigma "sticks" to the families of the afflicted as well. When Dorothy was locked up, Chara's schoolmates harassed her so relentlessly about her mother's incarceration that she spent much of her time in tears in the counselor's office. After Dorothy was released, a letter appeared in the local newspaper in response to coverage of Dorothy's clemency. Her children, the writer asserted, were now fated to wind up behind bars themselves. Had she remained in prison, they would have been better off; she might have offered them an object lesson in the consequences of a misstep.

One might expect a presidential decree to have some solvent power. That has not been Dorothy's experience. She went back to the hospital where she had previously worked, but was told that her conviction barred her from returning to the health-care field. She visited the employment office and told a counselor that she was interested in working with young people. He informed her that her conviction made her ineligible.

Employment bans affecting ex-offenders vary from state to state, but can cover a wide range of jobs, including health care, education, even working as a plumber. The old saw "There's always work at the post office" doesn't apply to those who have done time; some states—including Alabama—bar those with a record from any public employment. Some extend the ban to any field, such as real estate, that requires a state license. Post-9/11 security measures have expanded felony restrictions even further: airport baggage handlers and shoeshine-stand attendants lost their jobs, as did truck drivers who transported hazardous material.

Most states allow private employers to deny jobs not only to those with criminal records but also to people who were arrested for a crime, even if they were not convicted. With information about criminal history now often available on the Internet, employers are finding it increasingly convenient to exercise this option. Even when employers don't bother to check, lying about a conviction is rarely an option: probation officers often visit clients' job sites to check up on them.

The results of all this are predictable. Two-thirds of incarcerated parents were employed prior to their incarceration, but one survey of California parolees found that between 70 and 90 percent were unemployed. Some studies have determined that a criminal record diminishes one's employment prospects for life. "Many inner-city families not only experience incarceration because they are poor," the anthropologist Donald Braman has observed, "but they are also poor because they experience incarceration."

As the pressures and restrictions placed on returning prisoners have increased, recidivism rates have accelerated as well. In 1985, 70 percent of parolees successfully completed their supervision. By 1998, the number had dropped to 45 percent. Nearly two-thirds of released prisoners will be rearrested within three years, and nearly half of the parents currently in state prison were on parole or probation at the time of their most recent arrests.

Researchers use the term "churning" to describe the phenomenon of individuals cycling in and out of prison, often for technical violations of parole rather than new crimes. "Churned" is also an apt description of how children feel when their families are dissolved and reconstituted over and over.

Dorothy remembers watching other prisoners walk out the

door, only to return within months or even weeks. "They used to say, 'It's so hard out there,'" she said, "and I'd say, 'I just can't see it being hard once you get out there.' But now that I'm out here, I'm glad I'm not a user, not into any kind of criminal activities, because I can see how it happens. They put nothing out here once they turn us loose out of this cage."

Turning to those fields from which she was not formally barred, Dorothy submitted one application after another. She was, however, required to disclose the fact that she had a felony conviction. The phone sat silent. Informal barriers to employment may affect returning prisoners even more powerfully than do the explicit: researchers have found that only 20 percent of employers will consider hiring an applicant with a criminal history. The average annual income of former prisoners is less than $8,000.

A friend suggested that Dorothy skirt the multiple barriers to employment by starting her own business, so she began researching the licensing requirements for opening a day-care center in her home. Her conviction, she learned, ruled that out as well. She has thought about going back to school and pursuing a degree in counseling, but her conviction makes her ineligible for financial aid. She is barred from public assistance as well.

That Dorothy has been denied the opportunity to work has only added to her children's burden. A few months after my visit, Dorothy lost her house and moved into Natasha's already-crowded home, where she shares a bedroom with Natasha's three children. Chara, at the time of my visit, had been working off and on as a home health aide and sharing her paycheck with her mother, professing herself glad to do so. But it had not been easy for a young mother trying to gain her own footing. "I thought she would come home and everything would be OK," Chara said, "but she can barely take care of herself."

Both Chara and Phillip have traded the fantasy of being cared for by their mother for one in which they are able to provide for her. Chara hopes one day to help her mother build her dream house "from the ground up." Phillip dreams of being Donald Trump; of earning enough money that Dorothy would not have to "do anything except be my mom."

For her part, Dorothy has found returning to the task of being her children's mom rockier than she had expected. She did manage to get them back into school; she bought Phillip a belt and took him to the barber. By the time I met him, however, he still had not made it past the ninth grade.

"I feel like my mother owes me for what I been through, but she don't," Phillip said, in a confused jumble of past and present tense. "That's why I'd get mad about any little thing, 'cause I felt like she owed me something. . . . I'm trying to figure that out right now—to stop stressing mom out just 'cause I'm thinking she owes me. Like when she went to prison, she took my life. And she get back home and she wants her life, but my life's still stuck, so I feel like she owes me a lot."

Phillip's confusion is not so hard to fathom. Someone must owe him for all he has been forced to relinquish; from whom other than his mother can he safely demand an accounting? And if his mother owes him his childhood back, she might one day pay. It is a grievance that is also a form of hope—a hope destined for continued disappointment.

Sometimes, Phillip's bitterness so overwhelms him that he tells his mother, "I wish you'd have stayed in prison." Dorothy is wounded by his outbursts, but also understands them.

"I get so mad with him, but then I feel like, you know, he is my baby, and I know he's hurting," she said. "My son loves me, but he's just a hurt child."

As soon as Dorothy got home, by contrast, Natasha—a poised and polished thirty-year-old with a sleek bob and hazel eyes—picked up the college education she had set aside in order to care for her siblings six years earlier. When I met her, she was working full-time as an insurance agent and going to school at night, studying pre-law. She planned to go on to law school and become a criminal-defense attorney.

The difference between her and her siblings, Natasha told me, is that she had her mother through her teenage years— those years in which her adult self took shape. She remembers Dorothy as the kind of mother who, if you didn't come home on time, sat on the front porch and called your name until you appeared, thoroughly embarrassed, but safe in the knowledge that your absence had been noted. Natasha got ambition during those years, and has held on to it since. When her mother came home, she did more than put down the load she had carried and pick up where she had left off. She launched herself forward, into the life she wanted. Her younger brother was still trying to get back to where he had been, an effort that has kept him from moving forward into adulthood.

Phillip and Chara adore each other, and they often spend long afternoons in each other's company. They rarely talk about the years without their mother. Sometimes, though, they talk about what might have been. If Dorothy had not gone to prison, Phillip will speculate, he would be at Notre Dame by now, playing football. Chara would not have had a child as a teenager, and would be working as a cosmetologist, maybe opening her own shop.

At twenty, Chara was tall and slim, with cropped hair and eyebrows shaped into a graceful arch. The words MS. DOROTHY were tattooed on one calf—"big, so everyone can see"—and NEICKO, her son's name, on her wrist. Her face gained and lost years in the course of a sentence. Half the time, she was a classically sullen late adolescent, slumping on the sofa and answering her mother in monosyllables. When she spoke about her childhood, she straightened abruptly, her face illuminated, bouncing in her chair like a child.

"I had a *nice* life," she said of her family's early years together. "Oooh, we did so much! She was steady taking us to the zoo, to the park. We went to New Orleans, where we rode the ferry and the captain let the kids drive the boat. She'd take us to the mall, take us out to dinner. We'd do simple stuff, but it was fun stuff, 'cause we were with our mom."

Chara may not have been as vocal as Phillip about her mother's absence, but she felt it just as deeply. "When somebody takes a parent away, you feel like you don't have nobody," she said. "You feel like, 'Hey, I'm left all alone in the world, so I can do whatever I want.'"

What did Chara want? To talk with her mother about boys; to prepare with her mother for her first period and primp together for the prom. But Chara had done her own calculations: she would be thirty-two years old by the time Dorothy came home. She started skipping school, hanging out, drinking, and resisting Natasha's efforts to impose any kind of discipline— "If it wasn't my mama's voice, I didn't wanna hear it."

When Dorothy first returned, Chara relished her mother's efforts to get her wayward children in line. But it wasn't long before the "nagging and fussing" began to grate on her.

"I guess she hadn't been around us in so long that, in a way, she didn't know her kids," Chara said. "She didn't know what she was coming home to. She came home to some troubled kids. We're teenagers now, not little babies that she left behind, so our life is not gonna be back normal like it was before she left."

"Prissy, I'm home now," Dorothy would say, using Chara's childhood pet name, when she saw her daughter sinking into a depression. "You don't have to feel that way." But the darkness lingered.

Like her brother, Chara had responded to the news of her mother's sentence with a feeling of dissociation—"My mama gonna be gone for twenty years, I'm gone too. My body's still here, but my mind and my heart is gone. My soul is gone." Also like Phillip, Chara made a halfhearted suicide attempt after her mother returned, locking herself in her room with a fistful of Tylenol. Dorothy banged on the door until she beat it open and took Chara to the hospital, where a doctor offered her antidepressants and suggested she talk about her feelings.

Dorothy often tells her daughter the same thing, but having stifled her pain for so many years, Chara has not found it easy to follow this instruction. The inclination to protect her mother is hard to relinquish as well. A motherless girl is vulnerable to men—"They felt like, 'Hey, she ain't got nobody, nobody don't care about her, so we can do whatever we want with her,' " Chara said—and there are things that happened to Chara that she does not want Dorothy to know about, for fear her mother would blame herself. As she talked about some of the things that happened in Dorothy's absence, Chara shook with sobs that she gaspingly struggled to quiet; her mother was in the next room, one closed door away.

Chara has plans now: to go to college, get her cosmetology license, eventually become a nurse. Finding the strength to realize those dreams is proving to be a challenge. "You can't really go back to those years that you lost," Chara said. "You have to try to move forward again; to look toward the future. But it's hard to look toward the future when you still got pain holding you back."

AT 3RD STREET AND AVENUE C on the Lower East Side of Manhattan, a corner storefront has been converted into a dense warren of cubicles, offices, and conference rooms. The unprepossessing space houses La Bodega de la Familia, a carefully orchestrated experiment aimed at making reentry work by tapping the strengths of families. Through a combination of case management, direct service, and relentless faith in the prospect of redemption, La Bodega aims to move not just returning prisoners but their families and community out of the shadow of the prison and toward a more stable future. Working closely with parole and probation, La Bodega has succeeded in integrating into the system itself the understanding that no offender is an island; that prisoners not only come from but also return to families.

When founder Carol Shapiro took over the storefront property in 1996, it was an abandoned *bodega,* or corner grocery, which had functioned as a hub of the neighborhood drug trade. Photos from that era show a bullet-pocked façade with clusters of young men standing out front. A police officer had been shot and wounded at the site, and another man had been killed. Today, bright murals cover the same walls, and the center of activity has moved from the street outside to the office itself, which hosts a steady stream of neighborhood residents seeking job training, drug treatment, or simply conversation.

The premise of La Bodega's work is that a criminal

justice–involved family may, like the building itself, have a troubled history and the scars to show for it, but it is also a natural source of strength waiting to be tapped. The storefront location is deliberate, making La Bodega a visible presence on a busy block, but much of the work takes place not in the office but in the living rooms and kitchens of the Lower East Side, where case managers pay weekly visits to parolees, probationers, and their families. Eight years into its work, La Bodega has saturated the neighborhood, serving virtually every substance-abusing parolee and probationer who returns to the fifty-six square blocks that comprise its service area. By working to make the support it offers the norm rather than the exception, La Bodega has essentially become part of the landscape—as was the corner store/drug depot it supplanted.

Starting from the premise that "families are the experts on their own lives," La Bodega offers returning prisoners and their relatives case management, walk-in services, and a twenty-four-hour crisis hotline. By pumping in resources at the crucial moment of reentry, the program aims to stimulate diminished family economies and spark self-sufficiency. Bodega caseworkers steer clients to community resources—drug treatment, job training, medical care, and housing—but also help them mine resources within the family itself. It may be a client's mother who gets him through the door of La Bodega, a cousin who finds him a job, a sister who calls his case manager if she suspects he has relapsed.

The work at La Bodega is at once idea-driven and off-the-cuff pragmatic: case managers ask clients what they need and help make it happen. If a client calls to say he found needles in his brother's bed, a case manager will drop by and talk to the brother about rehab. If a husband is having a hard time finding work with a fresh-out-of-Riker's résumé, La Bodega might help the wife get a job in the meantime.

If Bodega staff and administrators recite the program's guiding tenets with an almost cultlike fervor, that may be because, in the face of the staggering array of post-prison difficulties their clients face—poverty, unemployment, addiction, mental illness, HIV/AIDS—they have come up with a formula that works. An evaluation of the program found that illegal drug use among participants declined by nearly half, from 80 to 42 percent, and cocaine use from 42 to 10 percent. Bodega clients were half as likely to be arrested and convicted of new offenses as were members of a control group.

Bodega mastermind Carol Shapiro was a small and energetic woman with short red hair; a narrow, strong-featured face; and long turquoise earrings that bobbed along with her enthusiastic narrative. In the quiet, airy office that houses Family Justice— the Manhattan nonprofit that Shapiro founded in 2001 to refine and disseminate the Bodega model—her tiny brown-and-white papillon, Bosco, noisily announced visitors and jealously guarded his owner's attention.

Shapiro visited her first jail at sixteen, after a high school teacher piqued her interest with a lecture on disparities in who is released on bail. A correctional candystriper at the tail end of the 1960s, Shapiro borrowed her mother's car and drove out to the local jail, where a welcoming warden invited her to visit with the inmates. Astonished to discover how many were there for using drugs or resisting the draft, Shapiro began formulating what would become an abiding ambition—"to change policy and practice in American criminal justice."

Shapiro volunteered behind bars through college and then graduate school, in law and social policy. Advanced degrees in hand, she took a job working for the New York City Department of Corrections as an assistant commissioner, running drug-treatment programs, electronic monitoring, and boot camps. The boot-camp graduations put family on her radar.

"I'm so proud of José," a graduate's mother might tell her. "This is the first thing he's ever graduated from. But when he's home, he steals from me. I'm taking care of his kids. Sometimes he disappears for days on end. I worry. But I love José."

"You hear enough of these stories," Shapiro said, "and you start to think, 'Well, what about the family? Why aren't we paying attention to these natural resources, but also to the supports that families may need if they're going to help their loved ones?'"

Shapiro left the DOC and, in 1994, began raising money for what she was calling a neighborhood drug-crisis center. Shapiro knew that most of New York's prisoners came from a handful of "feeder neighborhoods," which not only supplied a large portion of the state's prisoners but also reabsorbed them. Shapiro focused her attention on Manhattan's Lower East Side, a neighborhood that—according to the researchers who evaluated La Bodega—is so saturated with drugs that residents say it is impossible not to be affected in one way or another. More than half of the drug users the researchers interviewed had themselves grown up in drug-using households. Criminal justice involvement had become the norm in the neighborhood, and legal employment the exception.

Shapiro saw strengths on the Lower East Side as well, a foundation on which to build. The neighborhood was stable and relatively cohesive. Despite a recent spate of gentrification, it had a large population of long-term residents—multigenerational families with a history and a stake in the community. It also had more than its share of programs and resources, albeit uncoordinated.

Shapiro's years working inside "the system" left her with a commitment to working with, rather than against, the multiple bureaucracies that are omnipresent in neighborhoods like the Lower East Side. Government, Shapiro observed, "is so intrusive in poor people's lives, through child welfare, TANF, public health, justice, you name it. If you can get government to treat families respectfully, to engage them, then you can change outcomes in a very profound way."

People coming out of prison often describe multiple systems—child welfare, mental health, drug treatment, parole or probation—pulling their family in different directions and imposing conflicting demands. La Bodega takes this on by drawing up an "ecomap" for each client—a visual representation of the complex web of systems and institutions in which many poor families are entangled. The ecomap allows a Bodega case manager to see potential conflicts coming; the relationships Bodega has established with city institutions let him get on the phone and avert them.

The partnership La Bodega has developed with the New York parole department is particularly valuable. As caseloads nationwide have grown from an average of forty-five per officer in the 1970s to an average of seventy today—reaching into the hundreds in some big cities—parole officers have increasingly focused their efforts on supervision and enforcement rather than support and rehabilitation. In New York, the parole department has assigned six officers to work exclusively with Bodega clients and their families, practicing a form of old-school supervision that goes beyond urine tests and curfew checks. Bodega case managers accompany parole officers to pre-release visits at the prisons. Parole officers join case managers at family meetings. Perhaps most importantly—and surprisingly—La Bodega has hammered out an agreement with parole in which technical violations don't automatically mean a return to jail or prison. If someone relapses, Shapiro said, everyone just tries harder.

Listen to the talk of a prisoner whose release date is imminent. It is comprised less of wishes—hot meals and warm baths—than of promises: to stay clean this time, get a job and settle down, make a home for his children and a place for himself. Prisoners often walk out the gates with a powerful sense that they owe a debt to their families. This restorative impulse is too often thwarted by the barriers and restrictions that make it virtually impossible for many returning prisoners to fulfill their obligations to family and community. Nourished, it can prove a powerful force for personal and community recovery.

On paper, the Lower East Side is a neighborhood of single-parent families—women and children getting by on their own, the men lost to drugs or prison or second and third families. Men in this neighborhood speak adoringly of their "mommies" but reference paternity with the less-intimate term "father figure." La Bodega works with this reality, but also sees something more complicated—would-be dads dancing around the edges of reconstituted families, longing for a place they're not sure they've earned.

For case managers trained to see strengths rather than deficits, this will to parent—which often builds force inside prison, only to dissipate in the harsh light of post-release reality—represents a powerful opportunity. For men coming out of prison, a connection to children can be a strong motivator to stay clean and out of trouble. For children, a bond with a father can offer the sustenance they need to stay away from drugs and delinquency themselves.

Bodega case manager Hector Gonzalez grew up in the housing projects of the Lower East Side. By the time Gonzalez was six, his father, Hector Sr., was deep into drugs. Gonzalez remembers his aunt taking him on long drives to visit his father in a huge gated building that looked like a castle. Family members told him his father was on vacation. Gonzalez pretended to believe them.

By the time Gonzalez's father got out of prison the last time around, Gonzalez's parents had divorced, but that didn't stop Gonzalez from wanting a father. The surprise was that he got one. Hector Sr. went from prison to an inpatient drug-treatment center, stayed two years, and came out clean. Gonzalez remembers visiting the facility for barbecues and basketball games, sometimes for entire weekends. He loved seeing his father happy and respected, a mentor to the younger men in the program.

Gonzalez had fought a lot during the years when his father was in prison and using drugs; spent time in detention or with the school counselor. Once Hector Sr. got clean, he got his son in line. "He was pretty strict, 'cause he didn't want me to go through the same things he had, but he was understanding," Gonzalez remembers. "Now I had a father in my life—somebody that could hear me out. I kinda struggled, but I still did good."

When Gonzalez was fourteen, his father told him that he had HIV. Gonzalez remembers his father breaking the news gently, the two of them crying together. Hector Sr. died a few months later.

Gonzalez's father was in his life consistently for only a few years, but the impact has been lasting. "I base a lot of what I do on him," said Gonzalez, who went on to college and graduate school in social work. "He showed me that you could come from the streets, make mistakes, but also try to get your life together. Even though he went through all those bad experiences, he shaped a good future for me."

His father's transformation left Gonzalez with a faith he brings to his work with his clients at La Bodega. "A theme that recurs is that they want to be there for their children," Gonzalez said, "and I think they could be." Gonzalez's job is to channel that desire; to help his clients stabilize their lives so they can contribute to, as well as rely on, their families.

Clients dropped in to see Gonzalez all afternoon, both scheduled and unannounced. His conversational manner was friendly but directive: his admiration for a new pair of sneakers segued seamlessly into questions about the care of an invalid mother, or concerns about a nephew who was drifting into trouble. Gonzalez works hard to find jobs for his clients; men who can't provide may feel they have no place in their children's lives. He works with parole officers and drug treatment programs to help clients stay clean and free. When there's trouble with a child's mother, he does his best to mediate. He'll listen endlessly to the hard-luck stories of the men who drop by to see him, gently steering them past their frustration toward obligation and opportunity.

Samuel, thirty-seven, has been a Bodega client since 1998. His halting transition from addict and dealer to working father has affected two sets of children—his two biological children, who live with their mother and are now tentatively welcoming their father back into their lives, and his girlfriend's four children, who have come to know Samuel as a steady presence who helps them with their homework and keeps them off the corner.

Samuel grew up on the Lower East Side, married young and divorced quickly, then moved back with his mother. He picked up a cocaine habit, lost his job, and drifted into dealing. His ex-wife promised he could spend time with his kids any time he got clean, but Samuel kept on using.

Samuel bounced in and out of prison until 2002. When I met him, he had been out, and clean, for over two years. Drugs, he'd decided, were "stupid, childish"; prison was "for suckers." Now he wanted to find out what it felt like to pay rent, keep a job, be a responsible father.

At La Bodega, Samuel's case manager helped him find on-call custodial work and talked with him about his family. He's off her formal caseload now but around all the time anyway. When he's working, he drops by La Bodega once a week; when he's not, he stops by every day or two.

Many men return from prison to find their families reconfigured, with a new man at the table and no place left for them. Some respond with anger; others disappear. With La Bodega's help, Samuel has learned to approach his family with respect and humility. His son is fourteen now, and his daughter is thirteen. They have a stepfather who has raised them since they were small. Every time he gets the chance, Samuel thanks his children's new father for feeding and clothing them, for teaching them to ride a bike.

The previous year, he saw his children at Thanksgiving, Christmas, and over the summer. They were old enough that he could talk with them about the decade when he went missing; he could apologize, try to explain, and ask them what they wanted from him. He and his ex-wife are planning to sit down soon and work out a more regular visitation plan. She's told him she'll give him the benefit of the doubt, but made it clear he's on parental probation.

In the meantime, there are his girlfriend's four children— aged six, ten, eleven, and twelve—whose father left them to start a second family. Samuel helps them with their home- work—multiplication, division, vocabulary words—but draws the line at doing it for them. He's feeling his way; this everyday fatherhood is new to him.

The kids aren't allowed to hang out in front of the building, and Samuel limits his own sidewalk time as well. "I speak to a friend, how you doing, we laugh, OK, bye, see you later," he said. "I give a person fifteen, twenty minutes. Anything after that, you see cops coming up and down the streets. I'm not with that anymore."

In a neighborhood where even chatting on the sidewalk feels risky, La Bodega is an island of uninhibited talk. It is here that Samuel warms up for the difficult conversations with which he is working his way into his two families. His case manager, he explained, opened the floodgates. "She grabbed me. I don't know how. She didn't grab me physically, but she made me open up, and it just came out.

"It feels good," he said, of his new life and identity. "I don't have to worry about a number anymore: '04R6285, step up.' No. My name is Samuel, and I have a social security number that I go by, and that's the way it's gonna stay."

7

LEGACY

DAVID'S EARLIEST MEMORY IS of finding himself caged.

His mother, Candace Bettencourt-Ventra, had been arrested on a drug charge. David was taken to a children's shelter in Orange County, California, and placed in a crib from which he was too small to climb. So he peered through the rails, rails that felt like bars, trying to figure out where he was.

"I remember crying all the time in that crib," said David, a burly thirty-six-year-old whose face and arms were covered in blue-ink tattoos that mapped his transit through California's juvenile and adult correctional systems. When I met him, David was awaiting trial on assault charges for an altercation on the freeway. If convicted, he faced up to six more years in prison.

"I cried a lot because no one was around me," David said of that first trip to the children's shelter. "When someone came, I stopped. Then when they left I'd start crying again. For some reason I always remember that."

David's next memory is of being in a foster home. He thinks it was a couple of years later. "The family I was with wasn't my family."

A cycle was beginning—one that would last until he grew

old enough to do time himself. Sometimes family members would take David in when his mother was arrested, or retrieve him from foster care, only to ship him off to the children's shelter when they tired of shouldering his mother's responsibilities. Eventually, he'd wind up back with Candace. Then she would get arrested again and he'd find himself back in transit.

David went back to the children's shelter over and over—at seven, eight, nine, ten, eleven. "I've been locked up since I was three," he said. Technically, the children's shelter was not a juvenile jail; that facility was situated next door. But the children slept in what David described as "two-man cells" along a long corridor. The doors locked from the outside. The windows were covered with wire mesh. When the children were taken outside, they played beneath barbed wire.

" 'It's to keep bad people out, not to keep you in,' " David remembers the staff telling the children. The distinction meant less than the fact of the fence.

"Why should I pay for this?" David wondered each time he found himself on the wrong side of barbed wire. He still isn't sure what "this" is.

As many as half of the male children whose parents have been incarcerated will wind up behind bars themselves. One in ten of the children of prisoners will be locked up before they reach eighteen. Local studies have mapped more specific patterns. Researchers in Oregon, for example, followed 206 boys from high-crime neighborhoods from 1983 to the present. In the fourth grade, 9 percent of the boys had a mother who had been arrested; 22 percent had a father who had been arrested; and 2 percent had both. By eighteen, half of the boys whose father had been arrested and 80 percent of those whose mother, or both parents, had been arrested had themselves been arrested twice or more. (By way of comparison, 20 percent of boys from the same neighborhoods who had not experienced parental arrest had been arrested twice or more themselves.) Another study, in Sacramento, California, found that among nine- to twelve-year-old children who had been arrested, 45 percent had an incarcerated parent.

The relationship between parental incarceration and juvenile crime is not a new one. A study of delinquent boys in Massachusetts reformatories in the 1930s and '40s found that two-thirds had a father with a criminal record. Of these, 40 percent had a grandfather with a record.

The notion of an intergenerational cycle of crime has tremendous cultural and political currency. It appears in grant proposals for programs that aim to serve the children of prisoners, and in testimony in support of legislation aimed at restructuring the criminal justice system in one way or another. But negative expectations have a power of their own, and the concept of an "intergenerational cycle" is no exception. The same analyses that win dollars for programs can also heighten the already-burdensome stigma of having a parent in prison.

The history of professional theorizing on intergenerational criminality is reason enough for caution. In his 1969 study *The Child Savers: The Invention of Delinquency*, Anthony M. Platt chronicles a widely held nineteenth-century view of criminality as innate, biological, and hereditary. The work of the influential Italian pseudoscientist Cesare Lombroso—who posited the existence of a "criminal type" distinguishable from the rest of us by "observable physical anomalies" such as big ears, a heavy jaw, and a crooked skull—was appropriated and expanded upon by American theorists such as Arthur MacDonald, who offered this elaboration on the Lombrosian "born criminal" to a U.S. audience in 1893:

> Their moral degeneration corresponds with their physical, their criminal tendencies are manifested in infancy by onanism, cruelty, inclination to steal, excessive vanity, impulsive character. The criminal by nature is lazy, debauched, cowardly, not susceptible to remorse, without foresight; fond of tattooing. . . . As the born criminal is without remedy, he must be continually confined, and allowed no provisional liberty or mercy.

Biological theories of crime were founded on the idea of a "hereditary taint" so powerful that the only solution was to ensure that "certain classes of vicious persons could be hindered from propagation." These insights inspired anthropologists to produce elaborate studies of criminally inclined families. One such researcher claimed to have identified an Indiana clan of more than 5,000 members, "interwoven by descent and marriage. They underrun society like devilgrass. Pick up one and the whole five thousand would be drawn up."

Blaming this infestation on the "old convict stock" transported from England generations earlier, the researcher proposed a solution: "We must get hold of the children." Subsequent reformers took up the challenge, offering varied and imaginative proposals for achieving that end. One criminologist proposed "a methodized registration and training of such children, or these failing, by their early and entire withdrawal from the community!" Another went a step further, proposing, in the name of "scientific crime prevention," that "we can direct and control the progress of human evolution by breeding better types and by the ruthless elimination of inferior types, if only we are willing to found and to practice a science of human genetics."

These notions did not remain in the realm of theory. In the latter half of the nineteenth century, hundreds of thousands of urban children were shipped to the countryside on "orphan trains" to provide free labor to farm families, on the theory that removing impressionable children from the bad influences of their impoverished families was the only way to keep the "dangerous classes" from reproducing themselves and overrunning the cities.

The last century may not have taken us as far from this world-view as we would like to believe. The 1990s saw a rash of federally funded research aimed at pinpointing a "crime gene," in the hope that hereditary criminality, promptly identified, could be curbed through the use of pharmaceutical prophylactics. This research included a study in which black and Latino boys as young as six, whose older brothers had been adjudicated as delinquents, were injected with fenfluramine (the primary ingredient in the banned diet drug fen-phen) in the hope that the drug would curb their predicted—though as-yet-unmanifested—aggression.

Today, the abiding notion that the apple does not fall far from the tree—combined with the contemporary pseudo-science of racial profiling—leaves many children of incarcerated parents feeling as if they are indeed marked with a hereditary taint. Many young people report being singled out by police because of their family background. Many also face family members, teachers, or others who are quick to warn them that they will wind up just like their incarcerated parents.

"I was labeled a gang-banger before I was actually in a gang," said Marlene, whose father was sentenced to fifteen years in federal prison when she was nine years old, "because of my father's affiliation and my family history."

Police in the neighborhood where Marlene grew up used special databases to track juveniles who they believed were affiliated with local street gangs—a contemporary version of the "methodized registration" proposed by the nineteenth-century visionaries. Marlene believes that because her father and other family members had been arrested for gang activity, her name was added to the list. "I would get in a fight at school and the gang task force would come instead of the regular police," she said.

Calculations of "intergenerational criminality," it is worth noting, are based on arrest and incarceration rates for the children of offenders rather than criminal acts per se. If these children are in fact targeted at higher rates than their peers, that fact alone would account for part of the "cycle."

Denied any provisional mercy, Marlene developed what she called an " 'I don't give a fuck' attitude" and began living up to the label already assigned her. Soon she was locked up in juvenile hall herself. "Through that experience," she said, "me and my father got really close."

The determinism that was explicit in nineteenth-century criminology is reflected in the self-image of juvenile detainees today. "I got my dad and brother and cousins locked up," wrote one participant in a writing workshop inside a California youth facility. "Even when I was in my mom's stomach, she was locked up, and when I was born she was locked up, so I feel like I was born to the system. . . . I figure it's like a never-ending curse that can't be stopped and keeps on getting passed down."

"It's kind of funny how the majority of our family is always in the system somehow," wrote another. "It's like being locked up runs through our genes."

There is little question that the notion of an "intergenerational cycle" can easily be misused to perpetuate ugly stereotypes and self-fulfilling prophecies. There is also little question that such a cycle does in fact exist. The challenge is finding a way to understand and address it that does not ultimately—through labeling, stigmatizing, and penalizing children whose parents have broken the law—perpetuate it.

"Cycle" may in fact be too elegant a word to describe the process by which some children are dragged into, rather than actively pursuing, the paths their parents have worn. Imagine a family caught in a turning gear and you may get closer to the brutality of the forces a child must fight if he wants to travel into uncharted territory.

David saw no fork in the road. He began stealing cars, using drugs, fighting, once pulling a machete on an undercover police officer. By the time he hit his early teens, he was regularly deposited at juvenile hall rather than the adjacent children's shelter. At the shelter, he remembered, there had been a little store, from which he could earn a soda for good behavior. There was no such shop inside juvenile hall. Other than that, he didn't notice much difference. One institution had prepared him for the next.

David witnessed his mother's arrest several times. Once, he was sitting in a holding cell in the foyer of juvenile hall, awaiting an appearance in court. Candace showed up to attend his court date. From his cell, David watched police search his mother, who had an outstanding warrant, and find syringes on her. Then they handcuffed her and brought her into the same block of cells in which her son was being held, where she stayed until deputies arrived to transfer her to the adult jail. Humiliated and helpless, David kicked and beat the door of his cell until his mother was removed.

Another time, when David was twelve or thirteen, police kicked down the door of his family's apartment and charged into his bedroom.

"What are you doing here?" an officer asked, surprised, as David emerged from beneath his blankets. The officer knew David from the street, had arrested him before—as he had David's mother and stepfather—but had not made the connection between him and his family.

"I live here," David explained. "These are my parents."

David, when I met him, was burly, lumbering, tattooed, and muscular—"body armor," his mother called this imposing carapace. But something about him seemed immediately vulnerable, and visibly unprotected—a child who was still unable to contain his hurt. The officer who recognized David had come for his mother, but he took the son, too; being in a drug house—his own house—constituted a violation of his probation.

Inside juvenile hall, David worked out frenetically, building his legs into "big old blocks" in preparation for flight. He managed to escape from juvenile hall once, by climbing over the fence, and fled boys' ranches on several other occasions, but he never stayed free for long.

As his mother's addiction progressed, David's home life deteriorated. At one point, Candace had been a functioning heroin addict, holding a job and maintaining an apartment. Eventually, she lost her job, then her home. Finally, she began to prostitute herself. David picked up his mother's drug habit and started getting kicked out of school. The family lived out of motel rooms. With the exception of the police, no one seemed to notice.

About 20 percent of the children of the most acutely criminal parents—those who rack up the greatest number of arrests—exhibit serious "conduct problems" as adolescents. They lie, or steal, or get into fights—problems that are often associated with adult criminality and incarceration. Another way of looking at them is as flags, warnings to the world about trouble at home. David waved frantically.

"When I would get kicked out of school, nobody would ever ask, 'How are things at home?'" David said. "Here I was going to junior high school from a motel room while my mom's prostituting. That's not normal."

The signals missed or ignored, the hand withheld, are as central as the fact of parental criminality itself to the so-called intergenerational cycle. Arlene Lee of the Federal Resource Center for Children of Prisoners suggested that instead of using the term "cycle"—with its implications of fate, of predestination—we look at the trajectory that leads some children of prisoners into criminality themselves, and seek opportunities to interrupt it.

"If we do absolutely nothing," she said, "then yes, there is the distinct possibility the child of an incarcerated parent will end up going through our child welfare system, needing special education and mental health services, ending up in the juvenile justice and adult systems. If we do something, we can move them in a different direction—and we don't always have to do something huge."

Lee recalled a child she met in rural Kentucky whose father

had been sentenced to prison for a white-collar crime. That same year, another boy in the same third-grade class lost his father to cancer. The community took up collections and held bake sales to support the family that had lost a provider to illness. The family that had lost a father to incarceration was evicted from their home and went on welfare, but the community offered no response.

The best way to "do something," Lee proposed, is not to label the children of incarcerated parents "at risk" and focus on them as a potential threats, but to "look at them like any other child whose parent has been involved in some tragedy and left the child without the necessary supports, and then look at what each individual child needs as a result. Instead we judge them, and I think we set them up."

David's first juvenile arrest was for driving a stolen car. So was his first arrest as an adult. He spent sixteen months in state prison. Next came two years for robbery, then three years for possession of methamphetamine.

The early Romans tattooed slaves and criminals so they could easily be identified. In prison, David covered his own face in ink "because I thought I was never gonna get out or be good or do anything good. So I put these on my face, and then I beat down a corrections officer with his own billy club." That act of despair earned David a transfer to California State Prison–Corcoran—which made headlines and inspired lawsuits during his stay when correctional officers staged "gladiator" fights between rival gangs in the exercise yard, then fired shots into the crowd to quell the ensuing chaos—and four years in the Security Housing Unit, or SHU, where he was confined to his cell twenty-three hours a day.

· · ·

I returned from meeting David to find a message from his mother confirming an appointment the following week. Candace was calling from her San Jose office at Friends Outside, a statewide organization that supports prisoners and their families, where she worked as a drug and alcohol counselor and ran a juvenile justice program. She was sorry it had taken her a day to return my call; she had been "in the field," but was looking forward to our meeting. Her voice was relaxed, flawlessly professional. She left her work and cell phone numbers, repeating both. I wondered what David's life would be like now if he had grown up with this woman as his mother.

When I met Candace at her office the following week, she was furious at her younger son Michael. "What you taught me is how to fail," he had told her the night before. But Candace doesn't see herself as a failure.

"My sons like to hold me hostage," said Candace, fifty-three, making a petulant face and whiny noises in imitation. She was a large woman with wavy red-gold hair past her shoulders, deep pink lipstick, and darker liner. Her unheated office in the converted Victorian that housed Friends Outside was chilly on a January morning. In olive-green loose-cut pants and a matching short-sleeved shirt, she rocked back and forth in her desk chair and ate M&Ms, which she kept in bulk in a desk drawer. A wall of framed diplomas and certificates declared her an alcohol and drug counselor, an internationally certified alcohol and drug counselor, a certified prevention specialist.

Candace knows she hurt her children and has tried to make it up to them, she said. But now she was ready for them to put the past behind them, as she believes she has, so they could all move forward together.

"He's not responsible for what happened to him or how he

was raised," she said of her resentful younger son. "What he's responsible for is his choices today."

Candace's voice was deep and gravelly. "So I just told 'em this year, 'Ten years I've been making my amends to you, but cash cow is over and you get yourself on your own two feet. Every day that I stay clean is an amends to you. Every day that I'm not in the penitentiary or selling drugs or selling my ass or breaking the law or having a disconnected phone is an amends to you. If I can pull myself out from where I've been, so can you. You're not gonna hold me hostage with guilt and shame and embarrassment anymore."

Candace may be frustrated, but she is not, in fact, done making amends. As we spoke, Michael was asleep at her house, beneath a blanket she had tossed him in silence after their argument the night before. He was living in Southern California but had come up for an appointment with Candace's dentist—she picks up the bills—and to visit his cats, whom Candace was caring for until Michael found a place where he could keep them. Her credit cards were maxed out with Michael's textbooks, David's bail.

Candace grew up in Southern and then Northern California. She was a bright girl and an enthusiastic athlete—the tetherball champion of her elementary school—who went by the nickname "Candy." Her parents were both deaf—hardworking people who communicated with their hearing children through sign language.

When a boarder moved into their home and began molesting Candace, it was easy for him to take advantage of her parents' disability. Sometimes Candace's assailant would threaten her in her parents' uncomprehending presence. He told her he would choke her if she revealed his secret; that no one would believe her and she'd be taken away. At night he would put a pillow over Candace's face and nearly smother her, promising to follow through if she ever talked.

Candace started running away overnight, sometimes for a couple of days. She would hide in her "fort," a hollowed-out blackberry bush. "It was huge, but you had to be real small to get in there without getting scratched, and it was mine, and I was safe. I would sit in my little safe place and watch my sister and brother in the back of a police car while they drove up and down the street looking for me."

Finally, Candace decided she could no longer keep the abuse secret. Candace's deep voice rose in pitch as she told this part of her story, becoming again that of a frightened girl. She left her bedroom and went into the living room, where her parents were playing cards with her abuser.

"I don't feel good," she told her mother, who asked her what was wrong.

Candace took her mother into the bedroom and tried to tell her: "I'm sore."

"Did you fall on your bike?" her mother asked.

Finally, Candace managed to describe to her mother what had been done to her. Her mother went into the kitchen, picked up a knife, and drove the perpetrator from the house. Then she told her husband what had happened. His daughter was lying, he answered. But the man never came back.

When Candace was nine, her father left the family. Candace's mother took a job at a dry cleaner and struggled to support the children on her own. Candace remembers coming home from school to an empty house, empty cupboards. After a while, she stopped coming home.

Formerly an A student, Candace failed the fifth grade. Her

mother came in for a conference and signed her F-filled report card without question. Candace was sending up flares. As David's would a generation later, they rose and fell unheeded.

"How fucking stupid can you be?" Candace asked, still wounded by her long-ago invisibility. "These are teachers and they don't see. I had straight A's and now I'm failing school. There's gotta be something underneath that. But they didn't see, and they failed me, and that was the end of school for me."

The first time Candace was arrested, she was ten years old. She was hiding in a parked car and someone called the police. When the officers asked her what she was doing, she told them she didn't want to go home. They responded by taking her down to the police station and leaving her in a holding cell while they waited for her mother to come get her.

"How do you like it?" an officer asked her.

"I don't care, it's safe," Candace remembers thinking. To the officer, she said nothing. At ten, she had already begun to internalize the lessons that would later be instilled in David: that those in authority represented threat, not rescue; that a cell could feel like home.

In her search for refuge, Candace was setting off along a well-worn path. Many women prisoners first encounter the criminal justice system as adolescents, after running away from home in the wake of abuse. From there, the transition to the adult justice system is seamless—as it would be for Candace, and later for David.

By the eighth grade, Candace had been arrested for selling marijuana and sent to the California Youth Authority. When she refused a mandatory gynecological exam, no one asked her why. Instead, she was placed in solitary confinement until her mother won a court order exempting her from the exam.

A couple of months later, Candace discovered she was pregnant. She wasn't surprised; she had set out to conceive before she began her sentence, in an effort to win permission to marry her sixteen-year-old boyfriend. Instead, her mother informed her that the baby would be adopted. No one suggested that Candace might have a choice. She spent four days in labor, then gave birth in shackles. Her mother took the baby to paternal relatives in Texas. Candace never saw her daughter again.

After that, Candace was in and out of juvenile facilities. She got deeper into drugs—a trajectory that led briskly from codeine-laced cough syrup to heroin—in a mostly successful effort to "either change the way I felt or not feel at all."

She married at sixteen—by then she had been declared an "emancipated minor" and did not need her mother's permission—and soon gave birth to David. By the time he was old enough to walk, she was old enough to go to adult prison.

David was in the Security Housing Unit at Corcoran when he heard, after a long silence, from his mother. Candace wrote that she was clean, staying in a sober living environment—a housing complex devoted to those in recovery. She wrote that there was a better life out there without drugs and prison. To David, this came as news.

"I didn't think that was for me or my family," he said. "Not anything that could happen to us. I'd never thought about other people and other families, how they don't go through it. I just thought, well. Our life."

David had seen his mother near death as a result of her drug use. He didn't expect her transformation to last. But the letters kept coming. She was staying clean, Candace wrote. She had a job, an apartment.

David was and is deeply angry at his mother—"She ruined my life," he said more than once—but the devastation that drugs had wreaked on his family made her new example all the more powerful.

"My mom was a pretty bad dope fiend," David said, making the term sound almost an endearment. "If she could get clean, anybody could."

At Corcoran, David's cellmate was shot in the eye during one of the prison-yard melees. David himself was forced into combat more than once. Meanwhile, his mother was writing him long letters describing a life that was peaceful, productive—one he had never experienced and could barely imagine. On one level, he resented Candace's happiness. On another, he wanted a part of it.

When David was released, Candace was at the gate. "It went right through my head that you weren't going to be there," he said when he saw her.

"I'm here," she said.

"God, Mom," he told her once they were on the road, "I can't really believe you've been clean, and you're showing up, but I don't think I can do it."

Candace assured him that he could. David pointed to his tattoos. The blue ink that covers David's face includes the number 5150—the police code for crazy—over one eyebrow, and a teardrop beneath one eye. Ornate patterns wind their way down his arms and around both hands, past where any sleeve could obscure them. When you tattoo your face and hands, you are making both a statement and a prediction: that you never expect to find yourself in a setting where you will prefer to appear unmarked. David's goals may have been shifting, but the ink was indelible.

"Tattoos aren't against the law," Candace told her son. "That's not why you're going in and out of prison. You're going in and out 'cause you're a dope fiend like I am. If you stop using, you won't have to break the law. I know it sounds hard, but it's that simple."

Under the conditions of his parole, David was required to return to Orange County, where he had been arrested. But he told his parole officer—who had been a juvenile parole officer when David was a teenager and remembered him and his family—about the changes Candace had made. He needed his mother's help, David told the parole officer. He had no one else.

Because the mother was rehabilitated, the p.o. took a chance on the son. He removed David from "high control"—the strictest form of parole—and allowed him to move to San Jose. It was, David said, "the first time I noticed anybody really caring."

In San Jose, Candace took her son into her new apartment, bought him clothes and a car, and kept him fed while he looked for work. David doesn't remember long heart-to-hearts with his mother; he didn't ask for advice about how to stay clean, nor did she offer it. Instead, he said, "She showed me. She led by example. I started to see that there is life outside of prison."

In prison, David had been diagnosed with bipolar disorder and intermittent explosive disorder (a label that seems little more than a description). As a requirement of his parole, he took medication. He went to Narcotics Anonymous meetings and got a job in construction; he married and had two daughters. The marriage did not last, but David—who has since remarried—remained close to his children.

David didn't expect to stay out of prison, but he did anyway. Eventually, he felt so stable that he stopped taking his medication. Before long, the blackout rages were back—fits of anger so intense he could not remember, much less control, his actions.

David has been in therapy; has learned new names for the fury and despair that overtake him. "I have trust issues," he said, "and abandonment issues, which are just really surfacing today. Probably because I'm not on drugs anymore, and I'm more level-headed than before. I'm trying to figure out why I am the way I am, and so I have to search myself, and." His sentences often ended this way, not trailing off but stopping abruptly midway, as if he had hit a wall.

David was clearly proud of his mother's transformation, and grateful for her support. He believed he would not be free if not for her help and her example. But it is more complicated than that.

"She's got ten years clean and sober, she's a drug counselor, she thinks she's infallible now, and she's not," he said. "She keeps saying she did the best she could with what she had and blah blah blah, I'm here for you today. That's fine and dandy, but the system, her, they made me what I am today. And right now I'm looking at six years in prison."

The system, her, they made me what I am. The trouble David was born into—a drug-addicted family—is to him inseparable from the purported solution: serial incarceration. David's mother's drug use left him vulnerable and alone. Her arrest and incarceration made him more so. David responded predictably: drug use, violence, incarceration. The system intended to reform *him*—like the one that set out to penalize his mother—responded predictably as well, reinforcing what he had learned in a drug-abusing household.

In David's telling, the hurts he experienced at home blurred with those of prison life, all part of a continuum of harm and endangerment. "The system and my parents taught me that I can't trust anybody," he said. "'Cause in prison you can't trust anybody, and, you know, along with me not being able to trust my own family members to keep me safe and stuff. And the state made me that way because I never could trust them. They never did offer help, did anything good, and so it made me into the person I am today. I truly do believe that."

While David was off his meds, he stopped working at his construction job and hooked up with a local chapter of the Hells Angels, picking up a new tattoo to mark the affiliation. Three months before I met him, he got into a motorcycle accident, flying into the back of an SUV at seventy miles an hour. When that didn't kill him, he tried to overdose on heroin.

During that same period, he got into the fight for which he was awaiting trial. Another driver, whom David said he "apparently" cut off, started tailgating him, screaming and flipping him off. David slammed on his brakes, causing the other driver to rear-end him. The men got out and fought beside the freeway. David was arrested.

When I met David, his trial was several months off. If he were to go back to prison, he said, he wasn't sure he'd let his children visit. He never saw his mother when she was in jail or prison—at first, he had no one to take him; later, his own criminal history made him a "security risk" and precluded him from doing so—and wasn't sure he'd want his girls to see him behind bars. He said he didn't want his daughters to go through what he had. That was about all he was willing to say about them.

"I try not to think about it," he said of what it might mean to his girls if he went back to prison. "You know. Till it happens."

It is perfectly possible to emerge from a childhood marked by parental crime and incarceration and live a "normal life"; many, even most, children do. But to pull it off, one must extract oneself from the gears of the social machinery, acquiring in the process the scars that such an operation inevitably entails.

The first time I met David's younger half brother, Michael, he picked an elegant courtyard restaurant in Sacramento, where he was then living, filled with businessmen and tourists; ordered carefully; dressed seriously. At thirty-two, Michael had spent five years in the Marines; worked as a loan officer for a mortgage company; and was enrolled in community college, where he was fulfilling a long-standing dream of playing college football.

"I figured out that I'm blessed to be as intelligent as I am," he declared early in our conversation. "I had nothing my whole life. Nobody gave me anything. But still I came up with some rational conclusions in my life, good decisions. That's why I feel so good to be who I am, that I've done what I've done. It's all been based upon my own initiative and reasoning."

Little had come easily to Michael—the list of those whom he felt had unfairly thwarted his prospects included not only his mother but a jealous job interviewer, a crooked client, a disrespectful football coach, and an insensitive fourth-grade teacher. "People out there really don't care about other people, I don't believe," Michael asserted. But Michael was also a reformer, full of well-thought-out theories about why things are as they are, and blueprints for change.

"Sending people to jail for victimless crimes—for abusing themselves—doesn't produce a solution," Michael insisted. "I've thought a lot about this, and the reality is, the laws are not designed to be solutions. The laws only perpetuate what it is that they think they are trying to prevent."

Michael recalled the day the police came and took away his mother, stepfather, and older brother. He was left behind with a deaf and elderly grandmother who he said was unable to care for him.

"Eleven years old, I was on my own," Michael said. "I starved, to be honest with you." He started staying out until eleven at night, paging through *Soldier of Fortune* magazine at the 7-Eleven to avoid coming home to an empty refrigerator.

"When you send somebody to jail" for using drugs, Michael has since concluded, "you're sending a very bad message to their children. That message is that the law and the government don't care about the integrity of the family. They only care about levying their punishment and exercising their authority, rather than exercising reason and giving people hope. When you send somebody to jail, you're taking somebody that's in a bad situation and putting them in a worse situation. And you're providing no hope not only to the person going to jail, but the family that has to endure it, and all the stigma that comes with it."

Formerly a successful student, Michael managed to get himself to school in the morning during his family's absence, but his performance deteriorated: "Who wants to do schoolwork when your mother doesn't come home?" He got into a fight with a classmate who mocked his ragged clothing, and he was kicked out of the gifted class. He was sending up flares. No one answered.

At the end of his seventh-grade year, Michael went by himself to a field meet at school. By chance, his older brother's probation officer was there with his two children. He saw Michael on his own and recognized him, remembering that his mother and stepfather were both locked up. The next thing Michael knew, someone had contacted his father, who lived a few counties over, and told him to come retrieve his son.

Michael had a rough time at his father's house. His father worked twelve hours a day and spent most of his free time chasing women, according to Michael. The two fought, and Michael's father kicked him out more than once. But Michael wasn't hungry anymore, and he made it through school. The parole officer's brief intervention—the simple fact that he *saw* Michael, and not just as a potential criminal—was rescue enough. It was, Michael said, a rare instance in which "the system worked."

Like David, Michael was and is angry at his mother. At one point, when he was in the Marines, he stopped communicating with her entirely, resuming contact only once she got clean. He is still, according to Candace, inclined to berate her when things go wrong in his life. But, also as with David, it was his mother to whom Michael turned when he hit his lowest point as an adult.

He had finished his tour with the Marines and ended an important relationship. After four years in the tightly knit military community, he moved to Sacramento, where he knew no one. His loneliness triggered a depression so severe that he found himself one day with a rifle in his hands, asking, "Is this all there is?"

"I was willing to do anything to alleviate the pain I was feeling," Michael said. What he did was call his mother, who sent him to a Naranon meeting—a support group for those who have lived through a family member's addiction. From there, he was referred to a Co-Dependents Anonymous meeting, where he talked about his family and cried before strangers. Michael stayed only long enough to pull himself back from the precipice, but he remembers and repeats the lessons he learned about family dysfunction, the power of shame, and being his own worst enemy. His mother, it turned out, had known what he needed.

Each time I spoke with Michael, he was worrying about David. Michael remembered his older brother as a "very handsome, very intelligent, very athletic" kid, and he was furious that David had drifted so far from that remembered image; that his handsome face was almost completely obscured by his many tattoos; that he was facing yet another prison term.

"If you keep a dog on a chain, that dog is going to become vicious," Michael said. "My brother was sent to Corcoran prison. They were killing people there. Nobody knows what he's gone through. Even me.

"I was a fighter," said Michael, who believes he avoided his brother's path in part by learning from David's mistakes. "Some people, like my brother, were told they were bad, were treated bad, and became bad."

Michael worries now about his nieces, wonders whether they will find what they need to grow.

"She's just so beautiful, and extremely intelligent," Michael said of his older niece. "But I can already see how the pain that her father experienced is affecting her. It's built in our DNA."

Michael may well be right; pain all too often is handed down from one generation to the next. But the corollary assumptions—that criminality itself is writ in the DNA; that pain cannot be healed—are belied not only by Michael's own story, but by the one his mother ultimately wrote.

What brought Candace back from the brink? The story she tells is multifaceted, but the skeleton is simple: she got old, and tired of all the self-destruction. Then she got help.

As her addiction deepened, Candace began to prostitute herself for drugs—a line she had never expected to cross. Her mother died of colon cancer while Candace was in prison, and Candace was not able to attend the funeral. After her mother's death, Candace found herself with no visitors, no one to put money on her commissary account, no one waiting at the gate each time her release date came around. She had lost track of her children. She felt herself, as they say in rehab circles, hitting bottom.

Back on the street, she ran into a police sergeant she'd known, and despised, for years. He had recently found religion and acquired a new sense of mission. "I've been watching you slowly but surely destroy yourself for years," he told Candace. He gave her a card with the address of a church where he said she might find solace. Candace went, thinking she could wrangle some drug money out of the do-gooders, but left empty-handed. All the same, the cop had planted a new idea: "If I really wanted it, I guess there were people who would help me."

Candace went back to prison, but this time she decided to try to stay off drugs, which were easily available within the prison economy. She enrolled in a prison workshop designed to boost self-esteem and encourage better choices. When she got out, she put herself in rehab.

The spot she found was in an outpatient program. Most of the participants were there because the courts had sent them, and most of them were loaded. If Candace wanted drugs, she could buy them in the parking lot. Candace stayed off hard drugs, but she kept on drinking and smoking marijuana. Before long, the heroin cravings were back, as powerful as ever.

This time, instead of heading down to the corner, Candace went to see her parole officer. She confessed what she'd been up to and suggested he send her back to prison. Instead, he got on the phone and found her a bed in a residential drug-treatment facility. Ten years later, Candace still sends him a Christmas card.

In residential treatment, Candace saw a therapist and talked about parts of her childhood she'd kept buried for decades. "What brought me to some clarity," she said, "was realizing that every time I blamed the perpetrator [the man who had molested her], he was still victimizing me. I thought, 'Oh my God, I'm destroying my life, abandoning my kids, for him?' That's when I said, 'I'm going to change this. I'm not going to keep giving him the power to destroy me.'"

Candace started going to twelve-step meetings, church, any place that would have her. The support bolstered her confidence, but not enough to stop her from going on a methamphetamine binge with a fellow rehab graduate once she completed her program.

Again, Candace turned to the system she had for decades considered her enemy. When she called her p.o. and told him what she was doing, he asked her to come in, promising not to send her back to prison if she did. Candace hung up the phone and thought about her children. David was in prison. Michael was in the military and refusing to speak to her. She wanted to be high, but more than that, she wanted a connection with her sons.

"At the time," she said, "I don't know that I had anything to offer, except that I wanted a relationship with them. That's all I knew. I wanted to be hugging them and talking to them and looking at them. I wanted to be around them."

Candace went down to the parole office. Her p.o. kept his promise: her warrant was voided. When she saw that, said Candace, "I knew that I was on the right path, that the right players were being put in front of me, and because I was looking, I could recognize that when it was there."

This sense of destiny, of blessed convergence, is endemic to the successfully rehabilitated. What is notable about Candace's account is that when she reached that moment of readiness, the "right players" were all connected in one way or another with the criminal justice system. If that was due in great part to proximity—enforcers were the representatives of the larger society whom Candace was most likely to encounter—that fact only underscores the tremendous opportunity that law enforcement and corrections represent, if thoughtfully administered.

It is also worth noting how often Candace faltered on the way to recovery, and how often she was given another chance. Those chances may have come late, but come they did, as many as she needed. The same would likely not hold true today, when sentencing policy is driven by sports metaphors and chances are strictly rationed.

In the years since Candace made her circuit through the California courts, twenty-five states have passed some form of "three strikes" law mandating long sentences for repeat offenders. California's version requires sentences to be doubled for any felony for those with a prior serious or violent felony conviction, and mandates twenty-five-to-life for a third felony, down to and including shoplifting. A survey of California's second- and third-strikers found that nearly two-thirds were locked up for nonviolent offenses, and that more were serving life sentences for drug possession than for second-degree murder, assault with a deadly weapon, and rape combined.

"Strikes" laws vary from state to state, but all are predicated on the notion that there is a predetermined moment at which an individual can be declared permanently irredeemable. Anyone looking at Candace during her three decades of addiction might well have declared her beyond redemption. But Candace changed her life—not because she was facing some magic number of "strikes," but because she was ready, and because she found help.

In August of 2004, David went to trial. He was convicted of assault, sentenced to four years in prison, and given his second strike.

Candace, who was there in the courtroom, rose from her seat and demanded to be allowed to speak. A marshal told her if she did not stop disrupting the courtroom, she would have to leave. Deputies had already taken David away. The judge, however, consented to hear Candace and scheduled another hearing for the following week.

Candace returned to court armed with a photo album filled with pictures of David and his daughters: David in the hospital, his newborn clutching his finger; David leaning in as his elder daughter blew out birthday candles; dressing her up in a pumpkin suit for Halloween; standing in front of a Christmas tree wearing an elf's hat; reading to his daughter; teaching her to ride a bike; dozing on the couch with her cuddled up next to him.

David, Candace told the judge, had been abandoned, neglected, exposed to drugs, and passed from hand to hand. He had grown up without a father but was committed to being one. He had successfully met the requirements of his parole, was attending counseling and taking his medication again, and had had no other problems in five years out.

"On paper, he's just a number," Candace told the judge, "but he's a human being, and he's my son. He wears a mask to cover up the hurt he's been through, but I know what kind of person he really is."

The judge reconsidered, sentencing David to a year in the county jail and five years' probation. David's attorney told Candace it was the first time in his career he had seen such a thing happen. David's older daughter visits him every week.

THROUGHOUT HER YEARS OF addiction and incarceration, Candace told herself tall tales about the life she was making for her boys. When she dropped acid the night before Easter, she convinced herself it would help her make the most fanciful Easter eggs on the block. When a teenaged David came to her for heroin, she shared her stash, telling herself she was protecting him from the street, where he might get arrested or buy a contaminated batch. When the stories failed her—when she was locked up for long stretches, leaving her sons to fend for themselves—she simply forced herself not to think about her children.

That strategy wouldn't last long in Oregon, where reformers inside and outside the Department of Corrections (DOC) are implementing a gradual but potentially profound shift in the operation and even purpose of the state's prison system. The DOC has entered into a collaboration with other state and non-profit agencies known as the Children of Incarcerated Parents

Project. The initiative aims to improve the long-term prospects of the children of incarcerated parents—and help inmates succeed post-release—by fostering family bonds.

Men and women in Oregon prisons have access to parenting classes developed specifically for them by the Oregon Social Learning Center, and special visits where they receive feedback from a family therapist. Mothers at the Coffee Creek Correctional Facility, outside Portland, can participate in an on-site Early Head Start program, where young children spend twice-weekly three-hour stretches with their mothers in a preschool-like setting. The national program Girl Scouts Beyond Bars operates at Coffee Creek, allowing mothers and daughters to participate in bimonthly troop meetings inside the prison. Oregon inmates may also be eligible for on-site drug-treatment programs in dedicated housing units, where they spend fourteen hours a day in addiction treatment, counseling, education, and job training. On the outside, the DOC has developed a partnership with the Portland Relief Nursery to provide case management and family support to children, their caregivers, and their parents upon release.

Various prisons around the country run individual programs similar to those in Oregon. What makes Oregon unusual is that these efforts are coordinated at the state level and written into law. Senate Bill 133, approved by the Oregon legislature in 2001, requires state agencies to collaborate to support and strengthen the relationships between prisoners and their children. The result is that Oregon's prisons have become a place where it is increasingly difficult—for inmates and officials both—to put the children out of mind or to place faith in fairy tales about their lives.

Inside the Oregon State Correctional Institute in Salem, the

Parenting Inside/Out class meets weekly in a fluorescent-lit classroom. On the December morning when I visited, a dozen men in stiff blue denim sat around a conference table. The room was bare, save for a few failing potted plants, and the light through the windows was filtered by bars. A roll of toilet paper sat on the table, in case of tears.

Each prisoner had before him a teddy bear of one sort or another. Most of the bears were propped on the table, some facing their caretakers, others away. A man with a long ponytail and a goatee cradled his white polar bear against his chest as if he were not conscious of doing so, resting his head lightly on the bear's soft crown.

Rex Newton, the psychologist who runs the men's parenting class, was gray-haired and energetic, nutty-professorial in tasseled loafers and pleated khaki pants. Over the twelve-week session, Newton guides his students through lessons and role-plays that take on child development, discipline and play, role modeling, letter writing, and communicating with their children's caregivers. Much of the men's education, however, takes place outside the classroom, where they must care for the bears around the clock, enlisting a "babysitter" if they so much as take a shower, as a way of rehearsing for parental duties they are currently barred from exercising.

The bears have evoked some derision in this maximum-security facility, and occasional bouts of ill-advised comedy. One man's bear was kidnapped and replaced with a ransom note, much to the dismay of its caretaker, who gave the perpetrator a stern lecture about the respect due a neighbor's progeny. But the men in the parenting class have maintained a steadfastly serious attitude toward their plush charges—an attitude they said they have managed over time to instill in their fellow inmates. Several men bragged about the comebacks they had devised for use against those who mocked their devotion as "gay"—retorts that generally involved asserting that real men take care of their kids.

William was a baby-faced man with slicked-back light-brown hair, a neat goatee, and tattoos of women snaking down his arms. His brown teddy bear sat perched on a pile of papers, wearing a white baby's cap and tiny sunglasses. William was head of the inmate-led Children of Incarcerated Parents Program, which organizes fund-raisers to support the parenting program and spruce up the visiting room. He sought the post after his wife informed him that his six-year-old boy and a neighborhood girl had gotten in trouble for vandalizing the girl's father's Camaro. The man called the police in an effort to scare the children. The girl was cowed into repentance. William's boy remained defiant. "I don't care," he told his mother. "I want to go to prison like my dad."

"When she told me that," William said, "I broke down and cried for the first time. That was when I saw that I had to do something to reach out from here."

Children, like adults, are drawn to tall tales when the truth is painful. They may convince themselves that a mother's arrest was a case of mistaken identity, or a father's offense an act of manhood, his sentence a badge of honor. One youth worker told me about a boy who insisted that his father had been imprisoned for a crime committed by an identical twin. Well-meaning caregivers sometimes collaborate in these fictions, telling children that Daddy is in the hospital or Mommy away at school.

The men in Rex Newton's classroom were determined to face the truth, and to bring their children with them. They described a common fear of looking up one day to find one's grown son walking across the yard, and said they had come to see taking responsibility for their crimes—and communicating that responsibility to their children—as a way of staving off that nightmare.

"Choices" was the buzzword in Newton's classroom, a term the men used repeatedly to explain how they wound up there, and how they planned to stay free once they left. It was a word they had learned to use with their children as well.

William said his two sons used to ask him during visits, "'Dad, can I beat up this cop and kidnap you and take you home?' I told 'em, 'No. This cop is a good man. Dad made a mistake. Dad did it.'"

Richard—a burly man with a ponytail and a beard—said the class had made him more sensitive to his children's emotions. "My oldest, when he plays, he hits hard. I can tell when he hits me that he's mad, because he feels that I abandoned him. I explain to him that it was because of the choices that I made. I broke the rules, and that's why I'm here."

Before he came to prison on drug-related charges, Richard ran a successful trucking business, earning more than he needed to support his family. "But what I've learned here is the importance of the bonding," he said. "Not only, 'I'm going to buy this, buy that,' but me being there."

Richard and his family lived across the street from a park, and his boys used to pester him to come along and play with them. Exhausted from work, he might push them on the swing for five minutes before heading back to the sofa. Once he started using drugs, even that ended.

"And right now . . ." he said. There was a long silence, followed by tears. ". . . I wish I could go over there and just play with them." The transition from self-confident narration to open sobbing was sudden, pivoting on the word "now." The roll of toilet paper flew across the room in Richard's direction. No one, including Richard, appeared the least bit uncomfortable with this open display of grief.

"There are days I sit in my cell and remember all the times they said, 'Come on Dad, let's go play.' I said no. And if I'd made different choices, I'd be there right now."

By the end of class, most of the bears had migrated into their fathers' arms, where they were cradled or tightly clutched. One man was carefully, even tenderly, combing his bear's tawny coat. The twelve-week session was drawing to a close, and as the class adjourned, Newton collected the bears, which he would mail to his students' children.

As they handed over their bears, several of the men were visibly anxious. When Newton unceremoniously dumped the bears into a large plastic bag, it struck me as unseemly, even dangerous, so convinced had I become that the bears were, if not real, then potent enough in their symbolism to merit more solicitous care.

The Coffee Creek correctional facility for women is in Wilsonville, Oregon, twenty miles south of Portland off Interstate 5. As I made my way from the freeway to the prison, shopping malls gave way to green pastures where horses grazed. The turnoff for the prison compound was marked by a stand of pines impressive enough that one visiting toddler had concluded that "Mommy lives in the jungle." A bike lane ended at the gate.

Coffee Creek had been open for just over two years at the time of my visit. Before that, Oregon's women prisoners were scattered about the state, many in wings that had been tacked onto men's prisons as the female population grew. When the DOC decided to consolidate its women prisoners, children's advocates lobbied to get the prison sited near Portland, where most of the state's prisoners come from and most of their children live.

It wasn't easy. Residents in Salem had dubbed the area around the men's prison there "felony flats." Wilsonville residents were not interested in picking up a similar designation, and fought to get Oregon to do what most states do—site the prison in the boondocks. In Wilsonville, DOC OUT signs appeared in store windows. Across the street from the proposed prison site, an irate neighbor decorated his front yard with eight upended school buses—donated by sympathizers across the state—in an effort to convey some sort of message about the unsuitability of placing a prison in a residential neighborhood.

The buses remain, but the prison went up anyway. Sean makes the drive twice a week, to bring his three- and four-year-old boys to spend the morning with their mother at the Early Head Start program, held in a portable building on prison grounds. With its wooden climbing structures, brightly decorated walls, and abundant educational toys, the setting draws children in immediately. Caregiver participants also get monthly home visits from Early Head Start staff, who coordinate health and educational services and help plan for a mother's release.

Sean—a skinny, soft-spoken man with mild hazel eyes, wearing jeans and a yellow Gore-Tex jacket—was a visiting-room veteran. This was his wife's third prison stint, for crimes he was not willing to detail except to say that she was bipolar and got into trouble when she went off her medication.

Sean was accustomed to organizing his life around his wife's absence. He worked part-time and arranged his schedule to accommodate his children's—including making sure he could take them to Early Head Start twice a week. He hoped the investment would pay off when his wife returned home. The program, he said, "keeps her focused on getting out and being a good mother, a productive member of society. When the mothers get to see their kids, they try to get better so they don't have to leave them again."

Shortly after Sean arrived, I asked his wife if she had a moment to speak with me. "My boys just got here," she said, then hurried out to the yard after them. For the next hour, the three played happily while Sean hung back and drank a cup of coffee.

Over and over, I was struck by what a keen sense the prisoners I met in Oregon had not only of their past failings as parents, but also of their own potential. Putting bars between a woman and her children may be enough to make her think about how she has hurt them, but if you offer her no means of making things better, that painful realization can lead right back to drugs. By allowing and encouraging prisoners to engage with their children, the Oregon model offers participants a sense of agency that makes facing the truth both bearable and productive.

All through Coffee Creek, I met women who had let go of the fictions that had helped sustain their addictions. "I was of the mind-set that, because I didn't steal from anybody, what I was doing didn't hurt anybody but myself," said a forty-five-year-old mother of four who had used and sold drugs for nearly three decades. "As far as the kid thing goes, I thought about the monetary value of it. They were happy because they had everything they wanted—except for a mother. When I got sentenced, the judge wrote on my papers that I was an extreme danger to my children. I didn't understand that at the time, but now I do. My children idolize me, and they were doing a lot of the same things I was doing. The only way I can rectify that is by setting a good example from here on out."

The following Saturday, I returned to Coffee Creek for a Girl Scouts Beyond Bars troop meeting. Several dozen women and children had taken over the white cinder-block visiting room for the biweekly, three-hour gathering. On alternate weeks, the women meet inside the prison and the girls convene on the outside.

On this rainy morning, a tiny, optimistic Christmas tree blinked its white lights in the corner of the room. Clusters of women and girls sat on the floor or at long tables, making beaded wreaths and "Ecuadorian stars" from wood and yarn. A cadre of college-aged volunteers joined a red-haired troop leader in Girl Scout green and tan in circling the room, showering mothers and children alike with the kind of exaggerated praise normally reserved for the very young.

Promptly at eleven a.m., inmates and their visitors began to gather up yarn, sticks, tape, and beads, leaving the white linoleum floor once again pristine and institutional. A few girls scrambled to finish their wreaths as the troop leader instructed the group to "circle up" and sing "Happy Birthday" to Angel, a soon-to-be seven-year-old who beamed silently from her mother's lap.

After circle time, mothers and children shared box lunches of sandwiches and chips. Then it was time to go. As the women lined up to leave through one door and the girls through another, an eight-year-old in a red track suit leaned heavily into the shoulder of a ponytailed volunteer, tears streaming down her cheeks as she waved good-bye to her mother across the room.

"Say Merry Christmas to your mom," the volunteer instructed. The girl complied, nearly inaudibly. She couldn't stop crying.

"Say it louder," the volunteer coached her weeping charge. "Be nice. She's not going to see you for a while."

There is little question that the Girl Scouts and other programs offered at Coffee Creek are excellent examples of their kind; the women went out of their way to tell me so. But as the girls filed out in a glum line—hauling huge bags of bottles and cans that their mothers' keepers had donated so the girls could recycle them to help fund the program—I couldn't help but hear the trumpeting of the elephant in the living room: the fact of incarceration itself.

While the Oregon Department of Corrections was developing its family focus, the population under its control was growing at a rate that outpaced even the rest of the prison-happy nation. In 1994, Oregon voters passed Measure 11, a constitutional amendment that quadrupled the sentences for many crimes, including first offenses. The result is that more and more Oregon children are going longer and longer stretches with "programming" substituting for the daily presence of a parent. In 1993, Oregon had about 6,500 prisoners. Today that number has nearly doubled, to more than 12,000. The Oregon Office of Economic Analysis has predicted that it will reach 15,000 by 2012.

Dondralyn, a mother of two, had been a restaurant manager before she got involved in planning a robbery to garner some extra cash. The fact that her plans never came to fruition didn't do much for her under Measure 11; when I met her, she had served seven years of a mandatory ten-year sentence. Inside Coffee Creek, she worked eight-hour days answering phones for the Oregon Department of Motor Vehicles at its prison-based call center, earning $155 a month. "It's the best opportunity ever for a lot of the women here," she said without irony.

Dondralyn helped develop the parenting curriculum at Coffee Creek, and spoke enthusiastically of the institution's "family focus." She sees her children, who have been raised by a great-aunt, twice a year, when someone in her family is able to bring them.

The Oregon experiment highlights an inescapable paradox: the laudable enterprise of working to strengthen family bonds behind bars can only be undertaken wholesale because we have separated so very many children from the parents who now sit in prison classrooms, nodding solemnly as they are told how much their children need them.

In the lobby of Coffee Creek, a literature rack offered visitors a wealth of helpful brochures: A PERFECTLY FITTED BICYCLE HELMET: 7 EASY STEPS TO FOLLOW. KEEP YOUR BABY SMILING . . . PREVENT NURSING BOTTLE MOUTH. LIFE IS GOOD. BUCKLE UP RIGHT. This last brochure featured a tanned, blond young man windsurfing across a turquoise bay. There was something wrenching about this cheery library—as if these children had been left to live in a world where all that stood between them and health and happiness was a properly fitted bike helmet; as if their parents' incarceration had left them vulnerable to nothing more than tooth decay.

Tucked away among the mass-market brochures was a document produced specifically for prison visitors by the Oregon Department of Corrections: HOW TO EXPLAIN JAILS AND

PRISONS TO CHILDREN: A CAREGIVER'S GUIDE. Suggestions included having children whose families have been splintered by incarceration keep a written list of the names and addresses of their scattered siblings and parents (a form was included to aid in this exercise), and helping them predict when their parent might be coming home by searching for their release date on the DOC website.

The idea of saving the next generation by rehabilitating not just individuals but entire families is tremendously compelling. But must it happen at such a cost, in such a setting?

Ben De Haan—the man behind the Oregon experiment— says no. A slight and dapper man in a blue cable-knit sweater over a collared shirt, De Haan was copying messages from his cell phone onto a pile of paper napkins when I met him at a Starbucks on a suburban strip halfway between Portland and Coffee Creek.

"Prisons are the bluntest of social instruments," announced De Haan, who ran Oregon's child welfare and then corrections departments before leaving to found the Children's Justice Alliance, a nonprofit that is coordinating much of the work currently being done around prisoners' children in the state. "They are absolutely necessary, but hopelessly overused."

I asked De Haan a question many people I've interviewed have danced around—either because they were loath to admit that anyone should be in prison, or because they hesitated to say definitively that anyone should not: how many is too many? What is the right number of prisoners?

De Haan hesitated, but his hesitation was different from that I had previously encountered: he was doing the math in his head. Half, he answered finally. "If you took the prison population ten years ago"—before Measure 11 kicked in—"that would be about where you would want to be." If they were properly prepared and offered adequate post-prison supports, De Haan insisted, half of Oregon's prisoners could go home to their families right now with no threat to public safety.

Even that, De Haan contended, wouldn't solve the problems we've created by overusing the prison system—problems he predicted would "have the half-life of plutonium. Even if we are successful at dealing with it on the sentencing level, we'll be dealing with the effects for generations to come."

"Prisoners are disenfranchised from their communities," De Haan said. "They lose contact and relationships with their families and their children. They're exposed to very high levels of violence in prison—to HIV, Hepatitis C, you name it. Lightweight offenders are exposed to career criminals. If you leave people in prison too long, you're acculturating them in a deviant set of values, and you're spending a lot of money to do it."

The side effects of prison, De Haan argued, are themselves contagious: "One of the most reliable predictors of whether a kid will engage in criminal behavior is whether he has a criminal parent. To the extent that you exacerbate criminal tendencies in the parents, you're paving the way for a youngster to follow the parent into criminality."

De Haan reached these conclusions after spending most of his career in what he called "the dark underbelly of public policy—putting people in prison and taking away their children." At twenty-three, just out of college, De Haan took a job as a child-protection worker. A series of promotions followed, and eventually De Haan was named to head the child welfare department. From there he moved to the Department of Corrections, first as deputy director and then as director.

In 1996, when De Haan began to look into the subject, Oregon, like most states, did not even ask incoming prisoners whether they had children. De Haan started asking. Twenty thousand Oregon children, he found, had a parent in prison. Most of the mothers, and about half of the fathers, expected to resume caring for their children upon their release, but half of the mothers and 70 percent of the fathers who had that expectation had not had a single visit during the previous month. Forty-one percent of kids in foster care in Oregon had an incarcerated parent. Forty-six percent of juvenile detainees had a parent who had been convicted of a crime. Sixteen- and seventeen-year-olds confined to youth facilities were provoking fistfights in the hope of earning a disciplinary transfer to the adult system, where they could be with family. Thirteen percent of juvenile detainees were parents themselves.

De Haan and Claudia Black—his deputy at the DOC and now at the Children's Justice Alliance—began testing a new hypothesis: that integrating family support into the correctional mission would be a "two-for-one deal." The best way of guaranteeing the safety and nurturance of children, they ventured, was to give them competent, engaged parents. And fostering prisoners' commitment to, and ability to care for, their children would give them a powerful motivation to succeed once they were released.

"Think about how central being a parent is to our lives," De Haan observed, "how it motivates us, causes us to act one way or another. To presume to motivate prisoners towards changing their lives and not include in that calculus their relationship with their children is bizarre."

De Haan and Black got the legislature on board by presenting some numbers: "Every time someone leaves our prison system and fails," De Haan asserted, "it costs the taxpayers fifty-seven thousand dollars. That doesn't take into account prosecution costs, the chances of putting another kid in foster care, all those other collateral expenses. At a time when we have an out-of-control, aberrant criminal justice system, it provides a glimmer of hope when you can say, 'Here's an option that saves money, is humane, and is demonstrated to be effective.'"

The work being done in Oregon is based on a recognition that children need their parents—and also that many prisoners will need significant supports in order to give their children the care they need. Without question, prisons and jails around the country should follow Oregon's lead, placing family at the center of the correctional enterprise. But such initiatives are no substitute for ensuring that resources that support family bonds are also available outside prison walls, in settings that might spare children the primal trauma of separation, and parents the destructive experience of confinement.

At the Oregon Social Learning Center, director Mark Eddy told me he and his colleagues had tried to launch a parenting curriculum similar to the one they later developed for the Oregon Department of Corrections for the parents of "at-risk" children in the public schools, but chronic funding problems kept it from taking hold. "Embedding" his program in the corrections system, Eddy reported, solved this problem in a single stroke.

That Eddy and his colleagues are seizing this opportunity to provide needed services is only to their credit. But when money pours into prisons at the expense of other publicly funded institutions—including those as fundamental as schools—it creates a powerful countercurrent that works against the larger goal of keeping kids from winding up as second- or third-generation convicts.

As we have come to rely ever more heavily on incarceration, we have lent velocity to a cycle that overtakes not just individual families but entire communities. Researchers talk about "million-dollar blocks"—urban microcosms so impacted by incarceration that such is the bill for maintaining their missing residents. Needless to say, the children who live on those blocks have their own ideas about how those millions might better be used.

These young people regularly refer to, blame, live within what David called "the system." The term encompasses prisons—the ones to which their parents are sent, and the juvenile institutions to which they themselves are often consigned—but "the system" as kids experience it has a broader reach than that. Walking through poor neighborhoods—neighborhoods bereft of jobs, playgrounds, stores, sports fields—one sees large numbers of young people standing around doing absolutely nothing. This forced idleness, almost incapacitation, evokes nothing so much as being inside a prison.

The legal scholar Randall Kennedy has written about the ways in which "criminogenic social conditions" contribute to the concentration of crime in particular neighborhoods—and, by extension, families. Racism, Kennedy observed, has "given energy to policies and practices (such as racial exclusion in housing, impoverished schooling, and stingy social welfare programs) that have facilitated the growth of egregious, crime-spawning conditions that millions of Americans face in urban slums and rural backwaters across the nation." These conditions—conditions that persist or worsen from one generation to the next, and that are exacerbated when social resources are concentrated disproportionately on enforcement—play an important role in the perpetuation of criminality between generations.

"In my community, all the resources for kids, like the rec centers, are gone or shut down," said Antonia, whose mother was in and out of jail and prison throughout her childhood. "I think there should be a program to help kids cope with the fact that their mother is arrested. I know I needed something.

"I would have liked to go camping," Antonia elaborated. "Horseback riding. Rock climbing. At a young age, that's when you develop your talent. Drawing. Singing. Dancing. Acting. Something like that would have shown me that there is more in the world than bad stuff. You need to know you can go through bad stuff, get out of it, and do so much more. Be so much more."

Michael asked me to imagine what the money spent to incarcerate his brother and his mother over the decades might have meant had it been used instead to support his faltering family. "The system is always looking to build itself, grow itself, and that is draining the resources of society," he said. "If somebody has a drug problem, why spend money sending them to prison and creating a family of convicts? Why not spend that money on turning that family into a successful family?"

The legacy of prison is not simply something handed down within families. Our intemperate use of incarceration has made it a collective legacy passed on from one generation to the next. If current incarceration rates remain unchanged, one out of every seventeen children born at the beginning of the twenty-first century will find him- or herself in prison.

Individually, of course, the legacy of prison can be overcome—and it is, every day, by young people who struggle mightily, against powerful forces, to secure for themselves a future of their choosing. Collectively, however, we cannot hope to shed this legacy until we begin rethinking, in a broad and fundamental way, our approach to crime and punishment.

CONCLUSION

SOME HAVE CALLED OVERINCARCERATION the civil rights issue of the twenty-first century. It may also be the children's issue of our time. Many of the things we worry about on behalf of children—poverty, single- or no-parent families, homelessness, unemployment, juvenile delinquency—are exacerbated by, if not directly attributable to, parental incarceration. And parental incarceration, unlike many of the risks children face, is the direct result of state action. This distinction makes it a powerful starting place—an opportunity to improve children's lives by rethinking policy.

Individuals make the choice to break the law. But we, collectively, have decided that the only or best response to a huge array of illegal acts, violent and otherwise, is to remove those who commit them from their families and communities—and to do so in ways that are virtually guaranteed to broaden and deepen the resultant harm to children.

Children do better when their families do better. Any well-planned effort to improve the prospects of those who fall under the jurisdiction of the criminal justice system is likely to improve those of their children as well. But those that explicitly take family connections into account hold particular promise for restoring a social fabric rent by crime and punishment both.

The programs and initiatives profiled in the preceding chapters—efforts grounded in children's needs and experiences—represent a starting place. But at the moment, they exist in piecemeal form, scattered across the nation, serving a small percentage of the families who need them, and often with no reliable source of funding from one year to the next.

Approaches that work need not be the exception. Every neighborhood in the country might be patrolled by police who had the specialized training and access to resources that police in New Haven have. Every grandparent could have access to the support that those in Little Rock are offered. All children should be offered the opportunity to visit their parents in environments like the Children's Center at Sing Sing. All returning prisoners could receive the services that are available to those who come home to the Lower East Side of Manhattan. Bringing such initiatives to scale might sound costly, but it would consume only a small portion of the billions currently being spent on unnecessary or overlong prison terms. If doing so succeeded in curtailing crime, as evidence from individual programs indicates it would, it could generate substantial savings in the long run.

There will always, however, be prisons—and children will always lose parents to them. In their widely used child welfare treatise *Beyond the Best Interests of the Child*, Yale Child Study Center founder Albert J. Solnit and his colleagues proposed a new standard for determining the placement of children who had been removed from their parents' care. They called this standard "the least detrimental alternative," a term they felt placed a child's interests at the forefront while also acknowledging that "a child whose placement must be determined in legal controversy has already been deprived of her 'best interests.'" Similarly, decisions about crime and punishment will sometimes necessarily run counter to a child's interests. When the arrest and incarceration of a parent are genuinely necessary, it remains our responsibility to seek a "least detrimental alternative"—to take steps to protect and support children at every step of the process, from arrest through reentry.

My conversations with the children of prisoners across the country—and with those who work with them—have led me to several conclusions as to how to begin that process:

Develop arrest protocols that support and protect arrestees' children. Training police officers to understand and address children's fear and confusion when a parent is arrested is an important first step. At a minimum, police could be instructed to inquire about minor children, and to rely—unless there is evidence that to do so would place a child at risk—on the arrested parent as a first source of information about potential caregivers. This would minimize the possibility both of children being left alone and of children entering the child welfare system unnecessarily.

Keeping in mind that safety is the first priority, the following steps might also be considered when appropriate and feasible: avoiding the use of sirens and lights in nonemergency situations, to reduce the fear and/or shame children may experience; having an officer take children into another room and explain to them what is happening, and what will happen next; allowing an arrestee to talk with children and say good-bye, and walking her out of sight of the children before handcuffing her.

When it is not possible or appropriate for an arrestee to do so, officers might be trained to offer children an age-appropriate explanation (e.g., "Mom needs to take a time-out and we will be taking her someplace where she can do that. You have not done anything wrong. We will make sure your mother is safe, and Grandma will be here to make sure you are safe.")

"Mirandize" children. The 1966 Supreme Court *Miranda* decision established the principle that police officers have an obligation to inform arrestees of the rights guaranteed them under the Constitution. Children also deserve to have fundamental rights—the right to be kept safe, to know where a parent is being taken and how to reach him, to receive care and support in a parent's absence—both communicated and respected. When children are not present at the time of a parent's arrest, police officers should leave behind a printed list of children's rights and the means for realizing them (i.e., information on where the parent is being held, visiting hours and procedures, local resources for locating care and support). When young children are involved, their rights should be communicated via their caregivers.

Consider children's needs at sentencing. When Andrew Fastow and his wife Lea were both charged in connection with the Enron scandal, they and their lawyers made their children's needs central to plea negotiations. The result was staggered sentences, so that the children would not be left parentless. Rather than being decried as special treatment, similar consideration should routinely be extended to children of lawbreakers whose collars are other than white.

Devise and implement sentences that encourage accountability to children. There is little evidence that incarcerating parents encourages them to live up to their responsibilities toward their children. In fact, it is literally impossible for them to assume many of those responsibilities while they are behind bars. Alternative sentences should be looked to not only for their capacity to rehabilitate, but also to allow and encourage parents to fulfill their obligations to their children.

Include a family impact statement in pre-sentence investigation reports. Parole and probation officers are frequently required by the court to prepare a pre-sentence investigation report (PSI), traditionally aimed at helping judges understand the background, and potential for rehabilitation, of those who come before them. In recent decades—as indeterminate sentencing has given way to mandatory sentencing, and judicial discretion has waned—the PSI has come to focus increasingly narrowly on the offense alone. The PSI should be restored to its traditional purpose, and a new component added: a family impact statement, which would include an assessment of the potential effect of a given sentence on children and families, and recommendations for the "least detrimental alternative" sentence in this context. The PSI should also include recommendations aimed at placing prisoners in facilities that are as close as possible to their children, and at providing services and supports to children during a parent's absence.

Create a child-centered visitation policy. Contact between children and parents should be construed as a child's right rather than an inmate's privilege. Visiting should not be withheld for disciplinary reasons, except when safety demands such a restriction. Children should not be subjected to "window visits." Facilities, such as county jails, that rely on such visits should set up separate visiting programs where children can see and touch their parents. Prisons should design and run their visiting rooms with children's needs and sensibilities in mind, and/ or operate separate children's centers. Opportunities for extended contact—on-site weekend visits, summer camps, weekend furloughs—should be supported and extended.

Abolish the phone tax. Prisoners' families should not be forced to subsidize the state and private industry through exorbitant collect-call rates. Inmates should be permitted to buy market-rate phone cards at commissary, and collect calls should be billed at standard rates.

Ensure equity between relative and non-relative caregivers. One way to do this is to establish subsidized guardianship programs, through which relative caretakers receive the supports and services associated with foster care without having first to relinquish custody of their grandchildren, and without threatening the legal standing of the parent-child relationship. Grandparents who are old and in poor health should have access to additional supports, such as respite care and help with transportation.

Create specialized units within child welfare departments. Children of prisoners have the same needs as other foster children for love and continuity in the absence of a parent, but they also have needs specific to their situation: contact with parents who can only call collect and who may be housed hundreds of miles away; honest communication about, and help in understanding, their parents' incarceration. In those cases where a foster care placement is deemed necessary, children should receive services from social workers who have been trained and given resources to address these needs. These units might—as does the Children of Incarcerated Parents Program of the Administration for Children and Families in New York—arrange and provide transportation for visits; offer social workers training that includes how to address the risk of termination of parental rights; run a collect-call line for incarcerated parents; and work with families to prevent foster care placement.

Consider "differential response" when a parent is arrested. Differential response laws—now on the books in more than ten states—allow child protective services departments to respond to families in crisis by offering support, often through referrals to community-based agencies, without opening a formal investigation. Evaluations of differential response programs have found that children were made safer sooner than those who received a traditional child welfare response, services were delivered more quickly, and workers believed the approach was more effective. Differential response offers a promising model for how child welfare departments might support families struggling with the incarceration of a parent. Workers could interview caregivers, incarcerated parents, and older children to determine their needs, and offer referrals to services, without the risk of sanction and long-term separation that a formal investigation can trigger.

Reexamine the Adoption and Safe Families Act. Dependency cases involving children whose parents are incarcerated should be looked at on an individual basis, and viable families preserved, whether or not sentences exceed the ASFA time lines. ASFA should be revised to allow for such flexibility. State statute in Nebraska prohibits filing a termination proceeding "if the sole factual basis for the [termination] petition is that . . . the parent or parents of the juvenile are incarcerated." This statute could provide a model for federal legislation revising ASFA.

Unless and until that happens, better use should be made of what flexibility the law already allows. Under ASFA, exceptions to the time lines for termination are permissible under two circumstances: when a court determines that "reasonable efforts" have not been made to support reunification, or when it finds that termination is not in a child's best interest. Given the minimal efforts that are generally made to maintain contact and plan for reunification between incarcerated parents and their children—and the obstacles even the most energetic social workers face when they do try to support reunification—terminations in cases involving an incarcerated parent ought to receive automatic scrutiny under the "reasonable efforts" clause. When children enter foster care simply because of parental arrest, rather than evidence of abuse or neglect, these cases deserve careful consideration under the "best interests" clause.

At the same time, arrested parents whose children are in, or may enter, the dependency system should receive complete information about ASFA, its potential impact on parental rights, and their own rights and responsibilities within it, prior to any plea bargain that could lead to a sentence long enough to trigger the ASFA time lines.

Designate a family services coordinator at prison and jail facilities. Prisoners whose children are in foster care may have a hard time even locating those children, much less arranging visits from behind bars and fulfilling the multiple mandates required for reunification. Investing in a staff member whose job it is to facilitate family contact and support reunification could result in significant child welfare savings and decreased recidivism.

Train staff at institutions whose constituency includes children of incarcerated parents to recognize and address these children's needs and concerns. Any institution dealing with vulnerable youth—including schools—will likely serve numerous children of incarcerated parents. In many cases, children do not feel able to talk about this aspect of their experience. If they express their grief instead through anger or defiance, they find themselves disciplined, labeled, and often eventually jailed. When adults are sensitive to the needs—not to mention the existence—of the children of prisoners, they are better prepared to offer support instead of stigma, and help avert this cycle.

Provide access to specially trained therapists and counselors. Some of the same issues that can make counseling valuable to children of prisoners—repeated loss, heightened fear of authority, discomfort in institutional settings, difficulty in forming trusting relationships—can also make providing that care particularly challenging. Children need access to therapists or other counselors who have the experience and training to surmount these barriers.

Create opportunities for children of incarcerated parents to communicate with and support one another. The shame that young people experience when a parent is locked up is intensified when they harbor the misperception that they are alone in their experience. The company of other children who have similar histories—whether in support groups, recreation programs, or summer camps—can allow young people to unburden themselves of a painful secret, learn they are not to blame for their family troubles, and perceive themselves as having potential.

Revise child support law and policy to reflect the reality of parental incarceration. As dissenting justices in a Wisconsin Supreme Court decision that upheld a $25,000 child support order against an incarcerated father observed, "Child support orders that are beyond a non-custodial parent's ability to pay are not in the best interests of the child." While most states make no exception to child support rules for parental incarceration, a few have instituted policies that serve as useful models. A North Carolina statute, for example, allows a child support order to be suspended without interest if a parent is incarcerated. In Oregon, an administrative rule requires that, if an incarcerated parent requests a modification in a child support order, the order be reduced to zero for the period of incarceration, and sixty days after, based on the parent's inability to pay. Similar policy on a national level would serve not to relieve incarcerated parents of their obligation to support their children, but to make sure they do not accrue levels of debt that are so high as to impede them from doing so once they are released.

Support family reunification pre- and post-release. Prison and jail family services workers could develop pre-release plans for incarcerated parents and refer them to community agencies that can help them with housing and employment upon their release. Probation and parole departments should shift resources from supervision to support and consider operating family services units dedicated to serving probationers and parolees who are working to reestablish themselves as parents.

Remove legal barriers to successful reentry. Long after a sentence is served, the collateral consequences of a criminal record make the basic tasks of parenthood—providing food, clothing, shelter, and care for one's children—difficult or impossible. At the same time, researchers have found that abiding family bonds are the strongest predictor of successful reentry. Removing felony restrictions on employment, housing, TANF, and food stamps is crucial to giving struggling families a chance to rebuild.

Save 5 percent for families. Each state, and the federal government, should allocate 5 percent of its corrections budget to efforts to support prisoners' families both during and after a parent's time in prison. This investment will likely be more than recouped via reduced recidivism and lower rates of intergenerational incarceration. In the meantime, trimming excessive sentences would produce the immediate savings to fund such an initiative.

If we mean to improve the prospects of the children of incarcerated parents, we must move simultaneously along two tracks. First, we must work to mitigate the harms of parental incarceration as much as possible—as the above recommendations aim to do. Second, we must look closely at whom we incarcerate, why, and for how long, and move toward a system of sanctions and supports—including a much heavier reliance on alternatives to incarceration—that will rehabilitate individuals and restore, rather than fragmenting, families.

Current sentencing laws should be reviewed explicitly in terms of their impact on children and families, and those that cause unnecessary harm without measurably enhancing public safety should be revised or repealed. The most valuable interventions on behalf of children might take place before a parent ever sees a jail cell. Diversion programs, drug treatment, restorative justice initiatives, and other rehabilitation-focused alternatives to incarceration must be the starting place for any serious effort to improve the lives and prospects of children whose parents have run afoul of the law.

The children of drug offenders are far from the only ones who would benefit from such a shift. But they merit particular focus for two reasons. First, the harm to children represents the most powerful argument for some kind of governmental or societal response to drugs. To say that our drug laws demand revision is not to say that it is somehow acceptable that children grow up in drug-afflicted households. The stories children tell about life in such homes are heart-stopping. But the more one talks with these children, the clearer it becomes that the "solution" we have contrived to the very genuine problem of parental drug addiction exacerbates children's suffering, sinks them deeper into chaos, rather than offering some semblance of security or solace.

Children have long been used as a rhetorical weapon in the War on Drugs: *We need to lock these people up before they get our kids hooked on crack.* But "our kids" include prisoners' kids, in ever-increasing numbers. What might it mean to them to have Mom in treatment instead of behind bars; to have state intervention in her life make their own lives better?

Second, changes in drug laws are responsible for most of the growth in the prison population over the past three decades, and the resultant dissolution of millions of families. In particular it is the drug war, rather than an increase in female criminality, that has caused the population of incarcerated women—who are most likely to have been the primary caregivers to children—to increase more than sevenfold since 1980.

The denial of family bonds—as both a matter of law and a reality of daily life—was, as legal scholar Peggy Cooper Davis has observed, "a hallmark of slavery in the United States." It has also become a hallmark of our ever-expanding penal system. We have chosen to enforce the social order in a way that undermines the family structure of entire communities, causing or exacerbating the "family breakdown" for which we prefer to blame only the individuals affected.

Stories of family separation were central to the antislavery movement. Abolitionists decried slavery as a violation not only of personal integrity but also of family bonds, which, they asserted, were both protected by the Constitution and sacred in the eyes of God. "Proslavery men and women!" one abolitionist implored, "for one moment only, in imagination, stand surrounded by *your* loved ones, and behold *them*, one by one, torn from your grasp, or you rudely and forcibly carried from them—how, think you, would you bear it?"

It is a question worth asking ourselves today. One in thirty-three American children—and nearly one in eight African American children—will go to sleep tonight denied access to a parent's embrace, because that parent is incarcerated.

That these children are rarely taken into account by the multiple institutions that contain and control their parents is more than an oversight. It is a natural consequence of American individualism—an ethos that plays out in exaggerated form in a criminal justice system that insists on treating lawbreakers as if they were connected to nothing and attached to no one, and on using isolation as the primary instrument of justice.

This approach slams up against the unyielding truths of

child development: the hunger for attachment; the trauma of separation; the stubborn pull of the blood connection. Viewed through the lens of a child's experience, it threatens a right so central as to be not merely civil but human: the right to family.

The good news is that children can do much more than tell us where it hurts. They offer both the insight and the impetus we need to rethink criminal justice—to create a system that protects children, rehabilitates parents, and promotes public safety. A criminal justice model that took as its constituency not just individuals charged with breaking the law, but also the families and communities within which their lives were embedded—one that respected the rights and needs of children—might become one that inspired the confidence and respect of those families and communities, and so played a part in stemming, rather than perpetuating, the cycle of crime and incarceration.

We are able to lock people up in the numbers that we do only so long as we see them as useless—extraneous individuals whom our society simply does not need. But the majority of prisoners are mothers and fathers: they are needed in the most fundamental way. The parent-child bond, beyond its private importance to the individuals who share it, is a social asset that must be valued and preserved.

If we are to reassess our criminal justice system in terms of its aims, its impact, and its costs—and there is growing consensus that the time is overdue for such an accounting—we might start by trying to see it through a child's eyes. What a child so doggedly hopes for—his parent home and whole, equipped to care for him and assume a useful role in the larger society—is what our system ought also to aim for, and achieve.

NOTES

Introduction

2 Two-point-four million American children: e-mail correspondence with Christopher Mumola, Bureau of Justice Statistics, U.S. Department of Justice, November 29, 2004.

2 More than seven million: "Children of Incarcerated Parents: A Fact Sheet," Federal Resource, Center for Children of Prisoners, www.cwla .org/programs/incarcerated/cop_factsheet.htm.

2 2.1 million of our citizens behind bars: Paige M. Harrison and Allen J. Beck, Ph.D., "Prison and Jail Inmates at Midyear 2004," Bureau of Justice Statistics Bulletin, U.S. Department of Justice, April 24, 2005, 1.

2 a fivefold increase from thirty years ago: Ann Adalist-Estrin and Jim Mustin, "Introduction to Children of Prisoners," Facts and Issues: CPL 101, Children of Prisoners Library, Family and Corrections Network, Palmyra, VA, www.fcnetwork.org/cpl/CPL101-Introduction .html.

2 we have now outstripped Russia: "New Prison Figures Demonstrate Need for Comprehensive Reform," Sentencing Project, Washington, DC, May 2004.

2 nearly three-quarters of those admitted to state prisons: "Incarcerated America," Human Rights Watch Backgrounder, April 2003, 1.

3 the number of people behind bars for breaking the drug laws: ibid.

3 Overall, however, the picture drawn by researchers: See Katherine Gabel and Denise Johnston, M.D., eds., *Children of Incarcerated Parents* (New York: Lexington Books, 1995), and Ross D. Parke and K. Alison Clarke-Stewart, "The Effects of Parental Incarceration on Children: Perspectives, Promises, and Policies," in Jeremy Travis and Michelle Waul, eds., *Prisoners Once Removed: The Impact of Incarceration and Reentry on Children, Families and Communities* (Washington, DC: Urban Institute Press, 2003), 189–232.

3 they get poorer once a parent is arrested: Donald Braman, *Doing Time on the Outside: Incarceration and Family Life in Urban America* (Ann Arbor: University of Michigan Press, 2004), 82.

3 As many as half of all boys: telephone interview with Denise Johnston, M.D., Center for Children of Incarcerated Parents, December 20, 2004.

1. Arrest

9 the majority of police departments have no written protocol: Barbara E. Smith and Sharon Goretsky Elstein, *Children on Hold: Improving the Response to Children Whose Parents Are Arrested and Incarcerated* (Washington, DC: American Bar Association Center on Children and the Law, 1994), 161.

9 A national survey by the American Bar Association: ibid., 34.

9 confronted with drawn weapons: S. Phillips, "Programming for Children of Female Offenders," Fourth National Headstart Research Conference, Washington, DC, 1998, in "Children of Incarcerated Parents Project: Report to the Oregon Legislature on Senate Bill 133," December 2002, 2.

9 flashbacks to the moment of arrest: Christina Jose Kampfner, "Post-Traumatic Stress Reactions in Children of Imprisoned Mothers," in Katherine Gabel and Denise Johnston, M.D., eds., *Children of Incarcerated Parents* (New York: Lexington Books, 1995), 95.

10 drugs in their clothing or diaper: Smith and Elstein, *Children on Hold*, 141.

10 inside his own apartment during police raids: Leon Dash, *Rosa Lee: A Mother and Her Family in Urban America* (New York: Plume, 1996), 165.

10 in a less-intimidating vehicle: Smith and Elstein, *Children on Hold*, 71.

10 shelter or other civilian destination: ibid.

10 interfere with their ability to do their real job: ibid., 230.

10 "This is not a good place to watch children": ibid., 129.

11 for their smooth collaboration: ibid., 175.

14 like one-third of all incarcerated mothers: Christopher J. Mumola, "Incarcerated Parents and Their Children," special report, Bureau of Justice Statistics, U.S. Department of Justice, Washington, DC, August 2000, 4.

17 "I have taken and seen hundreds of children processed": Rick Gore, investigator, Yolo County D.A. Child Abduction Unit, "Law Enforcement Concerns and Issues."

17 "Most cops do not like to and will not take kids into protective custody": Clare M. Nolan, "Children of Arrested Parents: Strategies to Improve Their Safety and Well-Being," California Research Bureau, Sacramento, July 2003, 16.

17 "one more thing to do": ibid., 171.

17 getting off easy because they had children: ibid., 136.

18 agencies other than their own: Marcus Nieto, "In Danger of Falling Through the Cracks: Children of Arrested Parents," California Research Bureau, Sacramento, April 2002, 1.

18 there is in general no statutory mandate: Nolan, "Children of Arrested Parents," 1.

18 *White v. Rochford*, the 1979 case that established the precedent: Smith and Elstein, *Children on Hold*, 6.

19 a Florida two-year-old spent nearly three weeks alone: "Two-year-old Survives Almost Three Weeks Alone in a House," Associated Press, September 30, 2003.

19 teenage children of arrestees are commonly left to fend for themselves: *Leaving No Child Alone: A Training and Planning Guide for the Emergency Response to Children of Arrestees*, prepared for the Boston Police Department and the Coalition of Service Providers by Circle Solu-

tions, Inc., and the American Bar Association Center on Children and the Law, May 18–19, 1998, 26.

19 only 55 percent defined "minor" as all children under eighteen: ibid., 12.

2. Sentencing

30 according to court documents: In the U.S. District Court for the Eastern District of Louisiana, *United States of America vs. Danielle Bernard Metz, a/k/a "Boo,"* Presentence Investigation Report, Docket No. 92-00469-002.

32 According to a report from the Sentencing Project: Marc Mauer, Ryan S. King, and Malcolm C. Young, "The Meaning of 'Life': Long Prison Sentences in Context," Sentencing Project, Washington, DC, May 2004, 5.

32 needs of children: Center for Children of Incarcerated Parents, 1992; Kiser, 1991; Bloom and Steinhart, 1993; Barry, 1989, in Barbara E. Smith and Sharon Goretsky Elstein, *Children on Hold: Improving the Response to Children Whose Parents Are Arrested and Incarcerated* (Washington, DC: American Bar Association Center on Children and the Law, 1994), 3.

33 their numbers increased more than sevenfold: "Prison Statistics, Summary Findings," Bureau of Justice Statistics, U.S. Department of Justice, Washington, DC, June 30, 2003.

33 from rehabilitation to punishment: Marc Mauer, *Race to Incarcerate* (New York: The New Press, 1999).

37 According to the U.S. Sentencing Commission: Eric E. Sterling, "Sentencing Is Perverse in the War on Drugs," *Chicago Sun-Times*, April 30, 2000.

37 one federal judge complained publicly: "More Than They Deserve," *60 Minutes*, January 4, 2004.

37 Reporters from the *Minneapolis Star Tribune:* Joe Rigert, "Drug Sentences Often Stacked Against Women," *Minneapolis Star Tribune*, December 14, 1997.

49 "While incarceration forces offenders to answer to the state": Donald

Braman, *Doing Time on the Outside: Incarceration and Family Life in Urban America* (Ann Arbor: University of Michigan Press, 2004), 162.

49 "While it is common for family members to help one another out": ibid., 112.

55 "I hope that by the sentence you receive": Bill Voelker, "Metz Drug Gang Principals Get Lectures, Life Without Parole," *New Orleans Times-Picayune.*

56 the drug trade has accelerated rather than diminished: "Primer on Mandatory Sentences," Families Against Mandatory Minimums, Washington, DC, 1, www.famm.org/pdfs/Primer.pdf.

56 there were 11.4 million illegal drug users in the country in 1992: *1992 National Household Survey on Drug Abuse*, Substance Abuse and Mental Health Services Administration, www.hhhs.gov/news/press/pre1995 pres/930623.txt.

56 there were more than 19 million: "Overview of Findings from the 2003 National Survey on Drug Use and Health," Substance Abuse and Mental Health Services Administration, Rockville, MD, September 2004, 3.

56 one in six American teenagers was approached: ibid., 26.

56 Louisiana currently has the highest incarceration rate in the nation: Paige M. Harrison and Allen J. Beck, Ph.D., "Prisoners in 2003," Bureau of Justice Statistics, U.S. Department of Justice, Washington, DC, November 2004, 3.

56 New Orleans's per-capita homicide rate: Steve Ritea and Tara Young, "Violence Thrives on Lack of Jobs, Wealth of Drugs," *Times-Picayune*, February 8, 2004.

56 The state ranks sixth in the country: "DEA Briefs and Background, Drugs and Drug Abuse, State Factsheets, Louisiana," 2005.

56 Ongoing research by criminologists Dina Rose and Todd Clear: Dina R. Rose and Todd R. Clear, "Incarceration, Reentry, and Social Capital: Social Networks in the Balance," in Jeremy Travis and Michelle Waul, eds., *Prisoners Once Removed: The Impact of Incarceration and Reentry on Children, Families and Communities* (Washington, DC: Urban Institute Press, 2003), 313–42.

56 A major study by the RAND Corporation: Jonathan P. Caulkins, C.

Peter Rydell, William L. Schwabe, and James Chiesa, *Mandatory Minimum Drug Sentences: Throwing Away the Key or the Taxpayers' Money?* (Santa Monica, CA: Rand, 1997), 2.

56 The million-plus dollars: Mauer et al., "The Meaning of 'Life,'" 3.

57 budget crises have inspired: "Creating the Next Crime Wave," editorial, *New York Times*, March 13, 2004.

57 At least seven states: Vincent Schiraldi, "Finally, States Release the Pressure on Prisons," *Washington Post*, November 30, 2003, B03.

57 During the year ending in June 2004: Paige M. Harrison and Allen J. Beck, Ph.D., "Prison and Jail Inmates at Midyear 2004," Bureau of Justice Statistics, U.S. Department of Justice, Washington, D.C., April 2005, 2.

57 State prisons currently operate at an average of 16 percent above capacity: ibid.

58 federal offenders with no prior arrest or conviction: Ruben Castillo et al., "Recidivism and the 'First Offender,'" U.S. Sentencing Commission, Washington, DC, May 2004.

59 The psychiatrist Robert Coles has written: Robert Coles, *The Moral Life of Children* (New York: Atlantic Monthly Press, 1986).

60 the psychologist Jerome Bruner has warned: Jerome Bruner, "Do Not Pass Go," *New York Review of Books*, September 25, 2003, 46.

60 more than half of the prison population: David Cole, *No Equal Justice: Race and Class in the American Criminal Justice System* (New York: The New Press, 1999), 4.

60 and use drugs at a rate similar to that of whites: "Results from the 2002 National Survey on Drug Use and Health: Detailed Tables," Office of Applied Studies, Substance Abuse and Mental Health Services Administration, Department of Health and Human Services, 2003, and the 2000 U.S. Census, available at www.census.gov, in Tushar Kansal, "Racial Disparity in Sentencing: A Review of the Literature," Sentencing Project, Washington, DC, January 2005, 13.

60 mandatory minimums have exacerbated racial disparities in sentencing: Associated Press, "Sentencing-Guidelines Study Finds Continuing Disparities," *New York Times*, November 27, 2004.

60 Disparities have been documented: Celesta Albonetti, "Sentencing

Under the Federal Sentencing Guidelines: Effects of Defendant Characteristics, Guilty Pleas, and Departures on Sentence Outcomes for Drug Offenses, 1991–1992," *Law and Society Review* 31 (1997): 789–822, in Kansal, "Racial Disparity in Sentencing," 9.

61 black children are nine times more likely: Barry A. Krisberg, Ph.D., and the Honorable Carolyn Engel Temin, "The Plight of Children Whose Parents Are in Prison," *NCCD Focus*, October 2001.

61 Nearly one in eight African American children has a parent behind bars today: e-mail correspondence with Arlene Lee, Federal Resource Center for Children of Prisoners, November 28, 2004.

61 Because prisons are frequently sited in mostly white rural counties: Tracy Huling, "Building a Prison Economy in Rural America," in Marc Mauer and Meda Chesney-Lind, eds., *Invisible Punishment: The Collateral Consequences of Mass Imprisonment* (New York: The New Press, 2002), 208.

61 "The perception and reality of double standards": Cole, *No Equal Justice*, 11.

63 New York State's prison population had doubled: Anne J. Swern, "DTAP Thirteenth Annual Report," Drug Treatment Alternative-to-Prison Program (DTAP), Kings County District Attorney's Office, Brooklyn, NY, December 2003, 17.

63 the crack and heroin trades were booming: ibid., 1.

63 four years behind bars: "Crossing the Bridge: An Evaluation of the Drug Treatment Alternative-to-Prison (DTAP) Program," National Center on Addiction and Substance Abuse at Columbia University, New York, March 2003.

63 Ninety-two percent were employed: ibid.

63 The DA's own analysis: DTAP website, www.brooklynda.org/DTAP/DTAP.htm.

3. Visiting

76 Consistent, ongoing contact reduces the strain of separation: J. Creasie Finney Hairston, "Prisoners and Families: Parenting Issues During In-

carceration," paper presented at From Prison to Home conference, January 30–31, 2002.

77 A much-cited 1972 study: Norman Holt and Donald Miller, "Explorations in Inmate-Family Relationships," Research Division, California Department of Corrections, Sacramento, January 1972.

77 cutting visiting days from three or four to two: Mark Martin, "Visit Crunch for Inmates' Loved Ones," *San Francisco Chronicle,* May 9, 2004.

77 In a 2000 review of the literature: Terry A. Kupers, M.D., "Brief Literature Review re Prison Visiting," October 9, 2000.

78 fewer than half of parents in state prison had received even a single visit: Christopher J. Mumola, "Incarcerated Parents and Their Children," special report, Bureau of Justice Statistics, U.S. Department of Justice, Washington, DC, August 2000, 1.

78 three-quarters did so less than once a month: Ross D. Parke and K. Alison Clarke-Stewart, "The Effects of Parental Incarceration on Children: Perspectives, Promises, and Policies," in Jeremy Travis and Michelle Waul, eds., *Prisoners Once Removed: The Impact of Incarceration and Reentry on Children, Families and Communities* (Washington, DC: Urban Institute Press, 2003), 208.

78 held more than one hundred miles from home: Mumola, "Incarcerated Parents and Their Children," 5.

78 more than 5,000 of the state's approximately 7,400 incarcerated mothers are held in two facilities: "Where's Mommy? Mothers in the California Prison System in 2003," Center for Children of Incarcerated Parents, Pasadena, www.e-ccip.org/publication.html.

78 nearly half the parents in federal institutions: Mumola, "Incarcerated Parents and Their Children," 5.

79 Children will bang their fists or even heads against the glass: Barbara E. Smith and Sharon Goretsky Elstein, *Children on Hold: Improving the Response to Children Whose Parents Are Arrested and Incarcerated* (Washington, DC: American Bar Association Center on Children and the Law, 1994), 219.

81 Visitors often wait outside in line for hours: "Maintaining Family Contact When a Family Member Goes to Prison: An Examination of State Policies on Mail, Visiting and Telephone Access," prepared by the

Committee on Corrections, Justice Council, Florida House of Representatives, November 1998, vii, 5.

81 even a "diaper peek": Florida Corrections Commission 2001 Annual Report, www.fac.state.fl.us/fcc/reports/final1013visithtm#rec.

81 "emotionally enticing to the inmate": "Maintaining Family Contact When a Family Member Goes to Prison," 6.

81 as do those who are wearing the wrong clothes: ibid., vii, 4.

83 there is evidence that consistent visitation *enhances* security by motivating prisoners to follow the rules: Arlene Lee, "Children of Prisoners: Children of Promise, Educating Communities and Professionals About This Hidden Population of Children and Re-entry as a Family Issue," *Corrections Today* (publication pending).

83 A report to the Florida state legislature: "Maintaining Family Contact When a Family Member Goes to Prison," iii, 2.

83 "Security measures which are overzealously applied": ibid., x, 1.

86 families are charged a "connection charge": Donald Braman, *Doing Time on the Outside: Incarceration and Family Life in Urban America* (Ann Arbor: University of Michigan Press, 2004), 132.

86 as much as twenty times that of standard collect calls: Donald Braman and Jenifer Wood, "From One Generation to the Next: How Criminal Sanctions Are Reshaping Family Life in Urban America," in Travis and Waul, *Prisoners Once Removed*, 184, n. 6.

86 California nets more than $35 million each year: Jenifer Warren, "Inmates' Families Pay Heavy Price for Staying in Touch," *Los Angeles Times*, February 16, 2002, in Jeremy Travis, Elizabeth M. Cincotta, and Amy L. Solomon, "Families Left Behind: The Hidden Costs of Incarceration and Reentry," Justice Policy Center, Urban Institute, Washington, DC, October 2003, 6.

86 New York collects more than $20 million: Pat Duggan, "Captive Audience Rates High: Families Must Pay Dearly When Inmates Call Collect," *Washington Post*, January 23, 2000, A03.

86 In Florida, the legislature found: "Maintaining Family Contact When a Family Member Goes to Prison," iii, 1.

86 Many families have their phones disconnected: Braman, *Doing Time on the Outside*, 56.

88 Today, nearly six thousand D.C. residents are in federal and private prisons: David Crary, "Faced with Crowded Prisons, 11 States Opt to Ship Large Numbers of Inmates Out of State," Associated Press, January 15, 2004.

88 A fifteen-minute phone call to the Washington, D.C., area: Hope House website, www.hopehousedc.org/more.htm.

90 Hawai'i, for example, sends nearly half of its approximately 3,500 prisoners to private prisons: Ron Station, "Isle Inmates on Mainland Keep Moving Farther Away: Transferring Prisoners Saves the State Money, but Disconnects Them from Their Families," Associated Press, May 16, 2004; Gordon Y.K. Pang, "$1.2 Million More Sought to House Prisoners," *Honolulu Advertiser,* January 13, 2000.

91 Arizona sends prisoners to Texas: "Breakdown of Inmates Sent Out of State Because of Crowding Problems," Associated Press, January 15, 2004.

91 Hawai'i transferred some of its mainland prisoners: Ron Station, "Plan to Move Hawai'i Prisoners to Mississippi Draws Criticism," Associated Press, May 17, 2004.

91 Hawai'i is finding that the recidivism rate is higher: Crary, "Faced with Crowded Prisons."

91 Several prisons operate family literacy programs: "Services for Families of Prison Inmates," *Special Issues in Corrections,* National Institute of Corrections, February 2002.

92 housing more than two thousand men: Ted Conover, *Newjack: Guarding Sing Sing* (New York: Vintage, 2001), 61.

92 forty have been sited upstate: Lisa Freeman and Robert Gangi, "Following the Dollars: Where New York State Spends Its Prison Money," City Project, March 2000, 4, cited in Marc Mauer and Meda Chesney-Lind, "Introduction," in Mauer and Chesney-Lind, eds., *Invisible Punishment: The Collateral Consequences of Mass Imprisonment* (New York: The New Press, 2002), 6.

93 Two-thirds of the state's prisoners come from New York City: ibid., 2.

94 "a covenant, as important to us as marriage vows": Elizabeth Gaynes, "We Did It Ourselves: The Evolution of a Comprehensive Program

for Prisoners and Families," *America's Family Support Magazine*, Fall 2003, 29–30.

98 Researchers who evaluated Family Works: Kim A. Cattat and Dina R. Rose, "Family Works: An Evaluation of a Fathers-in-Prison Program, Executive Summary," Osborne Association, New York, August 2002, 19.

98 "the Children's Center may be an important tool in reducing the intergenerational cycle": ibid., 24.

106 "I felt a change": "Father Shares Love, Lessons, and Values Behind Bars," *Osborne Today*, Winter 2002, 1.

106 the U.S. Supreme Court upheld a Michigan policy: Anne Gearan, "Supreme Court Upholds Strict Prison Visitation Policies," Associated Press, June 1, 2003.

4. Grandparents

110 The cohort Theresa had joined so abruptly was large and growing: Lynne M. Casper and Kenneth R. Bryson, "Co-resident Grandparents and Their Grandchildren: Grandparent Maintained Families," Population Division, U.S. Bureau of the Census, March 1998, 6.

110 4.4 million children: "Children and the Households They Live In: 2000," Census 2000 Special Reports, U.S. Census Bureau, March 2004.

110 Half of all children with incarcerated mothers: Christopher J. Mumola, "Incarcerated Parents and Their Children," special report, Bureau of Justice Statistics, U.S. Department of Justice, Washington, DC, August 2000, 4.

114 as is depression: Casper and Bryson, "Co-resident Grandparents and Their Grandchildren," 3.

115 only about 200,000 of the 1.8 million children then living with relatives: Jennifer Ehrle Macomber, Rob Geen, and Rebecca L. Clark, "Children Cared for by Relatives: Who Are They and How Are They Faring?" New Federalism: National Survey of America's Families series, no. B-28, Urban Institute, Washington, DC, February 2001.

115 only about a quarter received financial support: Amy Billing, Jennifer Ehrle Macomber, and Katherine Kortenkamp, "Children Cared for by Relatives: What Do We Know about Their Well-Being?," New Federalism: National Survey of America's Families series, no. B-46, Urban Institute, Washington, DC, May 2002.

116 Nearly two-thirds of children being raised by single grandmothers live in poverty: Casper and Bryson, "Co-resident Grandparents and Their Grandchildren," 13.

116 "incarceration acts like a hidden tax": Donald Braman, *Doing Time on the Outside: Incarceration and Family Life in Urban America* (Ann Arbor: University of Michigan Press, 2004), 156.

126 the California legislature passed Assembly Bill 231: "Advocates for Battered Women and Women Prisoners to Demand Parole for Theresa Cruz," press advisory, California Coalition for Women Prisoners, San Francisco, March 10, 1998.

136 In her 1974 account of kinship networks in a poor black community: Carol B. Stack, *All Our Kin: Strategies for Survival in a Black Community* (New York: Harper Torchbooks, 1975), 46.

5. Foster Care

144 As the writer Nina Bernstein has observed: Nina Bernstein, *The Lost Children of Wilder* (New York: Pantheon Books, 2001), xiv.

144 doubling over the past two punitive decades: "Partnerships Between Corrections and Child Welfare, Part Two: Collaboration for Change," Annie E. Casey Foundation, Baltimore, March 2002, 3.

144 well over half a million: "The AFCARS Report: Preliminary FY 2001 Estimates as of March 2003," Children's Bureau, Administration on Children, Youth, and Families, Administration for Children and Families, U.S. Department of Health and Human Services, Washington, DC, March 2003.

144 At any given moment, 10 percent of the children of women prisoners: "An Overview of Statistics," Federal Resource Center for Children of

Prisoners, Washington, DC, www.cwla.org/programs/incarcerated/cop_factsheet.htm.

144 One study of children in long-term foster care: "Children of Criminal Offenders and Foster Care," Center for Children of Incarcerated Parents, presented at the 1999 Child Welfare League of America National Conference on Research, Seattle, WA, www.fcnetwork.org/reading/fostercare.html.

145 All fifty states have failed a federal foster care review: e-mail correspondence with Gina Russo, Communications Director, Pew Commission on Children in Foster Care, November 18, 2004.

145 According to Richard Gelles: "Too Fast for Families," Forum at the Center for an Urban Future, New York, January 19, 1999.

145 Children are significantly more likely to be abused: see Timothy Roche, "The Crisis of Foster Care," *Time*, November 13, 2000; Richard Wexler, testimony before the Subcommittee on Children and Families, Senate Committee on Labor and Human Resources, May 25, 1995.

146 They are also increasingly likely to land in institutions: "Partnerships Between Corrections and Child Welfare," 3–4.

146 the number of families willing: ibid., 3.

146 The longer a child stays in this kind of care: Lynne Marsenich, LCSW, "Evidence-Based Practices in Mental Health Services for Foster Youth," California Institute for Mental Health, Sacramento, March 2002, 12.

146 a Sacramento, California, study: Cynthia Seymour, "Child Welfare Policy, Program, and Practice Issues," *Child Welfare Journal of Policy, Practice and Program*, Special Issue: Children with Parents in Prison, September/October 1998.

147 Nearly half of all eighteen-year-olds: Richard Wertheimer, Ph.D., "Youth Who 'Age Out' of Foster Care: Troubled Lives, Troubling Prospects," research brief, Child Trends, Washington, DC, December 2002, 5.

147 In California, 65 percent transition directly into homelessness: Kevin Fagan, "Saving Foster Kids from the Streets," *San Francisco Chronicle*, April 11, 2004, 1.

147 A University of Chicago study: "61% of Foster Home Boys Have Rap Sheet by Age 17," *Chicago Sun-Times*, February 26, 2004.

147 One in five women prisoners: Denise Johnston, M.D., and Katherine Gabel, "Incarcerated Parents," in Katherine Gabel and Denise Johnston, M.D., eds., *Children of Incarcerated Parents* (New York: Lexington Books, 1995), 3–20.

149 the average term being served by parents in state prison: Christopher J. Mumola, "Incarcerated Parents and Their Children," special report, Bureau of Justice Statistics, U.S. Department of Justice, Washington, DC, August 2000, 6.

150 As early as 1944, the Supreme Court recognized: Lanette P. Dalley, "Policy Implications Relating to Inmate Mothers and Their Children: Will the Past Be Prologue?," *Prison Journal* 82 (June 2002), 234.

150 In a series of subsequent cases: ibid., 239.

150 One court noted: In re Brittany, 17 Cal. App. 4th 1399, 1402 (Cal. Ct. App. 1993), rev. den. 1993 Cal. LEXIS 6444 (193), in Amy Hirsch et al., "Every Door Closed: Barriers Facing Parents With Criminal Records," Executive Summary, Center for Law and Social Policy, Washington, DC, and Community Legal Services, Philadelphia, 5.

150 thirty-four states now have statutes in place: telephone interview with Philip Genty, Columbia University School of Law, December 9, 2004.

150 In Georgia, for example: Philip Genty, "Summary of State Statutes Survey," 2003.

150 Several states also identify parental incarceration as an "aggravating circumstance": Philip M. Genty, "Recent Developments in Child Custody Policy and Legislation: The Impact of ASFA upon Incarcerated Parents and their Families," *Family and Corrections Network Report*, no. 22, October 1999.

150 Under a New York statute: New York State Social Service Law s384b, in Timothy Ross, Ajay Khashu, and Mark Warnsley, "Hard Data on Hard Times: An Empirical Analysis of Maternal Incarceration, Foster Care, and Visitation," Vera Institute of Justice, New York, August 2004, 2.

151 Nationwide, 75 percent of foster care administrators say they do not

consider proximity: Barbara E. Smith and Sharon Goretsky Elstein, *Children on Hold: Improving the Response to Children Whose Parents Are Arrested and Incarcerated* (Washington, DC: American Bar Association Center on Children and the Law, 1994), 78.

151 If a social worker does not locate and arrange visits with an incarcerated parent: ibid.

151 only about 13 percent of prisoners' children in long-term foster care visit their incarcerated mothers: Yolanda Johnson-Peterkin, "Information Packet: Children of Incarcerated Parents," National Resource Center for Foster Care & Permanency Planning at the Hunter College School of Social Work, New York, May 2003, 4.

151 Transfers from one facility to another are common: "Partnerships Between Corrections and Child Welfare," 15.

151 Incarcerated parents who have child welfare cases: ibid., 16.

151 When the Child Welfare League of America surveyed: Seymour, "Child Welfare Policy, Program, and Practice Issues."

152 Researchers from the Vera Institute of Justice found: Ross et al., "Hard Data on Hard Times," 9.

154 incarcerated parents owe: Esther Griswold, Jessica Pearson, and Lanae Davis, "Testing a Modification Process for Incarcerated Parents," Center for Policy Research, Denver, December 2001, 11–12, in "Report of the Re-Entry Policy Council, Executive Summary," Re-Entry Policy Council, New York, January 2005, xix.

154 Should they subsequently manage to find legal work: Travis et al., *Families Left Behind*, 8.

155 Failure to pay can mean more prison time: Jessica Pearson, "Building Debt While Doing Time: Child Support and Incarceration," *Judges' Journal* 43, no. 1 (Winter 2004), 8.

155 In various surveys, half or more of child welfare supervisors: Smith and Elstein, *Children on Hold*, 82; Marcus Nieto, "In Danger of Falling Through the Cracks: Children of Arrested Parents," California Research Bureau, Sacramento, April 2002, 22.

156 Maintaining family contact is one of the most effective means of achieving successful reentry: Creasie Finney Hairston, "Prisoners and Their Families: Parenting Issues During Incarceration," in Jeremy

Travis and Michelle Waul, eds., *Prisoners Once Removed: The Impact of Incarceration and Reentry on Children, Families and Communities* (Washington, DC: Urban Institute Press, 2003), 260–61.

156   The average time spent in foster care: Barbara White Stack, "Federal Adoption Law Spurs Rise in Legal Orphans: Legislation Intended to Increase Adoptions Led to Increase in Kids with No Parents at All," *Pittsburgh Post-Gazette*, December 26, 2004.

157   there were some 129,000 children designated as "waiting": "National Campaign Urges Americans to Adopt," *Children's Bureau Express* 5, no. 6 (June 2004), Administration for Children and Families, U.S. Department of Health and Human Services.

157   The federal Department of Health and Human Services has taken on this problem: ibid.

164   compared to about half of the women: Jenifer Warren, "Prison System Fails Women, Study Says," *Los Angeles Times*, December 16, 2004.

164   Vera Institute of Justice researchers: Ross et al., "Hard Data on Hard Times," Executive Summary.

165   In the nineteenth century: Lucia Zedner, "Wayward Sisters," in Norval Morris and David J. Rothman, eds., *The Oxford History of the Prison: The Practice of Punishment in Western Society* (New York: Oxford University Press, 1998).

165   Today, there are prison nurseries in eleven states: "Services for Families of Prison Inmates," *Special Issues in Corrections*, U.S. Department of Justice, National Institute of Corrections Information Center, Longmont, CO, February 2002.

170   between 6 and 10 percent of women enter prison pregnant: Barbara Bloom, "Imprisoned Mothers," in Katherine Gabel and Denise Johnston, M.D., eds., *Children of Incarcerated Parents* (New York: Lexington Books, 1995), 23.

171   One study of combat veterans: Judith Herman, M.D., *Trauma and Recovery* (New York: Basic Books, 1992), 44.

171   Some research suggests: ibid.

171   meet the criteria for post-traumatic stress disorder: "Mental Health Treatment for Youth in the Juvenile Justice System," National Mental Health Association, Alexandria, VA, 2004, 1.

171 More than three-quarters of the women behind bars have been physically or sexually abused: Barbara Bloom, Meda Chesney-Lind, and
Barbara Owen, "Women in California Prisons: Hidden Victims of the
War on Drugs," Center on Juvenile and Criminal Justice, San Francisco, 1994.

171 Eighty percent of women in state prisons: Center for Substance Abuse
Treatment, Rockville, MD, 1999, in Stephanie S. Covington, "A
Woman's Journey Home: Challenges for Female Offenders," in Travis
and Waul, *Prisoners Once Removed*, 71.

174 "Parental love cannot be synthesized": Jonathan Kozol, *Rachel and Her
Children* (New York: Fawcett Columbine, 1988), 61.

174 The California prison system is home to about 7,400 mothers:
"Where's Mommy? Mothers in the California Prison System in 2003,"
Center for Children of Incarcerated Parents, Pasadena, May 2004.

176 In 1999, I interviewed and surveyed: Nell Bernstein, *A Rage to Do Better: Listening to Young People from the Foster Care System*, Pacific News
Service, San Francisco, May 2000.

6. Reentry

181 In 2004, nearly 650,000 Americans were released from prison: Serious
and Violent Offender Re-Entry Initiative website, Office of Justice
Programs, U.S. Department of Justice, www.ojp.usdoj.gov/reentry/
learn.html, in "Report of the Re-Entry Policy Council, Executive
Summary," Re-Entry Policy Council, New York, January 2005, xviii.

182 "Prolonged, repeated trauma, by contrast, occurs only in circumstances of captivity": Judith Herman, *Trauma and Recovery* (New
York: Basic Books, 1992), 74.

182 "Once we got out": Mauricio Rosencof, quoted in Lawrence Weschler,
"The Great Exception: Part I; Liberty," *New Yorker*, April 3, 1989, in
Herman, *Trauma and Recovery*, 90.

183 Craig Haney, a psychologist, has written about "prisonization": Craig
Haney, "The Psychological Impact of Incarceration: Implications for
Postprison Adjustment," in Jeremy Travis and Michelle Waul, eds.,

Prisoners Once Removed: The Impact of Incarceration and Reentry on Children, Families and Communities (Washington, DC: Urban Institute Press, 2003), 33–66.

184 U.S. District Judge Alex Howard declared at sentencing: Sam Hodges and Joe Danborn, "Dorothy Gaines Wins Her Freedom," *Mobile Register*, December 23, 2001.

190 Under the 1996 federal welfare reform law: Patricia Allard, "Life Sentences: Denying Welfare Benefits to Women Convicted of Drug Offenses," Sentencing Project, Washington, DC, February 2002, 1.

190 Drug offenders comprise one-third of all released prisoners: James P. Lynch and William J. Sabol, "Prisoner Reentry in Perspective," Justice Policy Center, Urban Institute, Washington, DC, September 2001.

190 their access to drug treatment may be limited: Allard, 26.

191 Senator Phil Gramm, the sponsor of the provision, explained: ibid, 11.

191 Public housing is closed to most people with felony convictions: Amy Hirsch et al., "Every Door Closed: Barriers Facing Parents With Criminal Records," Executive Summary, Center for Law and Social Policy, Washington, DC, and Community Legal Services, Philadelphia, 4.

191 Congress cut off financial aid: ibid., 6–7.

191 Another federal law requires states to suspend the driver's licenses: "A Catch-22 for Ex-Offenders," editorial, *New York Times*, April 6, 2004.

191 The number of deportations: U.S. Citizen and Immigration Services, cited in Jay Conui et al., "Justice Detained: The Effects of Deportation on Immigrant Families," Asian & Pacific Islander Youth Promoting Advocacy and Leadership (AYPAL) and the Data Center, Oakland, CA, March 2004, 9.

191 More than 47 million Americans: Jeremy Travis, "Invisible Punishment: An Instrument of Social Exclusion," in Marc Mauer and Meda Chesney-Lind, eds., *Invisible Punishment: The Collateral Consequences of Mass Imprisonment* (New York: The New Press, 2002), 18.

191 Thirteen million, or 6 percent of the population: ibid.

192 only one in ten receives any treatment: Jeremy Travis, Amy L. Solomon, and Michelle Waul, "From Prison to Home: The Dimensions and Consequences of Prisoner Reentry," Justice Policy Center, Urban Institute, Washington, DC, June 2001, 18.

192 Educational and vocational programs: ibid., 17.

192 In California, for example: ibid., 42.

192 a recidivism rate of nearly 80 percent: "Editorial: Improve Prison Education," *San Francisco Chronicle*, April 12, 2004.

192 "In the popular view, guilt is not merely a description of behavior": Howard Zehr, *Changing Lenses* (Scottsdale, PA: Herald Press, 1990), 69.

193 Employment bans affecting ex-offenders: Fox Butterfield, "Freed from Prison, but Still Paying a Penalty," *New York Times*, June 6, 2003; Travis, Solomon, and Waul, "From Prison to Home," 31.

193 some states—including Alabama—bar those with a record from any public employment: Travis, Solomon, and Waul, "From Prison to Home," 31.

193 Post-9/11 security measures: Lance Gray, "Jobs Decline for Ex-cons Since 9–11," Scripps Howard News Service, February 1, 2005.

194 Most states allow private employers to deny jobs: Paul Samuels and Debbie Mukamal, "After Prison: Roadblocks to Reentry," Legal Action Center, New York, 2004, 8.

194 Two-thirds of incarcerated parents were employed: Christopher J. Mumola, "Incarcerated Parents and Their Children," special report, Bureau of Justice Statistics, U.S. Department of Justice, Washington, DC, August 2000, 9.

194 one survey of California parolees: California Department of Corrections, 1997, in Travis, Solomon, and Waul, "From Prison to Home," 12.

194 a criminal record diminishes one's employment prospects for life: Travis, Solomon, and Waul, "From Prison to Home," 31.

194 "they are also poor because they experience incarceration": Donald Braman, *Doing Time on the Outside: Incarceration and Family Life in Urban America* (Ann Arbor: University of Michigan Press, 2004), 154.

194 In 1985, 70 percent of parolees successfully completed their supervision: Travis, Solomon, and Waul, "From Prison to Home," 5.

194 Nearly two-thirds of released prisoners will be rearrested: Patrick A. Langan and David J. Levin, "Recidivism of Prisoners Released in 1994," Bureau of Justice Statistics, U.S. Department of Justice, Washington, DC, June 2004, in Doug McVay, Vincent Schiraldi, and Jason

Ziedenberg, "Treatment or Incarceration?: National and State Findings on the Efficacy and Cost Savings of Drug Treatment Versus Imprisonment," Justice Policy Institute, Washington, DC, March 2004, 14.

194 nearly half of the parents currently in state prison: Mumola, "Incarcerated Parents and Their Children," 7.

195 only 20 percent of employers will consider hiring an applicant with a criminal history: Stephanie Armour, "Competitive Job Market Locks Out Former Offenders," *USA Today,* November 21, 2003.

195 The average annual income of former prisoners is less than $8,000: ibid.

202 An evaluation of the program: Eileen Sullivan, Ph.D., et al., "Families as a Resource in Recovery from Drug Abuse: An Evaluation of La Bodega de la Familia," Vera Institute of Justice, New York, 2002, 54.

202 Bodega clients were half as likely to be arrested: ibid., 50.

203 More than half of the drug users the researchers interviewed: ibid., 9.

203 Criminal justice involvement had become the norm: ibid., 8.

204 As caseloads nationwide have grown from an average of forty-five per officer: Amy L. Solomon, Michelle Waul, Ashley Van Ness, and Jeremy Travis, "Outside the Walls: A National Snapshot of Community-Based Prisoner Reentry Programs," Urban Institute, Washington, DC, January 2004, 120.

204 reaching into the hundreds: Joan Petersilia, "Probation in the US," *Perspectives* 30 (Spring 1998), part 1, in "Re-Entry Statistics," Re-Entry Policy Council, New York, January 2005, www.reentrypolicy.org/statistics-by-subject-matter.html.

7. Legacy

212 As many as half of the male children: telephone interview with Denise Johnston, M.D., Center for Children of Incarcerated Parents, December 20, 2004.

212 One in ten of the children of prisoners: "Partnerships Between Corrections and Child Welfare, Part Two: Collaboration for Change," Annie E. Casey Foundation, Baltimore, March 2002, 8.

212 Researchers in Oregon, for example, followed 206 boys: J. Mark Eddy

and John B. Reid, "The Adolescent Children of Incarcerated Parents: A Developmental Perspective," in Jeremy Travis and Michelle Waul, eds., *Prisoners Once Removed: The Impact of Incarceration and Reentry on Children, Families, and Communities* (Washington, DC: Urban Institute Press, 2003), 238.

213 Another study, in Sacramento: Cynthia Seymour, "Child Welfare Policy, Program, and Practice Issues," *Child Welfare Journal of Policy, Practice and Program*, Special Issue: Children with Parents in Prison, September/October 1998.

213 A study of delinquent boys: cited in Fox Butterfield, *All God's Children: The Bosket Family and the American Tradition of Violence* (New York: Perennial, 1996), 103.

213 The work of the influential Italian pseudoscientist Cesare Lombroso: Anthony M. Platt, *The Child Savers: The Invention of Delinquency* (Chicago: University of Chicago Press, 1969), 20.

214 "Their moral degeneration corresponds with their physical": *Abnormal Man* (Washington, DC: Government Printing Office, 1893), 44–45, in Platt, *Child Savers*, 22.

214 "certain classes of vicious persons could be hindered from propagation": Nathan Allen, "Prevention of Crime and Pauperism," Proceedings of the Annual Conference of Charities (PACC), 1878, 111–24, in Platt, *Child Savers*, 25.

214 One such researcher claimed to have identified an Indiana clan: Oscar C. McCulloch, "The Tribe of Ishmael: A Study in Social Degradation," Proceedings of the National Conference of Charities and Correction (PNCCC), 1888, 154–59, in Platt, *Child Savers*, 26.

214 "We must get hold of the children": ibid.

214 "a methodized registration and training of such children": "The Moral Imbecile," PNCCC, 1890, 244–50, in Platt, *Child Savers*, 28.

215 "we can direct and control the progress of human evolution": Ernest Hooton, *Crime and the Man* (Cambridge: Harvard University Press, 1939), 391, 396, in Platt, *Child Savers*, 27.

215 hundreds of thousands of urban children were shipped to the countryside: Linda Gordon, *The Great Arizona Orphan Abduction* (Cambridge: Harvard University Press, 1999), 3–37.

215 were injected with fenfluramine: Daniel S. Pine et al., "Neuroendocrine Response to Fenfluramine Challenge in Boys," *Archives of General Psychiatry* 54, no. 9 (September 1997), 830, 840, cited in Mitchel Cohen, "Beware the Violence Initiative Project—Coming Soon to an Inner City Near You," *Synthesis/Regeneration* 19 (Spring 1999).

219 About 20 percent of the children of the most acutely criminal parents: Eddy and Reid, "Adolescent Children of Incarcerated Parents," 234–36.

224 Many women prisoners first encounter the criminal justice system: Stephanie S. Covington, "A Woman's Journey Home: Challenges for Female Offenders," in Travis and Waul, *Prisoners Once Removed*, 71.

236 A survey of California's second- and third-strikers: Scott Ehlers, Vincent Schiraldi, and Jason Ziedenberg, "Still Striking Out: Ten Years of California's Three Strikes," Justice Policy Institute, Washington, DC, March 2004, 2.

247 In 1993, Oregon had about 6,500 prisoners: "Prisoners at Midyear, 1993," U.S. Department of Justice, Washington, DC.

247 Today that number has nearly doubled: interview with Ben De Haan, December 2003.

247 predicted that it will reach 15,000 by 2012: "Oregon Corrections Population Forecast, October 2002," Oregon Department of Administrative Services, Salem.

253 "criminogenic social conditions": Randall Kennedy, *Race, Crime, and the Law* (New York: Vintage Books, 1997), 24.

253 "given energy to policies and practices": ibid., 14.

254 If current incarceration rates remain unchanged: Thomas P. Bonczar, "Prevalence of Imprisonment in the U.S. Population, 1774–2001," Bureau of Justice Statistics, U.S. Department of Justice, Washington, DC, August 2003.

Conclusion

258 They called this standard "the least detrimental alternative": Joseph Goldstein, Albert J. Solnit, Sonja Goldstein, and Anna Freud, "Beyond

the Best Interests of the Child," in Goldstein et al., *The Best Interests of the Child: The Least Detrimental Alternative* (New York: The Free Press, 1996), 50.

260 When Andrew Fastow and his wife Lea were both charged: "Lea Fastow Sentenced to 12 Months in Prison in Enron Case," Reuters, May 6, 2004.

261 the PSI has come to focus increasingly narrowly: Jacqueline Sullivan, "The History of the Presentence Investigation Report," Center on Juvenile and Criminal Justice, San Francisco, www.cjcj.org/pubs/psi/psireport.html.

263 Differential response laws: Leigh Goodmark, "Promoting Community Child Protection: A Legislative Agenda," American Bar Association Center on Children and the Law, Washington, DC, 2002.

266 As dissenting justices in a Wisconsin Supreme Court decision: cited in Jessica Pearson, "Building Debt While Doing Time: Child Support and Incarceration," *Judges' Journal* 43, no. 1 (Winter 2004), 6–7.

266 A North Carolina statute: ibid., 9.

267 researchers have found that abiding family bonds: see Jeremy Travis and Michelle Waul, "Prisoners Once Removed: The Children and Families of Prisoners," in Travis and Waul, *Prisoners Once Removed: The Impact of Incarceration and Reentry on Children, Families, and Communities* (Washington, DC: Urban Institute Press, 2003), 10–12.

269 increase more than sevenfold since 1980: "Prison Statistics, Summary Findings," Bureau of Justice Statistics, U.S. Department of Justice, Washington, DC, June 30, 2003.

269 "a hallmark of slavery in the United States": Peggy Cooper Davis, *Neglected Stories: The Constitution and Family Values* (New York: Hill and Wang, 1997), 9–10.

269 "Proslavery men and women!": ibid., 105.

269 One in thirty-three American children: e-mail correspondence with Christopher Mumola, Bureau of Justice Statistics, U.S. Department of Justice.

269 nearly one in eight African American children: e-mail correspondence with Arlene Lee, Federal Resource Center for Children of Incarcerated Parents, November 28, 2004.

INDEX